THE WAR ON DRUGS

THE WAR ON DRUGS

HEROIN, COCAINE, CRIME, AND PUBLIC POLICY

James A. Inciardi

Division of Criminal Justice
University of Delaware

MAYFIELD PUBLISHING COMPANY

Palo Alto, California

Sponsoring Editor: Franklin C. Graham

Manuscript Editor: Claire Hunt Comiskey

Managing Editor: Pat Herbst

Production Editor: Jan deProsse

Art Director: Cynthia Bassett

Designer: Gary Head

Illustrator: Signature Design Associates

Production Manager: Cathy Willkie

Compositor: G & S Typesetters, Inc.

Printer and Binder: George Banta Company

Library of Congress Catalog Card Number: 86-061126

International Standard Book Number: 0-87484-743-5

Manufactured in the United States of America

10 9 8 7 6 5 4 3

Mayfield Publishing Company
1240 Villa Street
Mountain View, California 94041

This research was supported, in part, by HHS Grant #1-RO1-DAO-1827 from
the National Institute on Drug Abuse, by the American Participant Program
of the United States Information Agency, and by the Health Services Research
Center at the University of Miami School of Medicine. The opinions expressed
are those of the author and do not reflect the official policies of any government
or private agency.

TO CARL, HARVE, DR. DAVE

and our early days together in drug research

CONTENTS

PREFACE

The worlds of heroin, cocaine, and crime are peculiar worlds, populated by presidents and kings, diplomats and merchants, peasants and slaves, and by hookers, thieves, junkies, dealers, and other bizarre creatures of the streets. These are dangerous and tragic worlds where violence and death are commonplace, and many alien and exotic worlds, ranging from the secluded poppy fields of Southeast and Southwest Asia and the jungles of Amazonia to the streets of urban and rural America.

This book is a series of reflections on these worlds, observed from both near and far. Much of what is said in the book is based on street research in Miami and New York and on interviews with the heroin and cocaine users, dealers, and traffickers who live in these cities and the law-enforcement agents and government officials charged with controlling drug use and crime in the streets. As such, the data are both systematic and anecdotal. The research also includes observations and interviews in South America—in the drug-trafficking capitals of Colombia, Bolivia, Peru, and Ecuador, in the coca fields of the Andes Mountains, and in the jungle labs and drug-selling bazaars of Amazonia. In South America, the informants included peasant laborers, military officials and other foreign government representatives, North American and South American drug-enforcement agents, members of the U.S. diplomatic corps, and drug-abuse clinicians and researchers.

As a series of perspectives and reflections, this book is not intended to give a definitive statement on any of the topics it covers, although at times the opinionated nature of the commentary might seem to suggest this. But the perspectives and reflections are intended to provide an examination of the nature of American drug policy against the backgrounds of social and cultural change—where this policy has been, where it is now, and where it ought to be going.

In this behalf, Chapter 1, "From Dover's Powder to Ecstasy," traces the evolution of drug abuse in the United States from the early years of the eighteenth century to the present, focusing on many social and cultural events that served to shape the nature of drug-use and drug-control policy. Chapter 2, "Shit, Smack, and Superfly," provides an overview of heroin and cocaine trafficking and use—where the drugs come from, how they are refined and distributed, how they are prepared and used, and what effects they engender. Chapter 3, "The Vilification of Euphoria," gives a social history of the criminalization of drug use in the United States. Chapters 4 and 5, "The Drugs–Crime Connection" and "Hooker, Whore, Junkie, Thief," respectively, are empirical examinations of drug-related crime combined with attempts to demythologize some of the erroneous, but nevertheless enduring, misconceptions and ideas about drug use. Chapter 6, "From Tingo Maria to Teheran," examines the social, economic, and political implications of drug trafficking, and the Epilogue offers an approach for salvaging American drug-control policies.

One final note: The reflections and comments of many people who populate the worlds of heroin, cocaine, and crime are included throughout this book. Reported verbatim, they are uncensored and often tend to be rather graphic. All such quotations that are not footnoted as to the source are based on interviews that the author conducted.

ACKNOWLEDGMENTS

The total number of debts one incurs in writing a book is surprisingly large. My first acknowledgments must go to Dan J. Lettieri, Louise Richards, and Michael Backenheimer, who were project officers at the National Institute on Drug Abuse at various stages of the research; their support made this whole endeavor possible. For their imparted doses of criticism, sincere thanks must go to Carl D. Chambers, Paul J. Goldstein, Franklin C. Graham, Carolyn J. Inciardi, Anne E. Pottieger, and Richard C. Stephens. Thanks also to the academic reviewers, John C. Ball and David N. Nurco of the University of Maryland; and Richard R. Clayton of the University of Kentucky. Special thanks is due to Nancy Quillen who spent many weeks at the library and many hours on the telephone obtaining background information for this work. I am indebted as well to Rayburn Hesse and Robert R. Schwartz for the data they provided. Finally, I am indebted to Susan E. Loring for her critique of the first draft of the manuscript—page by page, line by line, and word by word—and to Jan deProsse, Claire Hunt Comiskey, Don Palm, Cynthia Bassett, and all the other people at Mayfield Publishing Company who helped to make this book possible.

James A. Inciardi
Key Largo
April 1986

THE WAR ON DRUGS

CHAPTER ONE

FROM DOVER'S POWDER TO ECSTASY
The Evolution of Drug Taking in the United States

The beginnings of most social phenomena are relatively easy to trace. American jazz emerged a little more than a century ago in the city of New Orleans. It was a fusion of the existing musical art forms of black America—the work songs, spirituals, and blues—combined with elements of white folk music, the rhythms of Hispanic America and the Caribbean, the melodies of French dances, and the instrumentation of the marching band. The environmental movement of the late 1960s and early 1970s was an outgrowth of the writings of biologist Rachel Carson, combined with a better understanding of the effects of pollution on ecosystems. The roots of today's attempt to rid American streets and highways of drunk drivers are also easily targeted. They began on a spring afternoon in 1980 when a 13-year-old California teenager was struck down and killed by a hit-and-run driver. Stunned by the fact that the driver of the automobile was not only drunk, but out on bail for his third drunk-driving offense, and unlikely to be punished for the killing, the child's mother launched the organization of Mothers Against Drunk Drivers (MADD) and initiated a campaign of public outcry. But the origins of other social trends can be more difficult to uncover. The roots of drug abuse are particularly obscure. The use of opium dates back at least to the ancient Greeks, and references to marijuana appear in early Persian, Hindu, Greek, Arab, and Chinese writings. Similarly, when the Spanish conquistador Francisco Pizarro stumbled upon the Inca empire in 1531, the chewing of coca had already been in Inca mythology for centuries. Even in the United States, a nation with a relatively short history, the onset of drug taking as a social phenomenon remains somewhat of a mystery.*

---

* *Note:* All undocumented quotations throughout this text are personal communications to the author collected during the course of field research in the United States and South America.

1

THOMAS DOVER, OPIUM, AND THE GREAT AMERICAN MEDICINE SHOW

Perhaps it all began during the eighteenth century with Thomas Dover, a student of British physician Thomas Sydenham. Known as the "English Hippocrates" and the father of clinical medicine, Sydenham had been a strong advocate of the use of opium for the treatment of disease. In fact, he was so committed to the clinical value of opium that sometime before his death in 1689 he stated that "among the remedies which it has pleased the Almighty God to give to man to relieve his sufferings, none is so universal and so efficacious as opium."[1]

Following the path of his mentor, Dover developed a form of medicinal opium. Known as *Dover's Powder,* it contained one ounce each of opium, ipecac (the dried roots of a tropical creeping plant), and licorice, combined with saltpeter, tartar, and wine.[2] It was introduced in 1709, the same year that Dover, also an adventurer and privateer, rescued castaway Alexander Selkirk from one of the desolate Juan Fernandez Islands off the coast of Chile, thus inspiring Daniel Defoe's *Robinson Crusoe.* Dover's Powder made its way to America and remained one of the most widely used opium preparations for almost two centuries.

The attraction of Dover's Powder was in the euphoric and anesthetic properties of opium. For thousands of years, opium had been a popular narcotic. A derivative of the *Oriental poppy*—known to most Americans as the flower that interrupted Dorothy and Toto in their journey along the yellow brick road to the wonderful land of Oz—it was called the "plant of joy" some 4,000 years ago in the "fertile crescent" of Mesopotamia. In Homer's *Odyssey,* the potion that Helen of Troy mixed "to quiet all pain and strife, and bring forgetfulness of every ill," is believed to have contained opium. There is even speculation that the "vinegar mixed with gall," mentioned in Matt. 27:34, as an offering to Christ on the cross contained opium.[3]

The introduction of Dover's Powder apparently started a trend. By the latter part of the eighteenth century, patent medicines containing opium were readily available throughout urban and rural America. They were sold in pharmacies, grocery and general stores, at traveling medicine shows, and through the mail. They were marketed under such labels as *Ayer's Cherry Pectoral, Mrs. Winslow's Soothing Syrup, McMunn's Elixer, Godfrey's Cordial, Scott's Emulsion,* and *Dover's Powder.* Many of these remedies were seductively advertised as "painkillers," "cough mixtures," "soothing syrups," "consumption cures," and "women's friends." Others were promoted for the treatment of such varied ailments as diarrhea, dysentery, colds, fever, teething, cholera, rheumatism, pelvic disorders, athlete's foot, and even baldness and cancer. The drugs were produced from imported opium, as well as from the white opium poppies that were being legally grown in the New England states, Florida and Louisiana, the West and Southwest, and the Confederate States of America during the Civil War.

The medical profession also fostered the use of opium. Dr. William Buchan's *Domestic Medicine,* first published in Philadelphia in 1784 as a practical handbook on simple medicines for home use, suggested for the treatment of coughs:

> A cup of an infusion of wild poppy leaves and marsh-mellow roots, or the flowers of coltsfoot, may be taken frequently; or a teaspoonful of the paregoric elixer (flowers of benzoin plus opium) may be put into the patient's drink twice a day. Spanish infusion (liquor combined with the syrup of poppy leaves) is also a very popular medicine in this case, and may be taken in the quantity of a teacupful three or four times a day.[4]

Buchan's treatise on home remedies, which was republished in several editions, also recommended tincture of opium for the treatment of numerous common ailments:

> Take of crude opium, two ounces; spirituous aromatic water, and mountain wine, of each ten ounces. Dissolve the opium, sliced, in the wine, with a gentle heat, frequently stirring it; afterward add the spirit, and strain off the tincture.[5]

Yet the mere appearance of Dover's Powder and other patent medicines in America was only minimally related to the evolution of drug taking; other more potent social forces had been of considerably greater significance. Along with Dover's opium concoction, similar remedies were initially shipped to the colonies from London, as were most of the medications of the period. They were available from physicians, or over the counter from apothecaries, grocers, postmasters, and printers, but only in modest quantities. When trade with England was disrupted during the Revolutionary War, a patent medicine industry emerged in the United States, spirited also by the state of eighteenth-century and early nineteenth-century *regular* medicine. The prevailing vogue in American medical therapy had stressed extreme bleeding and purging. It was medicine's "heroic" age, but suspicion of heroic therapy led many to seek out home remedies or "cures" available through their local general store.

These suspicions were further intensified with the rise of Jacksonian democracy and its antagonism toward intellectuals.

Expansions in the patent-medicine industry were also related to the growth of the American press. The manufacturers of the "medicines" were the first business entrepreneurs to seek national markets through widespread advertising. They were the first hucksters to use psychological lures to entice customers to buy their merchandise. They were the first manufacturers to help the local merchants who retailed their wares by going directly to consumers with a message about their products. In total national advertising, this segment of the drug industry ranked highest in expenditures. During the post-Civil War decades, some individual proprietors spent in excess of $500,000 each year for advertising. In the 1890s, for example, more than $1 million was spent annually for the promotion of *Scott's Emulsion.*[6] As to the number of different varieties of patent medicines available, an 1804 New York catalog listed some 90 brands of elixirs; an 1857 Boston periodical included almost 600; in 1858 one newspaper account totaled over 1,500 patent medicines; and by 1905 the list had stretched to more than 28,000.[7]

Curiously, the widespread presence of opium in patent medicines was not altogether understood by the majority of the public, for the so-called "patent medicines" were actually *unpatented.* The patenting of a drug required revealing its ingredients so that all might know its composition, but unpatented "patent medicines" kept their contents secret. In fact, in 1881 the Proprietary Medicine Manufacturers and Dealers Association was organized as an effective lobby for all interests in the trade. For almost three decades it fought against disclosure laws while Dover's Powder and the other popular opium-containing drugs sold in massive quantities.

Even though opium had been the only known product of the Oriental poppy for the longest time, in 1803 a young German pharmacist, Frederick Serturner, isolated the chief alkaloid of opium.[8] Serturner had hit upon *morphine,* which he so named after Morpheus, the Greek god of dreams. The discovery was to have profound effects on both medicine and society, for morphine was, and still is, the greatest single pain reliever the world has ever known. Then the hypodermic syringe was invented, and the use of morphine by injection in military medicine during the Civil War and the Franco-Prussian War granted the procedure legitimacy and familiarity to both physicians and the public.[9] Furthermore, hypodermic medication had its pragmatic aspects—it brought quick local relief, its dosage could be regulated, and it was effective when oral medication was impractical. The regimen, however, was used promiscuously, for many physicians were anxious to illustrate their ability to quell the

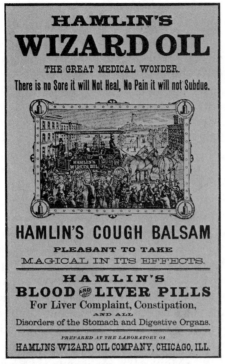

Hamlin's Wizard Oil, a nineteenth-century,
opium-based patent medicine

pain suffered by their patients, who, in turn, expected instant relief from
discomfort. Or as one commentator put it:

> There is no proceeding in medicine that has become so rapidly
> popular; no method of allaying pain so prompt in its action and
> permanent in its effect; no plan of medication that has been so
> carelessly used and thoroughly abused; and no therapeutic dis-
> covery that has been so great a blessing and so great a curse to
> mankind than the hypodermic injection of morphia.[10]

The use of morphine by needle had become so pervasive by the 1890s
that technology soon responded with the production of inexpensive equipment for mass use. In the 1897 edition of the Sears Roebuck catalog, for
example, hypodermic kits, which included a syringe, two needles, two

vials, and a carrying case, were advertised for as little as $1.50, with extra needles available at 25 cents each or $2.75 per dozen.[11]

In addition to the uncontrolled use of opium in patent medicines and morphine by injection, the practice of opium smoking also was prevalent. The Chinese laborers who were imported to build the railroads and work the mines in the trans-Mississippi West had introduced it to America. It was estimated that by 1875 opium smoking had become widespread, particularly among prostitutes, gamblers, and other denizens of the underworld, but also among more respectable men and women of the middle and upper classes.[12]

As to the full volume of the opium and morphine actually consumed during the nineteenth century, the picture is not altogether clear. The domestic production of opium was limited as a result of cultivation techniques that tended to yield a product considerably deficient in morphine, so one indicator of consumption could be drawn from import figures. According to data that the U.S. Public Health Service compiled in 1924, more than 7,000 tons of crude opium and almost 800 tons of smoking opium were imported during the four-decade period ending in 1899.[13] Estimates as to the number of individuals actually *addicted* to opium during the latter part of the nineteenth century tended to be compiled rather loosely, ranging as high as 3 million.[14] Yet other, more rigorously collected data for the period did indicate that the use of narcotic drugs was indeed pervasive. In 1888, for example, one examination of 10,000 prescriptions from Boston-area pharmacies found that some 15% contained opiates,[15] and that was only in Boston. In 1900, it was estimated that in the small state of Vermont, 3.3 million doses of opium were sold each month.[16]

THE DIVINE GIFT OF THE INCAS

Beyond opium and morphine, the patent-medicine industry branched even further. Although chewing coca leaves for their mild stimulant effects had been a part of Andean culture for perhaps a thousand years, for some obscure reason the practice had never become popular in either Europe or the United States. During the latter part of the nineteenth century, however, Angelo Mariani of Corsica brought the unobtrusive Peruvian shrub to the notice of the rest of the world. After importing tons of coca leaves to his native land, he produced an extract that he mixed with wine and called *Vin Coca Mariani*.[17] The wine was an immediate success, publicized as a magical beverage that would free the body from fatigue, lift the spirits, and create a lasting sense of well-being. Vin Coca brought Mariani immediate wealth and fame, as well as a medal of appreciation from Pope Leo XIII who used the drink as a source of comfort in his many years of ascetic retirement.

Across the ocean during the same years, John Styth Pemberton of Atlanta, Georgia, had been marketing *Triplex Liver Pills, Globe of Flower Cough Syrup,* and a number of equally curious patent medicines. Noting Mariani's great success, in 1885 Pemberton developed a new product that he registered as *French Wine Coca—Ideal Nerve and Tonic Stimulant.* It was originally a medicinal preparation, but the following year he added an additional ingredient, changed it into a soft drink, and renamed it *Coca-Cola.*[18]

Although the extracts of coca may have indeed made Pemberton's cola "the real thing," the popularity of Coca-Cola in the years hence was hardly a reason for considering it a national health concern, for the stimulant effects of the drink were at best mild. The full potency of the coca leaf remained unknown until 1860 when cocaine was first isolated in its pure form.* Yet little use was made of the new alkaloid until 1883 when Dr. Theodor Aschenbrandt secured a supply of the drug and issued it to Bavarian soldiers during maneuvers. Aschenbrandt, a German military physician, noted the beneficial effects of cocaine, particularly its ability to suppress fatigue.

Among those who read Aschenbrandt's account with fascination was a struggling young Viennese neurologist, Sigmund Freud. Suffering from chronic fatigue, depression, and various neurotic symptoms, Freud obtained a measure of cocaine and tried it himself. He also offered it to a colleague who was suffering from both a disease of the nervous system and morphine addiction, and to a patient with a chronic and painful gastric disorder. Finding the initial results to be quite favorable in all three cases, Freud decided that cocaine was a "magical drug." In a letter to his fiancée, Martha Bernays, in 1884, Freud commented on his experiences with cocaine:

> If all goes well I will write an essay on it and I expect it will win its place in therapeutics by the side of morphium and superior to it. I have other hopes and intentions about it. I take

---

* There seems to be considerable contradiction in the literature as to who first isolated cocaine, and when. Although most recent sources hold that it was Gardeke in 1844, a more persistent search suggests that it was Dr. Albert Niemann almost two decades later. See Carl Koller, "On the Beginnings of Local Anesthesia," paper presented at the annual meeting of the Brooklyn Ophthalmological Society, Brooklyn, New York, April 18, 1940.

COCA-COLA
SYRUP ❖ AND ❖ EXTRACT.

For Soda Water and other Carbonated Beverages.

This "INTELLECTUAL BEVERAGE" and TEMPERANCE DRINK contains the valuable TONIC and NERVE STIMULANT properties of the Coca plant and Cola (or Kola) nuts, and makes not only a delicious, exhilarating, refreshing and invigorating Beverage, (dispensed from the soda water fountain or in other carbonated beverages), but a valuable Brain Tonic, and a cure for all nervous affections — SICK HEAD-ACHE, NEURALGIA, HYSTERIA, MELANCHOLY, &c.

The peculiar flavor of COCA-COLA delights every palate; it is dispensed from the soda fountain in same manner as any of the fruit syrups.

J. S. Pemberton,
❧ Chemist, ☙
Sole Proprietor, Atlanta, Ga.

very small doses of it regularly against depression and against indigestion, and with the most brilliant success. . . . In short it is only now that I feel that I am a doctor, since I have helped one patient and hope to help more.[19]

In July 1884, less than three months after Freud's initial experiences with cocaine, his essay was published in a German medical journal and reprinted in English in the *Saint Louis Medical and Surgical Journal* shortly thereafter.[20] Freud then pressed the drug onto his friends and colleagues, urging that they use it both for themselves and their patients; he gave it to his sisters and his fiancée, and continued to use it himself. By the close of the 1880s, however, Freud and the others who had praised cocaine as an all-purpose wonder drug began to withdraw their support for it in light of an increasing number of reports of compulsive use and undesirable side effects. Yet by 1890, the patent-medicine industry in the United States had also discovered the benefits of the unregulated use of cocaine. The industry quickly added the drug to its reservoir of home remedies, touting it as helpful not only for everything from alcoholism to venereal disease but also as a cure for addiction to other patent medicines. Since the new tonics contained substantial amounts of cocaine, they did indeed make users feel better, at least initially, thus spiriting the patent-medicine industry into its golden age of popularity.

THE PECULIAR LEGACY OF BAYER LABORATORIES

Research into the mysteries of opium during the nineteenth century led not only to Serturner's discovery of morphine in 1806 but to the discovery of more than two dozen other alkaloids, including codeine, in 1831. Yet more importantly, in an 1874 issue of the *Journal of the Chemical Society,* British chemist C. R. A. Wright described a series of experiments he had carried out to determine the effect of combining various acids with morphine. Wright produced a series of new morphinelike compounds, including what became known in the scientific literature as *diacetylmorphine.*[21]

The discovery of both codeine and diacetylmorphine had been the outgrowth of an enduring search for more effective substitutes for morphine. This interest stemmed not only from the painkilling qualities of opiate drugs but also from their sedative effects on the respiratory system. Wright's work, however, went for the most part unnoticed. Some 24 years later, though, in 1898, pharmacologist Heinrich Dreser reported on a series of experiments he had conducted with diacetylmorphine for Friedrich Bayer and Company of Elberfeld, Germany, noting that the drug was highly effective in the treatment of coughs, chest pains, and the discomforts associated with pneumonia and tuberculosis.[22] Dreser's commentary received immediate notice, for it had come at a time when antibiotics were still unknown, and pneumonia and tuberculosis were among the leading causes of death. He claimed that diacetylmorphine had a stronger sedative effect on respiration than either morphine or codeine, that therapeutic relief came quickly, and that the potential for a fatal overdose was almost nil. In response to such favorable reports, Bayer and Company began marketing diacetylmorphine, under the trade name of *Heroin*—so named from the German *heroisch,* meaning heroic and powerful.

Although Bayer's Heroin was promoted as a sedative for coughs and as a chest and lung medicine, it was advocated by some as a treatment for morphine addiction. This situation seems to have arisen from three

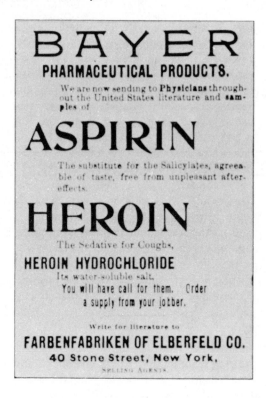

somewhat-related phenomena. The *first* was the belief that Heroin was nonaddicting. As one physician wrote in the *New York Medical Journal* in 1900:

> Habituation [with Heroin] has been noted in a small percentage of the cases. All observers are agreed, however, that none of the patients suffer in any way from this habituation, and that none of the symptoms which are so characteristic of chronic morphinism have ever been observed. On the other hand, a large number of the reports refer to the fact that the same dose may be used for a long time without any habituation.[23]

Second, since the drug had a greater potency than that of morphine, only small dosages were required for the desired medical effects, thus reducing the potential for the rapid onset of addiction. And *third,* at the turn of the twentieth century, the medical community did not fully understand the

dynamics of cross dependence. *Cross dependence* refers to the phenomenon that among certain pharmacologically related drugs, physical dependence on one will carry over to all the others. As such, for the patient
suffering from the unpleasant effects of morphine withdrawal, the administration of Heroin would have the consequence of one or more doses of
morphine. The dependence was maintained and withdrawal disappeared,
the two combining to give the appearance of a "cure."

Given the endorsement of the medical community, with little mention
of its potential dangers, Heroin quickly found its way into routine medical therapeutics and over-the-counter patent medicines.

ROCK OIL, DURHAM'S PURE BEEF LARD, AND THE QUEST OF FRANCIS BURTON HARRISON

By the early years of the twentieth century, the steady progress of medical
science had provided physicians with a better understanding of the long-
term effects of the drugs they had been advocating. Sigmund Freud had
already recognized his poor judgment in the claims he had made about
cocaine, the addiction potential and abuse liability of morphine had been
well established, and the dependence-producing properties of Bayer's
Heroin were being noticed. Yet these drugs—cocaine, morphine, and
Heroin—often combined with alcohol, were still readily available from a
totally unregulated patent medicine industry. Not only were they unregulated, but many were highly potent as well. *Birney's Catarrah Cure*, for
example, was 4% cocaine. *Colonel Hoestetter's Bitters* had such a gener-
ous amount of C_2H_5OH (alcohol) in its formula "to preserve the medicine" that the fumes from just one tablespoonful fed through a gas
burner could maintain a bright flame for almost five minutes.

To these and others could be added even more quack medications,
which, even though not necessarily dangerous to the patient's health,
were pushed on the unsuspecting and gullible public by enterprising and
imaginative hucksters. Perhaps the most curious of these was Samuel M.
Kier's *Rock Oil*. During the better part of the nineteenth century, salt was
typically produced from brine drawn from deep wells. Occasionally, the
utility of such wells was ruined when a black oily substance known as
"petroleum" found its way into the underground reservoirs. One Kentucky businessman secured a number of these abandoned "ruined" salt
wells, formed the American Medical Oil Company, and sold hundreds of
thousands of bottles of the greasy brine as *American Oil*, advertising it as

an effective remedy for almost any ailment. But Kier, the profiteering son of a Pennsylvania salt manufacturer, was even more enterprising. When oil began to flow in quantity from his underground salt deposits, he initiated an active campaign by giving testimony to the wonderful medicinal virtues of *Petroleum, or Rock Oil; A Natural Remedy; Procured from a Well in Allegheny County, Pennsylvania; Four Hundred Feet Below the Earth's Surface.* Kier's salespeople, equipped with ornamented wagons and ready supplies of the wonder oil, brought the legendary "medicine show" to rural and urban America, selling millions of half-pint bottles along the way.[24]

For decades, however, the task of bringing about change in the medicine industry seemed to have few results. As early as the 1870s, while some physicians were actively cashing in on the gullibility of the patient population, others expressed their reservations in print. The medical writings, however, went unnoticed for the most part, for few Americans other than doctors or pharmacists read the medical journals. Newspapers, on the other hand, were a haven for the patent-medicine industry, and most producers of the dubious drugs made sure that they would remain so. They invented a "red clause" that would appear in advertising contracts. "It is mutually agreed," the red type would indicate, "that this Contract is void, if any law is enacted by your state restricting or prohibiting the manufacture or sale of proprietary medicines."[25] Thus, the newspaper reader saw one column after another of patent-medicine advertising, with almost no questioning of the drugs' medical efficacy.

With the new century came a more progressive climate of opinion and a greater willingness to speak out for reform. The American Medical Association purged its journal of questionable advertising; the AMA Council on Pharmacy and Chemistry investigated the patent medicine industry; state chemists undertook analyses of the remedies; and all pooled their findings and turned them over to lay reporters. Then the muckraking journalists took over. William Allen White's *Emporia* (Kansas) *Gazette* ignored the infamous "red clause" and hosted a series of articles that pointed out the hazards of self-medication with patent medicines. At the same time, the *Ladies' Home Journal* extended the attack to the remedies high in alcoholic content. Yet the most provocative effort was "The Great American Fraud," a long series of articles written by Samuel Hopkins Adams that began in 1905 in the pages of *Collier's* magazine. Wrote Adams in his opening essay:

> Gullible America will spend this year $75 million in the purchase of patent medicines. In consideration of this sum it will swallow huge quantities of alcohol, an appalling amount of

Collier's
THE NATIONAL WEEKLY

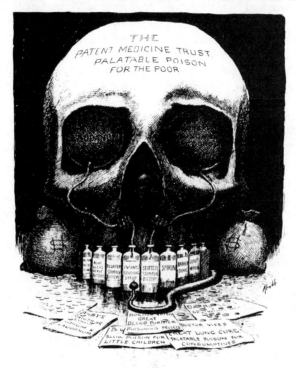

DEATH'S LABORATORY

Patent medicines are poisoning people throughout America to-day. Babies who cry are fed laudanum under the name of syrup. Women are led to injure themselves for life by reading in the papers about the meaning of backache. Young men and boys are robbed and contaminated by vicious criminals who lure them to their dens through seductive advertisement

DRAWN BY E. W. KEMBLE
[1]

opiates and narcotics, a wide assortment of varied drugs ranging from powerful and dangerous heart depressants to insidious liver stimulants; and, far in excess of other ingredients,
undiluted fraud. For fraud, exploited by the skillfulest of advertising bunco men, is the basis of the trade.[26]

In subsequent articles Adams exposed the institution of the "red clause"
and passionately described the powders and soothing syrups containing

heroin, opium, morphine, and cocaine as part of a shameful trade "that stupefies helpless babies and makes criminals of our young men and harlots of our young women."

Adams' commentaries in *Collier's* did not go unnoticed, but the final indictment leading to the downfall of the patent-medicine industry was totally unrelated to the problems described in "The Great American Fraud." On $500 supplied by a socialist periodical, a young novelist lived for seven weeks in the stockyards' meat-packing district of Chicago, gathering data among the welter of new emigrant nationalities who were struggling there to adjust to the New World. His name was Upton Sinclair, and his goal was to point out the evils of capitalist exploitation and to bring laborers under the wing of the Socialist party.

With the 1906 publication of Sinclair's account, *The Jungle*, public attention concentrated not on the scandalous miseries of the proletariat in capitalist America but on the lurid and nauseating details of Chicago's handling of the meat that the entire nation had been eating. It seems that deviled ham was actually minced tripe (stomach lining) dyed red, and much of the packers' lamb and mutton was goat. They kept down infestations of rats in the packing plants by baiting the unsuspecting rodents with poisoned bread. Then, dead rats, bread, and all typically went into the hoppers of oddments used for human consumption in sausages and other processed meats. And—what no reader could manage to forget—now and then an employee slipped on a wet floor, fell into a vat of boiling meat scraps, and "was overlooked for days, till all but his bones . . . had gone out to the world as *Durham's Pure Beef Lard*."

The Jungle shocked both Congress and America and represented the needed impetus for legislative reform. By mid-1906, the Pure Food and Drug Act was passed, prohibiting the interstate transportation of adulterated or misbranded food and drugs. The act brought about the decline of the patent-medicine industry because henceforth, the proportions of alcohol, opium, morphine, heroin, cocaine, and a number of other substances in each preparation had to be indicated. Thus, because of the mass media's having pointed out the negative effects of these ingredients, a number of the remedies lost their appeal. Moreover, it suddenly became difficult to market as a "cure" for morphine addiction a preparation that contained one or more other addicting drugs.

The new legislation merely imposed standards for quality, packaging, and labeling; it did not actually outlaw the use of cocaine and opiate drugs. The Harrison Act, sponsored by New York Representative Francis Burton Harrison and passed in 1914, ultimately served in that behalf and at the same time altered the nature of drug use in the United States once and for all.

The Harrison Act required all people who imported, manufactured, produced, compounded, sold, dispensed, or otherwise distributed co-caine and opiate drugs to register with the Treasury Department, pay spe-cial taxes, and keep records of all transactions. As such, it was a revenue code designed to exercise some measure of public control over drugs rather than to penalize the estimated 200,000 users of narcotics in the United States. In effect, however, penalization is specifically what occurred.

Certain provisions of the Harrison Act permitted physicians to pre-scribe, dispense, or administer narcotics to their patients for "legitimate medical purposes" and "in the course of professional practice." But how these two phrases were interpreted ultimately defined narcotics use as a crime.

On the one hand, the medical establishment held that addiction was a disease and that addicts were patients to whom drugs could be prescribed to alleviate the distress of withdrawal. On the other hand, the Treasury Department interpreted the Harrison Act to mean that a doctor's pre-scription for an addict was unlawful. The United States Supreme Court quickly laid the controversy to rest. In *Webb v. U.S.*,[27] decided in 1919, the Court held that it was not legal for a physician to prescribe narcotic drugs to an addict–patient for the purpose of maintaining his or her use and comfort. In *U.S. v. Behrman*,[28] decided three years later, this ruling went one step further by declaring that a *narcotic* prescription for an addict was unlawful, even if the drugs were prescribed as part of a cure program.* The impact of these decisions combined to make it almost im-possible for addicts to obtain drugs legally. In 1925 the Supreme Court emphatically reversed itself in *Lindner v. U.S.*,[29] disavowing the *Behrman* opinion and holding that addicts were entitled to medical care like other patients, but the ruling had almost no effect. By that time, physicians were unwilling to treat addicts under any circumstances, and a well-developed illegal drug marketplace had emerged to cater to the needs of the addict population.

SNOW PARTIES, GERMAN WAR PROPAGANDA, AND THE RISE OF THE CRIMINAL ADDICT

Many commentators on the history of drug use in the United States have argued that the Harrison Act snatched addicts from legitimate society and forced them into the underworld. As attorney Rufus King, a well-

---

* Although cocaine is not a narcotic, the Harrison Act and subsequent court decisions de-fined it as such. In much of the contemporary drug legislation at the federal level, cocaine is still listed as a narcotic.

known chronicler of American narcotics legislation, once described it, "Exit the addict–patient, enter the addict–criminal." [30] But this cause-and-effect interpretation tends to be a rather drastic oversimplification.

Without question, at the beginning of the twentieth century, most users of narcotics were members of legitimate society. In fact, the vast majority had first encountered the effects of narcotics through their family physician or local pharmacist or grocer. In other words, their addiction had been medically induced during the course of treatment for some other perceived ailment. Yet long before the Harrison Act had been passed, there were indications that this population of users had begun to shrink. [31] Agitation had existed in both the medical and religious communities against the haphazard use of narcotics, defining much of it as a moral disease. For many, the sheer force of social stigma and pressure served to alter their use of drugs. Similarly, the decline of the patent-medicine industry after the passage of the Pure Food and Drug Act was believed to have substantially reduced the number of narcotics and cocaine users. Moreover, by 1912, most state governments had enacted legislative controls over the dispensing and sales of narcotics. Thus, it is plausible to assert that the size of the drug-using population had started to decline years before the Harrison Act had become the subject of Supreme Court interpretation. Then too, the combined effects of stigma, social pressure, the Pure Food and Drug Act, and state controls had also served to create an underworld of drug users and black-market drugs. By 1914, a number of commentators had noted this change. Some, however melodramatically, targeted the subterranean economy of narcotics use:

> Several individuals have come to the conclusion that selling "dope" is a very profitable business. These individuals have sent their agents among the gangs frequenting our city corners, instructing them to make friends with the members and induce them to take the drug. Janitors, bartenders, and cabmen have also been employed to help sell the habit. The plan has worked so well that there is scarcely a poolroom in New York that may not be called a meeting place for dope fiends. The drug has been made up in candy and sold to school children. The conspiring individuals, being familiar with the habit-forming action of the drugs, believe that the increased number of "fiends" will create a larger demand for the drug, and in this way build up profitable business. [32]

By the latter part of the decade, other observers were noting that although the medically induced addict was still prominent, a new population had recently emerged.[33] It was an underworld population, composed principally of heroin and cocaine users who had initiated drug use as the result of associations with other criminals. Thus, it would appear that the emergence of the criminal addict was not simply the result of a cause-and-effect criminalization process—the Harrison Act's definition of narcotics use as criminal. Rather, it was likely the result of the effects of legislation *combined* with the creation of a new class of users who were already within the underworld.

Although accurate data on the incidence and prevalence of drug use have been available only recently, by the early 1920s readers of the popular media were confronted, almost on a daily basis, with how drug use, and particularly heroin use, had become a national epidemic. Estimates were placed as high as 5 million, with any number of explanations for the increased number of users. Some blamed it on the greed of drug traffickers, others on the inadequate personalities of the users. A few argued that it was a natural consequence of the Prohibition amendment.[34] Most observers generally agreed, however, that more legislation was the answer to the problem. As an editorial in the *Literary Digest* for June 10, 1922, stated:

> "Snow parties," which are said to have become so prevalent as to menace American civilization, will be made impossible by the Jones-Miller bill governing the manufacture, importation and exportation of habit-forming drugs, which has been passed by Congress and signed by President Harding. By striking at the source of supply, the bill goes to the root of the evil, and, in time, will eliminate it altogether.[35]

Snow, as the editorial suggested, referred to heroin and cocaine, and the Jones-Miller Act was a piece of federal legislation that set fines of up to $5,000 and imprisonment of up to 10 years for anyone involved in the unlawful importation of narcotics.

Even though the Jones-Miller Act had little impact, other than to further inflate the prices of heroin and morphine on the illicit drug marketplace, some people argued that the drug "epidemic" was a myth. One observer suggested that the exaggerated estimates were no more than German war propaganda. Referencing a rumor that those in charge of the draft during World War I would find no less than 500,000 addicts among the inductees, it was pointed out that of some 3.5 million men examined, only 3,284 were found to be addicts. By applying that ratio to 1920 census figures, it was concluded that 100,000 was likely a more accurate estimate, and that drug addiction had actually declined during the previous two decades.[36] Other data tended to support this seemingly outrageous conclusion. In 1924, Dr. Lawrence Kolb and Dr. A. G. Du Mez of the U.S. Public Health Service, after a careful examination of all the available survey data on drug use, estimated that there were probably only 110,000 addicts in the United States at the end of 1922, reflecting a considerable decline since the turn of the century.[37]

Whatever the correct figures, all agreed that narcotics use was indeed a problem in the United States. Where little agreement existed, however, was in the proper methods for handling it. Throughout the balance of the 1920s and the decade of the 1930s, three points of view dominated. The medical establishment argued that addiction was a physical disease and should be treated as such; the law-enforcement establishment saw addiction as a criminal tendency and favored harsh punishment for the sake of societal protection and deterrence; and then there was the political establishment. It believed that addiction could be simply legislated out of existence if enough comprehensive laws were passed. Each establishment worked in pursuit of its own position. Treatment facilities were opened, addicts were arrested and imprisoned, and new legislation was passed. By the early 1940s, narcotic addiction had all but disappeared in the United States. But it was not the result of medical, enforcement, or legislative efforts. World War II had intervened to cut off the supplies of opium from Asia and had interrupted the trafficking routes from Europe. As an editorial in *Time* put it in 1942, "The war is probably the best thing that ever happened to U.S. drug addicts."[38]

THE EVIL WEED OF THE FIELDS
AND RIVER BEDS AND ROADSIDES

The national concern over the use of narcotics during the 1930s was not focused solely on heroin, for another substance was considered by some to represent an even greater evil. One might expect that it was cocaine, since the drug's stimulant effects had been promoted in the United States well before the introduction of Bayer's Heroin. But this was not the case. After the passage of the Pure Food and Drug Act in 1906, cocaine use moved underground to the netherworlds of the jazz scene and the bohemia of the avant-garde. There it remained for decades, so much so that the Treasury Department's Bureau of Narcotics, a federal agency that has been prone to gross exaggeration, concluded in 1939 that, "The use of cocaine in the illicit traffic continues to be so small as to be without significance."[39] No, not cocaine, but rather the more insidious *marijuana,* alternatively called the "devil drug," "assassin of youth," and "weed of madness."

Marijuana, typically referred to a century ago as "cannabis" or "hashish," was introduced to the American public in essentially the same manner as were opium, morphine, cocaine, and heroin. A derivative of the Indian hemp plant *Cannabis sativa,* the drug appeared among the patent medicines hawked from the tailgates of medicine show wagons and was sold as a cure for depression, convulsions, hysteria, insanity, mental retardation, and impotence. Moreover, during the late 1800s such well-known pharmaceutical companies as Parke-Davis and Squibb produced tincture of cannabis for the family pharmacist to dispense. As a medicinal agent, however, the drug quickly fell into disfavor. Because of its insolubility, it could not be injected, and taken orally it was slow and generally ineffective. Moreover, its potency was variable, making dosage standardization difficult. Yet as a recreational drug, marijuana had its devotees. By the middle of the 1880s, every major American city had its clandestine hashish clubs catering to a rather well-to-do clientele.[40]

At the beginning of the twentieth century, what was referred to in Mexico as "marijuana" (also *marihuana* and *mariguana*) began to appear in New Orleans and a number of the Texas border towns. Having been used in South America and Central America for quite some time, it was a substance less potent than the hashish that was first smoked in the underground clubs decades earlier. Whereas hashish is the resinous extract of the hemp plant, marijuana is composed of the hemp plant's dried leaves, stems, and flowering tops.*

By 1920, the use of marijuana had become visible among members of minority groups—blacks in the South and "wetback" Mexicans in the Southwest. Given the social and political climate of the period, it is not at all surprising that the use of the drug became a matter of immediate concern. The agitation for reform that had resulted in the passage of the Harrison Act and the Pure Food and Drug Act was still active, and the movement for national prohibition of alcohol was at its peak. Moreover, not only was marijuana an "intoxicant of blacks and wetbacks" that might have a corrupting influence on white society, but it was considered

---

* The etymological roots of *marijuana* have been debated at length and still remain unresolved. Some maintain that the word comes from what the Aztec Indians referred to as "mallihuan," a term that imparted the idea of a substance that took possession of the user. A second position holds that *marijuana* is a corruption of the Portuguese "maranguango," meaning "intoxicating."

The Jaws of Death

A slinking thing with hellish sting,
The reptile known as Dope.
Its poison breath is living death
Beyond the pale of hope,
And in the blight of endless night
Its countless victims grope.

In stricken homes the reptile roams
On hearthstones bare and bleak.
Ambition dies in youthful eyes,
Slain by the noxious reek.
For Dope is strong and prospers long
Because the laws are weak.
By George E. Phair.

Atlanta Georgian, 27 February 1935

particularly dangerous because of its *alien* (spelled "Mexican") and un-American origins.

Through the early 1930s, state after state enacted antimarijuana laws, usually instigated by lurid newspaper articles depicting the madness and horror attributed to the drug's use. Even the prestigious *New York Times,* with its claim of "All the News That's Fit to Print," helped to reinforce the growing body of beliefs surrounding marijuana use. In an article head-lined "Mexican Family Go Insane," and datelined Mexico City, July 6, 1927, the *Times* reported:

A widow and her four children have been driven insane by eat-ing the Marihuana plant, according to doctors, who say that there is no hope of saving the children's lives and that the mother will be insane for the rest of her life.

The tragedy occurred while the body of the father, who had been killed, was still in a hospital.

The mother was without money to buy other food for the children, whose ages range from 3 to 15, so they gathered some herbs and vegetables growing in the yard for their dinner. Two hours after the mother and children had eaten the plants, they were stricken. Neighbors, hearing outbursts of crazed laughter, rushed to the house to find the entire family insane.

Examination revealed that the narcotic marihuana was growing among the garden vegetables.[41]

In other reports, the link between the antimarijuana sentiment and prejudice was apparent. On January 27, 1929, the *Montana Standard* reported on the progress of a bill that amended the state's general narcotic law to include marijuana:

There was fun in the House Health Committee during the week when the Marihuana bill came up for consideration. Marihuana is Mexican opium, a plant used by Mexicans and cultivated for sale by Indians. "When some beet field peon takes a few rares of this stuff," explained Dr. Fred Fulsher of Mineral County, "he thinks he has just been elected president of Mexico so he starts to execute all of his political enemies. . . ." Everybody laughed and the bill was recommended for passage.[42]

Although marijuana is neither Mexican opium nor a narcotic of any kind, it was perceived as such by a small group of legislators, newspaper editors, and concerned citizens who were pressuring Washington for federal legislation against the drug. Their demands were almost immediately heard by Harry J. Anslinger, the then recently installed Commissioner of the Treasury Department's Bureau of Narcotics in 1930. Whether Anslinger was simply a Neanderthal ultraright-wing conservative who truly believed marijuana to be a threat to the future of American civilization, or an astute government bureaucrat who viewed the marijuana issue as a mechanism for elevating himself and the Bureau of Narcotics to national prominence, is not fully clear. More likely, it was some combination of the two, and what followed, given what is now known about marijuana, Anslinger's crusade appears to have been the ravings of a madman.

Using the mass media as his forum, Anslinger described marijuana as a Frankenstein drug that was stalking American youth. In an issue of *American Magazine* he wrote, for example:

> The sprawled body of a young girl lay crushed on the sidewalk the other day after a plunge from the fifth story of a Chicago apartment house. Everyone called it suicide, but actually it was murder. The killer was a narcotic known to America as marijuana, and to history as hashish. It is a narcotic used in the form of cigarettes, comparatively new to the United States and as dangerous as a coiled rattlesnake. . . . [43]

Then there was Anslinger's "gore file," a collection of the most heinous cases, most with only the flimsiest of substantiation, that graphically depicted the insane violence that marijuana use engendered. For example, again from *American Magazine:*

> An entire family was murdered by a youthful addict in Florida. When officers arrived at the home, they found the youth staggering about in a human slaughterhouse. With an ax he had killed his father, mother, two brothers, and a sister. He seemed to be in a daze. . . . He had no recollection of having committed the multiple crime. *The officers knew him ordinarily as a sane, rather quiet young man; now he was pitifully crazed.* They sought the reason. The boy said that he had been in the habit of smoking something which youthful friends called "muggles," a childish name for marihuana. [44]

Much of the "gore file" also touched on the interracial fears of white society. For example:

> Colored students at the Univ. of Minn. partying with female students (white), smoking [marijuana] and getting their sympathy with stories of racial persecution. Result pregnancy.

> Two Negroes took a girl fourteen years old and kept her for two days under the influence of marihuana. Upon recovery she was found to be suffering from syphilis. [45]

As the result of Anslinger's crusade, on August 2, 1937, the Marijuana Tax Act was signed into law, classifying the scraggly tramp of the vegetable world as a narcotic and placing it under essentially the same controls as the Harrison Act had done with opium and coca products.*

IN SEARCH OF THE ROAD TO H

The crusade against marijuana during the 1930s had attributed to drug taking a level of wickedness that could only have been matched by the Victorian imagery of masturbation and its consequences. The 1940s all but ignored the drug problem, principally because if it were indeed a "problem," it was an invisible one—hardly a topic that should divert attention away from the events of a world at war. Then came the 1950s, a time when everything seemed right but in many instances was quite wrong.

Within three years after the close of World War II, the opium–heroin trafficking networks from Southeast Asia and Europe had been reestablished, and illicit narcotics once again began to reach American ports. During the opening years of the 1950s, the prevailing image of drug use was one of heroin addiction on the streets of the urban ghetto. As summarized by the distinguished author and journalist Max Lerner in his celebrated work *America as a Civilization:*

> As a case in point we may take the known fact of the prevalence of reefer-and-dope addiction in Negro areas. This is essentially explained in terms of poverty, slum living, and broken families, yet it would be easy to show the lack of drug addiction among other ethnic groups where the same conditions apply.[46]

Lerner went on to explain that addiction among blacks was due to the adjustment problems associated with their rapid movement from a depressed status to the improved standards and freedoms of the era. Yet

---

* For decades after the passage of the Maijuana Tax Act, Anslinger continued to write about the evils of marijuana, almost as if he had to justify the wisdom of the law. See, for example, Harry J. Anslinger and William F. Tompkins, *The Traffic in Narcotics* (New York: Funk & Wagnalls, 1953; Harry J. Anslinger and Will Ousler, *The Murderers: The Shocking Story of the Narcotics Gangs* (New York: Farrar, Straus, and Cudahy, 1961).

Lerner's interpretation was hardly a correct one, and not only about "reefer addiction" but also about the prevalence of drug abuse in other populations—rich and poor, white and black, young and old.

In the popular media a somewhat more detailed portrait of the problem was offered. *Time, Life, Newsweek,* and other major periodicals spoke of how teenagers, jaded on marijuana, had found greater thrills in heroin. For most, the pattern of initiation had been the same. They began with marijuana, the use of which had become a fad in the ghetto. Then, enticed in schoolyards by brazen Mafia pushers dressed in dark suits, white ties, and wide-brimmed hats, their first dose of heroin was given free. By then, however, it was too late; their fate had been sealed; they were already addicted.[47] Or as the saying went, "It's so good, don't even try it once!"

Hollywood offered a somewhat different image of the situation in the 1955 United Artists' release of *The Man with the Golden Arm*. The film was somewhat controversial in its day, for the Otto Preminger production had touched upon a topic that most Americans felt should remain in the ghetto where it belonged. In its actual content, like most films of the comfortable, conservative, prosperous, classless, sexless, and consensual paradise of the 1950s, it reflected majority attitudes and served to confirm established visions of reality. Cast in the role of a would-be professional musician, singer–actor Frank Sinatra was the hero of the story. Plagued by the evils of heroin addiction, he was unable to get his life together. Finally, however, through the help and understanding of his girlfriend Molly (portrayed by Kim Novak), he was saved from a life of pathetic degradation. As in the case of other media images of the drug scene, *The Man with the Golden Arm* offered only a contorted view, failing to probe even the most basic issues.

Within the scientific community, much of the literature and research was equally bizarre. As might be expected, most explanations of drug addiction focused on heroin in the ghetto. Young addicts were believed to be either psychotic or neurotic casualties for whom drugs provided relief from anxiety and a means for withdrawing from the stress of daily struggle in the slum. Among the more celebrated studies of the period was psychologist Isidor Chein's *The Road to H*. Concerning youthful addiction in New York City, Chein concluded:

> The evidence indicated that all addicts suffer from deep-rooted personality disorders. Although psychiatric diagnoses are apt to vary, a particular set of symptoms seems to be common to most juvenile addicts. They are not able to enter into prolonged, close, friendly relations with either peers or adults;

they have difficulties in assuming a masculine role; they are frequently overcome by a sense of futility, expectations of failure, and general depression; they are easily frustrated and made anxious, and they find frustrations and anxiety intolerable.[48]

By focusing on such maladies as "weak ego functioning," "defective superego," and "inadequate masculine identification," what Chein was suggesting was the notion of a psychological predisposition to drug use—in other words, an *addiction-prone personality.* The text went on to imply that the series of predispositions could be traced to the addict's family experiences. If the youth received too much love or not enough, or if the parents were overwhelming in terms of their affection or indulgence, then the child would develop inadequately. As a result, the youth would likely be unable to withstand pain and discomfort, to cope with the complexities of life in the neighborhood and community, to assess reality correctly, and to feel competent around others of more varied social experiences. Chein concluded that this type of youth would be more prone to trying drugs than others of more conventional family backgrounds.

The prevailing portrait of addiction in the scientific community, then, was one of passive adaptation to stress. Drugs allowed the user to experience fulfillment and the satiation of physical and emotional needs. This general view was also supported by sociological attempts to explain the broader concepts of deviance and delinquency. Given this predisposition, consider what became known in the literature as the "double-failure" hypothesis.[49] According to sociologists Richard A. Cloward and Lloyd E. Ohlin, double failures were ghetto youths who were unable to succeed in either the gang subculture or the wider legitimate culture. They embraced drugs, in turn, as a way of finding a place for themselves in society.

For those who lived in the ghetto, worked in the ghetto, took drugs in the ghetto, policed the ghetto, or in some other fashion actively observed or participated in ghetto life, the "addiction-prone personality," "double-failure," and other escapist theories of addiction were found humorous. On the contrary, the conduct of most addicts was anything but an escape from life. Much of their time was spent in drug-seeking behaviors, in meaningful activities and relationships on the street centers surrounding the economic institutions of heroin distribution. As the late urban anthropologist Edward Preble once put it, they were "taking care of business:"

The brief moments of euphoria after each administration of a small amount of heroin constitute a small fraction of their daily lives. The rest of the time they are aggressively pursuing a career that is exciting, challenging, adventurous, and rewarding. They are always on the move and must be alert, flexible, and resourceful. The surest way to identify heroin users in a slum neighborhood is to observe the way people walk. The heroin user walks with a fast, purposeful stride, as if he is late for an important appointment—indeed, he is. He is *hustling* [robbing or stealing], trying to sell stolen goods, avoiding the police, looking for a heroin dealer with a good *bag* [the street retail unit of heroin], coming back from *copping* [buying heroin], looking for a safe place to take the drug, or looking for someone who *beat* [cheated] him—among other things.[50]

"TIMOTHY LEARY'S DEAD . . ."

In many ways the 1950s had been a decade of waste. Caught up in a belief that the good life had arrived, Americans rushed to the suburbs to escape urban congestion. Throughout the country, tract-built developments sprouted as landscapes were bulldozed flat. This mass migration to the suburbs left the cities to deteriorate. An overwhelming reliance on the automobile, brought about by a sudden romance with the family car and the construction of a 40,000-mile interstate highway system, resulted in a breakdown in mass transportation and, in turn, pollution and congestion. These problems were most deeply felt in the central cities where the poor had been left behind.

Another problem was the racism that had persisted from earlier years. In the growing prosperity of the 1950s, blacks continued to face the legacy of Jim Crow. In the South, particularly, they were repeatedly the victims of mob murders, lynchings, and all forms of social disenfranchisement.

To compound these problems, American youth faced an enforcement of conformity, a transparency of sexual morals, and a set of cultural prescriptions and proscriptions that stressed achievement, prejudice, waste, compliance, and consensus, yet failed to explain or recognize the confusion and absurdity of it all. As a result of such contradictions, a teenage ethic emerged that made serious negative value judgments about the nature and meaning of life. As social critic Kenneth Rexroth warned in an early issue of *Evergreen Review:*

> Listen You—do you really think your kids are like bobby soxers in those wholesome Coca-Cola ads? Don't you know that

across the table from you at dinner sits somebody who looks on you as an enemy who is planning to kill him in the immediate future? Don't you know that if you were to say to your English class, "It is raining," they would take it for granted that you were a liar? Don't you know they never tell you nothing? that they can't? that . . . they simply can't get through, can't, and won't even try anymore to communicate? Don't you know this, really? If you don't, you're in for a terrible awakening.[51]

The enforced conformity, youth rebellion, racism, cultural values that had canonized both consumption and waste, and the numerous other problems in American society that had been festering during the 1940s and 1950s seemed to merge during the following decade, resulting in one of the most revolutionary periods in recent history. The 1960s was a time characterized by civil-rights movements, political assassinations, campus and antiwar protests, and ghetto riots.

Among the more startling events was the drug revolution of the 1960s. The use of drugs seemed to have leapt from the more marginal zones of society to the very mainstream of community life. No longer were "drugs" limited to the inner cities and half-worlds of the jazz scene and the underground bohemian protocultures. Rather, they had become suddenly and dramatically apparent among members of the adolescent middle-class and young-adult populations of rural and urban America. By the close of the decade, commentators on the era were maintaining that ours was "the addicted society," that through drugs millions had become "seekers" of "instant enlightenment," and that drug taking and drug seeking would persist as continuing facts of American social life.[52]

In retrospect, what were then considered the logical causes of the new drug phenomenon now seem less clear. A variety of changes in the fabric of American life had occurred during those years, which undoubtedly had profound implications for social consciousness and behavior. Notably, the revolution in the technology and handling of drugs that had begun during the 1950s was of sufficient magnitude to justify the designation of the 1960s as "a new chemical age." Recently compounded psychotropic agents were enthusiastically introduced and effectively promoted, with the consequence of exposing the national consciousness to an impressive catalog of chemical temptations—sedatives, tranquilizers, stimulants, antidepressants, analgesics, and hallucinogens—which could offer fresh inspiration, as well as simple and immediate relief from fear, anxiety, tension, frustration, and boredom.[53]

Concomitant with this emergence of a new chemical age, a new youth ethos had become manifest, one characterized by widely celebrated generational disaffection, a prejudicial dependence on the self and the peer group for value orientation, a critical view of how the world was being run, and mistrust for an "establishment" drug policy whose "facts" and "warnings" ran counter to reported peer experiences. On this latter point, it is no wonder that such mistrust had developed. Many teenagers and young adults across the nation had become recreational users of marijuana. For most, the psychological reactions they experienced included euphoria, fragmentation of thought, laughter, spatial and temporal distortions, heightened sensuality, and increased sociability. A few experienced fear, anxiety, and panic. Yet what most of the brokers of drug education were saying to users and their peers was something totally different—something reminiscent of Anslinger's pontifications during the 1930s' era of reefer madness. In fact, in the early 1960s Anslinger was still saying essentially the same things about marijuana:

> Those who are accustomed to habitual use of the drug are said eventually to develop a delirious rage after its administration during which they are temporarily, at least, irresponsible and prone to commit violent crimes. The prolonged use of this narcotic is said to produce mental deterioration. . . .
>
> Much of the most irrational juvenile violence and killing that has written a new chapter of shame and tragedy is traceable directly to this hemp intoxication.[54]

With statements such as these coming from the Commissioner of Narcotics, drug educators, and parents—statements that for the most part were contrary to experience and untrue—it is no wonder that the youth of the day turned deaf ears to the antidrug messages.

Whatever the ultimate causes, America's younger generations, or at least noticeable segments of them, had embraced drugs. The drug scene had become the arena of "happening" America; "turning on" to drugs for relaxation and to share friendship and love seemed to have become commonplace. And the prophet—the "high priest" as he called himself—of the new chemical age was a psychology instructor at Harvard University's Center for Research in Human Personality, Dr. Timothy Leary.

The saga of Timothy Leary had its roots, not at Harvard in the 1960s, but in Basel, Switzerland, just before the beginning of World War II. It was there, in 1938, that Dr. Albert Hoffman of Sandoz Research Laboratories first isolated a new chemical compound which he called D-lysergic acid diethylamide. More popularly known as *LSD*, it was cast aside in his laboratory where, for five years, it remained unappreciated, its properties awaiting discovery. On April 16, 1943, after absorbing some LSD through the skin of his fingers, Hoffman began to hallucinate. In his diary he explained the effect:

> With closed eyes, multihued, metamorphizing, fantastic images overwhelmed me. . . . Sounds were transposed into visual sensations so that from each tone or noise a comparable colored picture was evoked, changing in form and color kaleidoscopically.[55]

Hoffman had experienced the first LSD "trip."

Dr. Humphrey Osmond of the New Jersey Neuropsychiatric Institute neologized a new name for LSD. "Psychedelic," he called it, meaning mind-expanding. But outside of the scientific community, LSD was generally unknown—even at the start of the 1960s. This was quickly changed by Leary, and his colleague at Harvard, Dr. Richard Alpert. They began experimenting with the drug—on themselves, and with colleagues, students, artists, writers, clergymen, and volunteer prisoners. Although their adventures with LSD had earned them dismissals from Harvard by 1963, their message had been heard, and LSD had achieved its reputation. Their messages had been numerous and shocking to the political establishment and to hundreds of thousands of mothers and fathers across the nation.

In *The Realist,* a radical periodical of the 1960s, Leary commented:

> I predict that psychedelic drugs will be used in all schools in the near future as educational devices—not only marijuana and LSD, to teach kids how to use their sense organs and other cellular equipment effectively—but new and more powerful psychochemicals. . . . [56]

Elsewhere he wrote of the greatest fear that might be generated by psychedelic drug use, what he called "ontological addiction":

> . . . the terror of finding a realm of experience, a new dimension of reality so pleasant that one will not want to return. This fear is based on the unconscious hunch . . . that normal consciousness is a form of sleepwalking and that somewhere there exists a form of awakeness, of reality from which one would not want to return.[57]

And then, perhaps most frightening of all to the older generation, were Leary's comments to some 15,000 cheering San Francisco youths on the afternoon of March 26, 1967. As a modern-day Pied Piper, Leary told his audience:

> *Turn on* to the scene, *tune in* to what's happening; and *drop out*—of high school, college, grade school . . . follow me, the hard way.[58]

Leary's downfall came shortly thereafter, the result of conviction and imprisonment on drug-trafficking charges, followed by a period of time as a fugitive in Algeria and Afghanistan after a prison escape. But his demise was eulogized. At the opening of "House of Four Doors" on the album *In Search of a Lost Chord,* the Moody Blues sang: Timothy Leary's dead . . . he's on the outside, looking in." *

The hysteria over Leary, LSD, and the other psychedelic substances had been threefold. First, the drug scene was especially frightening to mainstream society because it reflected a willful rejection of rationality, order, and predictability. Second, there was the stigmatized association of drug use with antiwar protests and antiestablishment, long-haired, unwashed, radical "hippie" LSD users. And third, there were the drugs' psychic effects, the reported "bad trips" that seemed to border on mental illness. Particularly in the case of LSD, the rumors of how it could "blow one's mind" became legion. One story told of a youth, high on the drug, taking a swan dive in front of a truck moving at 70 mph. Another spoke of two "tripping" teenagers who stared directly into the sun until they were permanently blinded. A third described how LSD's effects on the chromosomes resulted in fetal abnormalities. The stories were never documented and were probably untrue. What *were* true, however, were the reports of LSD "flashbacks." Occurring with only a small percentage of the users, individuals would reexperience the LSD-induced state days, weeks, and sometimes months after the original "trip," without having taken the drug again.

Despite the lurid reports, as it turned out, LSD was not in fact widely used on a regular basis beyond a few social groups that were fully dedicated to drug experiences. In fact, the psychedelic substances had quickly earned reputations as being dangerous and unpredictable, and most

---

* Actually, Leary was not quite dead. By 1976 he had straightened out his legal problems and had become a free man. Since that time he has been "a cheerleader for scientific optimism," as he once put it. With the onset of the 1980s, Leary joined the ranks of the most highly paid speakers on the college lecture circuit, often debating G. Gordon Liddy of Watergate fame. Quite curiously, Liddy was once his nemesis, having organized a raid in 1966 that led to one of Leary's early drug arrests.

people avoided them. By the close of the 1960s, all hallucinogenic drugs had been placed under strict legal control, and the number of users was minimal.[59]

FROM BLACK BEAUTY TO KING KONG

Throughout the 1960s heroin remained the most feared drug, and by the close of the decade estimates as to the size of the addict population exceeded 500,000. Yet despite the hysteria about the rising tide of heroin addiction, LSD and the youth rebellion, Timothy Leary and the psychedelic age, and the growing awareness of drug abuse along the Main Streets of white America, no one really knew how many people were actually using drugs. In fact, the estimates of the incidence and prevalence of marijuana, heroin, psychedelic, and other drug use were, at the very best, only vague and impressionistic. Although the reliability of political polling had long since demonstrated that the social sciences indeed had the tools to measure the dimensions of the "drug problem," no one at any time throughout the 1960s had gone so far as to count drug users in a systematic way. Yet, several indicators existed. Studies were suggesting that the annual production of barbiturate drugs exceeded 1 million pounds, the equivalent of 24 one-and-one-half-grain doses for every man, woman, and child in the nation—enough to kill each person twice.[60] And for amphetamines and amphetamine-like compounds, the manufacturing figures came to some 50 doses per U.S. resident each year, with half the production reaching the illicit marketplace.[61]

The *amphetamines* were not new drugs, but their appearance on the street had been relatively recent. Having been synthesized in Germany during the 1880s, their first use among Americans had not come until World War II. Thousands of servicemen in all of the military branches had been issued Benzedrine, Dexedrine, and a variety of other types as a matter of course to relieve their fatigue and anxiety. After the war, amphetamine drugs became more readily available, and they were put to a wider assortment of uses—students cramming for exams, truck drivers and others who needed to be alert for extended periods of time, in weight-control programs, and as nasal decongestants. Yet as strong stimulants with pharmacological effects similar to those of cocaine, in time they became popular drugs of abuse.

As the 1970s began, the first item on the government's agenda for drug reform was the amphetamines, with Indiana Senator Birch Bayh conducting hearings. There was a parade of witnesses, and the worst fears about the drugs were confirmed—or so it seemed.[62] Bayh and his committee heard the horror stories of the "speed freaks" who injected amphetamine and methamphetamine, who stalked the city streets suffering from paranoid delusions and exhibiting episodes of violent behavior at the onset of their psychotic states. They heard, too, of the hundreds, thousands, and perhaps hundreds of thousands of children and teenagers stoned on "ups," "bennies," "pinks," "purple hearts," "black beauties," and "King Kong pills." By that time, systematic surveys of the general population had finally begun, with the first, conducted in New York, empirically documenting that amphetamine use and abuse were indeed widespread.[63]

Almost immediately, new legislation was proposed by the Bayh committee and pushed through by the Senate. Tighter controls were placed on the prescribing and distribution of amphetamines, and legitimate production was ultimately cut by 90%. In so doing, it was thought that the drug problem, at least in terms of the dangerous amphetamines, would be measurably solved.

But suddenly something seemed to go terribly wrong. The Senate, oftentimes a sacred repository of culture lag, in its infinite wisdom had totally ignored, or at least misunderstood, the very nature of the youth drug scene. True, many youths *were* getting stoned on amphetamines. And true, there *were* speed freaks out on the streets of America committing random acts of violence. But the actual numbers of amphetamine and methamphetamine "freaks" were comparatively few, and the frequency of their violent acts was even less. Moreover, the number of youths who had actually become dysfunctional as a result of amphetamine abuse was hardly what any sophisticated researcher or clinician would have called an epidemic. Most importantly, what the Senate missed was the fact that the amphetamine-using youth of America were "drug-use habituated." That is, it was not *amphetamines* that were important to them but drugs, *any* drugs. So, when the amphetamines dried up on the streets, the youthful users simply went to another widely available drug. They chose *methaqualone*—"sopors," "ludes," and "Captain Quaalude." Thus, one "drug problem" was simply replaced by another. But this time, rather than arriving in high school classrooms "stoned," users began showing up in hospital emergency rooms and county morgues.

Meanwhile, the heroin epidemic continued.

THE MANY LIVES OF CAPTAIN QUAALUDE

The U.S. Senate was not the *real* instigator of the methaqualone problem, for the crisis that followed was one in which everyone seemed to be at fault—the pharmaceutical industry, the medical profession, the Food and Drug Administration, the federal narcotics establishment, and the media. In 1972, the *Washington Post* focused the blame somewhat differently:

> The methaqualone boom should make an interesting case study in future medical textbooks: How skillful public relations and advertising created a best-seller—and helped cause a medical crisis in the process.[64]

Methaqualone was initially synthesized in India during the early 1950s as a possible antimalarial agent. When its *hypnotic* (sleep-producing) properties were discovered later in the decade, many hoped that as a *nonbarbiturate* methaqualone might be a safer alternative to the barbiturates.[65]

Barbiturate drugs had been available for the better part of the century. As potent central nervous system depressants, they were the drugs of choice for inducing sleep. Depending on the dosage level, they were also in common use for anesthesia, sedation, and the treatment of tension, anxiety, and convulsions. However, the barbiturates had their problems. They were widely abused for the "high" they could engender. Moreover, they produced addiction after chronic use, were life-threatening upon withdrawal, and could cause fatal overdoses—particularly when mixed with alcohol.

As an alternative to barbiturates, methaqualone was introduced in England in 1959, and in Germany and Japan in 1960. Despite extensive medical reports of abuse in these three countries, the drug was introduced in the United States under the trade names of Quaalude, Sopor, Parest, Somnafac, and later, Mequin. Although methaqualone was a prescription drug, the federal drug establishment decided that since there was no evidence of an abuse potential, it need not be monitored, and the number of times a prescription could be refilled need not be restricted. This, combined with an advertising campaign that emphasized that the drug was a "safe alternative to barbiturates," led to the assumption by the medical profession, the lay population, and the media that methaqualone was nonaddicting. Even the prestigious *AMA Drug Evaluations,* as late as 1973, stated no more than "long-term use of larger than therapeutic doses may result in psychic and physical dependence."[66]

The most effective advertising campaign was launched by William H. Rorer pharmaceuticals. Given the success of the catchy double-a in their antacid Maalox, they named their methaqualone product Quaalude. Their advertising emphasized that it was a nonbarbiturate. Free samples of Quaalude were shipped throughout the country, and physicians began overprescribing the drug.

Looking for a new and safe "high," users sought out methaqualone, and the drug quickly made its way to the street. Rather than a safe alternative to whatever they had been taking previously, street users actually had a drug with the same addiction liability and lethal potential as the barbiturates. What they experienced was a pleasant sense of well-being, an increased pain threshold, and a loss of muscle coordination. The "high" was reputed to enhance sexual performance. Although no actual evidence confirmed that effect, it is likely that the depressant effects of the drug in men were serving to desensitize the nerve endings in the penis, thus permitting intercourse for longer periods without climaxing. Moreover, like alcohol, the drug was acting on the central cortex of the brain to release normal inhibitions. Also common was "luding out"—attaining an intoxicated state rapidly by mixing the drug with wine.

In early 1973, after reports of widespread abuse, acute reactions, and fatal overdoses, Birch Bayh convened more Senate hearings, the problems with methaqualone were fully aired, and rigid controls over the drug were put into force.[67] Shortly thereafter, the abuse of methaqualone began to decline.*

"EVERYBODY SMOKES DOPE"

While legislators, clinicians, and drug educators struggled with the methaqualone problem, marijuana use grew apace. From 1960 through the end of the decade, the number of Americans who had used marijuana at least once had increased from a few hundred thousand to an estimated 8 million. Given such widespread use, in 1969 the government launched

---

* For those who missed the first wave of methaqualone abuse, another began in 1978 and persisted into the early 1980s. In 1980, some 4 tons of the drug were produced legally in the United States, and it is estimated that another 100 million tons were smuggled in, principally from Colombia. In 1982, when tight restrictions were placed on the importation of methaqualone powder from West Germany to Colombia, trafficking in the drug declined substantially. In 1984, all legal manufacturing of methaqualone was halted in the United States, and since that time the abuse of the drug has been, at best, modest.

an elaborate and determined effort to cut down the flow of marijuana into the United States. Known as "Operation Intercept," and based on the belief that Mexico was and would remain the primary source of marijuana for Americans, the effort was designed principally to tighten inspections of vehicles coming across the border from Mexico and to intercept smuggled drugs.[68]

Set for September 21, 1969, Operation Intercept was timed for the fall marijuana harvest. Along the 2,500-mile-long border, on land as well as in the sea and air, the surveillance network was intense, particularly so at the border crossings where vehicles and passengers could be individually searched. Within an hour after it all started, automobile traffic began to pile up as each vehicle waited to go through inspection. In no time, the backups were three miles long, and in some places they extended to six miles. Members of Congress and other officials immediately began to receive complaints—from Mexico because the effort was hurting tourism, from merchants on both sides of the border because it was affecting business, and from the American travelers who had spent many extra hours waiting to return home.

Twenty days later Operation Intercept was abandoned. Although the government deemed it a success, there had been no major seizures of marijuana. In fact, during the three weeks of the operation the actual seizures averaged 150 pounds per day, a rate no different from that which had existed earlier in 1969. Operation Intercept did have other effects, however. The temporary shortage that it created pushed up the street price of the drug; it led to increased imports of a more potent marijuana from Vietnam, and it stimulated the cultivation of domestic marijuana.*

By the early 1970s, marijuana use had increased geometrically throughout all strata of society. Expounding on this situation, a Miami attorney offered an interesting explanation of the prevalence of marijuana use in America:

> *Everybody smokes dope!*
> This profound statement should not be taken to mean that every *person* in the country smokes marijuana. It merely means: Policemen smoke dope. Probation officers smoke dope. Narcotic agents smoke dope (and sell it). *Judges smoke dope.* Prosecutors smoke dope. Plumbers, schoolteachers, princi-

---

* A State Department official indicated to the author in 1971 that, given the vast outflow of U.S. dollars into Mexico for wholesale purchases of marijuana, the real purpose of Operation Intercept was to stimulate the production of domestic marijuana and thus keep the dollar on this side of the border. This reasoning, however, has never been confirmed.

pals, deans, carpenters, disabled war veterans, Republicans, doctors, perverts, and librarians smoke dope. Legislators smoke dope. Even writers of articles on drug abuse smoke dope.

Everybody smokes dope! [69]

Given such pervasive use of marijuana, and arrests that were affecting the careers and lives of so many otherwise law-abiding citizens, legislation was introduced that reduced the penalties for the simple possession of the drug—first at the federal level and later by the states. In Alabama, judges were no longer required to impose the mandatory minimum sentence of five years for the possession of even one marijuana cigarette; Missouri statutes no longer included life sentences for second possession offenses; and in Georgia, second sale offenses to minors were no longer punishable by death.

Then there was the issue of "decriminalization"—the removal of criminal penalties for the possession of small amounts of marijuana for personal use. The movement toward decriminalization began in 1973 with Oregon, followed by Colorado, Alaska, Ohio, and California in 1975; Mississippi, North Carolina, and New York in 1977; and Nebraska in 1978. Given the fact that there were an estimated 50 million users of marijuana in the United States by the close of the 1970s, many hoped that decriminalization, and perhaps even the *legalization* of marijuana use, would become a national affair, but the "movement" suddenly stalled for a variety of reasons. [70] Principally, Congress had failed to pass legislation that would have decriminalized marijuana under federal statutes. The issue had not been salient enough throughout the nation as a whole to result in concerted action in favor of decriminalization. The lobbying on behalf of marijuana law reform had never demonstrated the power and influence necessary for repeal. Perhaps most important of all, marijuana had always been viewed as a drug favored by youth.*

---

* A rather curious but interesting indicator of the popularity of marijuana over the years is the number of different street terms that have been used to designate the substance. Over the last 100 years, no other drug has generated as many slang labels, including: A-bomb, Acapulco Gold, ace, African black, aunt mary, baby, bale, Bambalacha, bammy, banji, birdwood, black gunion, black moat, bo, bo-bo bush, bomb, bomber, boo, brick, broccoli, bud, bush, butter flower, California red, Canadian black, charge, Chicago green, coli, Colombian, creeper, dagga, dew, ditch weed, dogie, donjem, doobie, dope, dry high, erb, faggot, fatty, fingers, flowers, foo, fu, funny stuff, gage, Gainesville green, ganga, gangster, ganja, gauge, gigglesmoke, giggleweed, gold, golden leaf, gonga, goof, goofball, goofbutt, grass, green, grefa, greta, grifa, grillo, grunt, gunny, Hawaiian, hay, hemp, herb, homegrown, hooch, hop, humble, humble weed, Illinois green, Indian hay, Indian hemp, J, jane, jay smoke, Jersey green, jive, Johnson grass, johnnie, joint, joystick, joyweed, juane, juanita,

By the close of the 1970s and the onset of the 1980s, evidence indicated that marijuana use in the United States had actually declined. In 1975, surveys showed that some 30 million people were users.[71] By the early 1980s, this figure had dropped to 20 million, with the most significant declines among people ages 25 and under.[72] Perhaps the younger generation had begun to realize that although marijuana was not the "devil drug," "assassin of youth," or "weed of madness" that Harry Anslinger and his counterparts had maintained, it was not a totally innocuous substance either. Perhaps the change occurred because of the greater concern with health and physical fitness that became so much a part of American culture during the 1980s, or as an outgrowth of the antismoking messages that appeared daily in the media. Whatever the reason, it was clear that youthful attitudes had changed. Over the period from 1977 through 1984, the proportion of seniors in American high schools favoring the legalization of marijuana declined from 33.6% to 18.6%. Conversely, the proportion in support of continued criminal penalties increased from 21.7% to over 40%.*[73]

Despite the declining use and perhaps interest in marijuana within the youth culture, the drug remained in the news. A new organization calling itself The National Anti-Drug Coalition began a crusade against marijuana that was reminiscent of the reefer madness era of the 1930s.[74] "Prescription pot" became a reality in 1985 when the Food and Drug Administration gave approval to Unimed, Inc., a New Jersey research firm, to produce *Marinol*, a THC derivative effective for treating the nausea associated with cancer chemotherapy.[75] And in Oregon, a movement be-

---

juiana weed, keef, kick, kick sticks, kidstuff, kif, killer, killer weed, kilter, limbo, Lipton's, loco, loco weed, loveweed, lumbo, M, mach, maggie, margie, mari, mary, maryann, maryjane, maryjane superweed, mary warner, mary weaver, Maui, megg, merry, messerole, Mexican brown, Mexican green, Mexican locoweed, Mexican red, Mexican shit, M.J., mooca, moota, mooters, mootie, mota, mother, mu, muggles, muta, nickel, number, Panama gold, Panama red, panatella, pin, pod, poke, pot, punk, ragweed, rainy day woman, rama, reaper, red, red dirt, reefer, reeferweed, righteous bush, roach, root, rope, rough stuff, salt & pepper, sassfras, scissors, sinsemilla, skinny, smoke, snop, splay, spliff, splim, square grouper, stick, stinkweed, straw, stuff, stum, superpot, sweet lunch, sweet lucy, sweet maryjane, T, Tai weed, tea, Texas tea, Thai sticks, thirteen, thumb, tin, tripweed, twigs, twist, Vermont green, viper's weed, vonce, wackytabbacky, wackyweed, weed, weed tea, wheat, yerba, yesca, and Zacatecas purple.

*Surveys of high school seniors, conducted annually by researchers at the University of Michigan, indicate a changing trend in marijuana consumption since the mid-1970s. In 1975, for example, 40% of the students surveyed reported having used marijuana at least once during the previous year. This proportion steadily increased to 51% by 1979, but gradually declined back to 40% by 1984. At the close of 1985, however, there was a slight upturn to 41%; but this increase was far too small to be indicative of any future trend. (See *U.S. News & World Report*, 18 Nov. 1985, p. 16.)

gan to have the issue of marijuana legalization decided by state voters in the November 1986 election.[76]

Meanwhile, the heroin problem endured and cocaine emerged as a new drug of choice.

TIC, ROCKET FUEL, AND THE SPECTER OF THE LIVING DEAD

The propaganda campaigns that have periodically emerged to target specific drugs as the root causes of outbreaks of violent crime were not restricted to the Anslinger era of "reefer madness." More recently, PCP has emerged as the new "killer drug," which changes the user into a diabolical monster and a member of the "living dead."

PCP, or more formally *phencyclidine,* a central nervous system excitant agent having anesthetic, analgesic, and hallucinogenic properties, is not a particularly new drug. It was developed during the 1950s, and following studies on laboratory animals, it was recommended for clinical trials on humans in 1957.[77] Parke, Davis & Company marketed the drug under the trade name of Sernyl. Originally, phencyclidine was used as an anesthetic agent in surgical procedures. Although it was found to be generally effective, the drug often produced a number of unpleasant side effects—extreme excitement, visual disturbances, and delirium. As a result, in 1967 the use of phencyclidine was restricted to "veterinary use only." Under the trade name of Sernylan, it quickly became the most widely used animal tranquilizer.*

The initial street use of PCP (also known as horse tranquilizer, animal trank, aurora borealis, DOA, elephant, elephant juice, dust, angel dust, fairy dust, dummy dust, monkey dust, devil's dust, devil stick, hog, THC, Tic, tic tac, supergrass, rocket fuel, flakes, and buzz), appeared in the Haight-Ashbury underground community of San Francisco and other West Coast and East Coast cities during 1967. It was first marketed as the PeaCe Pill; hence, the name PCP quickly became popular.

Characteristic of the hallucinogenic drug marketplace has been the mislabeling and promotion of one substance as some other more desirable psychedelic, and for a time PCP occupied a conspicuous position in

---

* Dog and cat owners who request medication from a vet to sedate a pet during a plane or long automobile trip are generally given PCP.

this behalf. Samples of mescaline (the hallucinogenic alkaloid found in the peyote cactus) sold in Milwaukee, for example, were invariably PCP.[78] During the late 1960s and early 1970s, tetrahydrocannabinol (THC), the active ingredient in marijuana, was frequently sought after in its pure form as a prestige "fad" drug. Yet THC has *never* been sold on the street, for in its isolated form it is so unstable a compound that it quickly loses its potency and effect. During 1970, analyses of "street drugs" from the greater Philadelphia area revealed that PCP was a common THC substitute.[79] In an experiment undertaken in 1971, samples of alleged LSD, THC, mescaline, and PCP were secured from street suppliers in New York City's Greenwich Village. Laboratory analyses identified the THC and mescaline samples to be PCP, and the PCP sample to be LSD, with only the LSD sample having accurate labeling. In a second experiment carried out during early 1972 in Miami's Coconut Grove area, 25 individual samples of alleged THC were purchased from an equal number of street drug dealers. Under laboratory analysis, 22 of the "THC" samples were found to be PCP. One was Darvon (a prescription painkiller), another was an oral contraceptive, and the last a chocolate-covered peanut.[80] It was quickly learned that these apparent deceptions had been aimed at "plastic," or weekend, hippies and "heads"—those children of two cultures whose social schizophrenia placed them partially in the straight world and partially in the new underground, never fully being a part of either. In both the New York and Miami drug subcultures, however, and probably in most others, THC was simply accepted as another name for PCP, perhaps explaining why the latter drug was called "Tic" for more than a decade in many cities.

The stories describing PCP as a "killer drug" date to its first introduction to the street community. In 1969, for example, a New York City chief of detectives commented:

> Let me tell you, this stuff is bad, real bad. One dose of it and we're talking about some serious *instant addiction*. I keep telling these kids that if they keep playing around with that shit they are going to blow their fucking minds.[81]

Similarly, a number of news stories at approximately the same time described PCP as a synthetic drug so powerful that a person could become "high" simply by touching it—instantly absorbing it through the pores.[82] These early reports ran counter to both medical and street experiences,[83] and the drug quickly became relegated to the lengthening catalog of street substances that after their initial appearance received little public attention. Most of those using PCP during those early years were not found among the populations addicted to narcotic drugs. Rather, they were multiple-drug users manifesting patterns of long-term involvement with marijuana and/or hashish, combined with the experimental, social–recreational, or spree use of hallucinogens, sedatives, tranquilizers, and stimulants.

During 1978, the hysteria over PCP emerged once again, but this time in earnest. In one episode of the popular "60 Minutes" television series, CBS News commentator Mike Wallace described PCP as the nation's "number one" drug problem, reporting on bizarre incidents of brutal violence—reminiscent of Harry Anslinger's "gore file"—allegedly caused by the new "killer" drug. Shortly thereafter, a *People* magazine article touted PCP as America's most dangerous new drug—the "devil's dust." [84] In these and other reports, violence was always associated with PCP use, as well as its propensity to destroy the user's mind and hence to create new recruits to the growing army of the "living dead." During special hearings on August 8, 1978, a senator described PCP as "one of the most insidious drugs known to mankind," and a congressman declared that the drug was "a threat to the national security and that children were playing with death on the installment plan." [85] Then the syndicated columnist Ann Landers—the seemingly self-proclaimed expert on almost everything from aardvark to zymotechnics—offered the following comment about "angel dust" (PCP) as part of her 10-year campaign against marijuana use:

> Unless a teenager is a chemist, there is no way he can be sure of what he is ingesting. The possibility of getting angel dust sprinkled in with pot should be enough to scare even the dumbest cluck off the stuff for life. Angel dust can blow your mind to smithereens. [86]

Research during 1978 and 1979 quickly demonstrated that comments such as these may have been overstated. In 1978, when PCP was labeled by "60 Minutes" as the number one drug problem and responsible for more emergency room admissions than any other drug, estimates from the Drug Abuse Warning Network found PCP to account for only 3% of all reported drug emergencies.* Furthermore, ethnographic studies of

---

* The Drug Abuse Warning Network, more commonly known as DAWN, is a large-scale, data-collection effort designed to monitor changing patterns of drug abuse in the United States. More than 5,000 hospital emergency rooms and county medical examiners report regularly to the DAWN system. However, since a number of limitations are built into the DAWN data, the data are far from representative of the actual character of drug abuse in the United States.

PCP users in Seattle, Miami, Philadelphia, and Chicago demonstrated that the characterizations of users' experiences were slanted and misleading.[87] The studies found something quite different than the monster drug that the media presented as some live enemy making users lose complete control of rationality and being so overpowered by PCP that they helplessly and inescapably moved directly to either a psychotic episode, suicide, homicide, or a state of suspended confusion, which only an indefinite confinement in a mental hospital would hopefully reverse. Users were typically aware that PCP was a potent drug, and except for the few who sought a heavily anesthetized state, most used it cautiously. They aimed to control its effects. Although some had adverse reactions to the drug, violence was rarely a factor. In fact, among the more than 300 PCP users contacted during the studies, almost all were baffled by the connection of the drug with violent behavior. The only known episodes of violence occurred during "bad trips" when someone tried to restrain a user, and these were extremely unusual. Furthermore, the few who exhibited aggressive behavior typically had already developed a reputation for violence that was independent of PCP use.

None of this should suggest, however, that PCP is a harmless drug. On the contrary, hallucinations, altered mood states, feelings of depersonalization, paranoia, suicidal impulses, and aggressive behavior have been reported, only not to the extent that some commentators have suggested. In terms of the number of acute drug reactions involving PCP that resulted in a visit to a hospital emergency room, during 1983 some 6,200 incidents were reported to the DAWN system.[88] Almost half of these involved PCP in combination with some other drug, and curiously, the data reflected a striking regional variation. Of the some 6,200 cases nationwide, more than 3,000 were reported from the city of Los Angeles, a phenomenon that has been characteristic of PCP use since the mid-1970s.

In the 1980s, it appeared that PCP use had begun to decline. Among national samples of high school seniors surveyed annually, the proportions having used PCP at least once dropped from 13% in 1979 to 5% by 1984.[89] Moreover, the proportions who had used PCP during the 30-day period prior to the survey contact had declined from 2.4% to 1% over the same time in five years. In 1984 there were indications that additional changes had taken place, changes that appeared to be quite dramatic. More and more reports were appearing in the mass media describing the bizarre behavior that PCP users were exhibiting. PCP-related deaths had begun to increase, particularly in Washington, D.C., quickly rivaling Los Angeles as the national center for PCP use.[90] Moreover, the drug put so many of its users into Washington's Saint Elizabeth's Hospital in 1984 that with a grim irony PCP became known in that city as the "key to Saint

E's."[91] Yet despite the renewed media attention, all systematic attempts to study the alleged relationship between PCP use and violent behavior continued to conclude that only a very small minority of users committed bizarre acts while in a PCP-induced state.[92]

POSTSCRIPT

As America moved through the mid-1980s, both heroin and cocaine use persisted.* New drugs emerged (for example, "Ecstasy," a synthetic hallucinogen that was quickly outlawed),[93] and although the usage levels of some drugs declined, for the most part, substance abuse remained pervasive.

Given the changing character of drug use in the United States since the beginning of the current century, for those who had been studying it one conclusion seemed to be inescapable. Although the elimination of the use of dangerous drugs was a desirable goal, legislation alone was apparently not the answer. Except in the case of marijuana, law enforcement did seem to exert some control over the expanding number of users—for, after all, despite the many who initiated drug use simply because it *was* illegal, many more avoided it for the same reason. Yet legislation also created the greater problem of increased supplies of the very drugs it was trying to eliminate. Legal prohibitions removed the control of drug supplies from the hands of many to those of a select few. As a result, prices rose, as did black-market profits. What followed, then, was increased supplies when rising prices attracted additional traffickers, dealers, and other illicit entrepreneurs.

Notes

1. Charles E. Terry and Mildred Pellens, *The Opium Problem* (New York: Bureau of Social Hygiene, 1968), p. 56.
2. E. F. Cook and E. W. Martin, *Remington's Practice of Pharmacy* (Easton, Pa.: Mack Publishing Co., 1951).
3. Peter P. White, "The Poppy," *National Geographic,* Feb. 1985, p. 144.
4. William Buchan, M.D., *Domestic Medicine: or, A Treatise on the Prevention and Cure of Diseases by Regimen and Simple Medicines* (Philadelphia: Crukshank, Bell, and Muir, 1784), pp. 225–226.
5. Buchan, p. 520.

---

* Both heroin and cocaine are discussed in considerable detail in Chapter 2.

6. *Scientific American*, 5 Oct. 1985, p. 214.
7. James Harvey Young, *The Toadstool Millionaires: A Social History of Patent Medicines in America Before Federal Regulation* (Princeton, N.J.: Princeton University Press, 1961), pp. 19–23.
8. Jerome H. Jaffe and William R. Martin, "Narcotic Analgesics and Antagonists," in *The Pharmacological Basis of Therapeutics*, ed. Louis S. Goodman and Alfred Gilman (New York: Macmillan, 1970), p. 245.
9. See Roberts Bartholow, *A Manual of Hypodermatic Medication* (Philadelphia: Lippincott, 1891).
10. H. H. Kane, *The Hypodermic Injection of Morphia* (New York: C. L. Bermingham, 1880), p. 5.
11. *1897 Sears Roebuck Catalogue* (1897; rpt. New York: Chelsea House, 1968), p. 32 of insert on drugs.
12. Terry and Pellens, p. 73.
13. See Lawrence Kolb and A. G. Du Mez, "The Prevalence and Trend of Drug Addiction in the United States and the Factors Influencing It," *Public Health Reports*, 23 May 1924.
14. Terry and Pellens, pp. 1–20. See also H. Wayne Morgan, *Yesterday's Addicts: American Society and Drug Abuse, 1865–1920* (Norman: University of Oklahoma Press, 1974).
15. Virgil G. Eaton, "How the Opium Habit Is Acquired," *Popular Science Monthly*, 33 (1888), 665–666.
16. A. P. Grinnell, "A Review of Drug Consumption and Alcohol as Found in Proprietary Medicine," *Medical Legal Journal*, 1905, cited in Terry and Pellens, pp. 21–22.
17. Hector P. Blejer, "Coca Leaf and Cocaine Addiction—Some Historical Notes," *Canadian Medical Association Journal*, 25 Sept. 1965, p. 702.
18. E. J. Kahn, *The Big Drink: The Story of Coca-Cola* (New York: Random House, 1960).
19. Ernest Jones, *The Life and Work of Sigmund Freud* (New York: Basic Books, 1953), I, 81.
20. Freud's paper "Über Coca" (On Coca) has been reprinted in *Cocaine Papers by Sigmund Freud*, ed. Robert Byck (New York: New American Library, 1975), pp. 49–73.
21. C. R. A. Wright, "On the Action of Organic Acids and Their Anhydrides on the Natural Alkaloids," *Journal of the Chemical Society*, 12 July 1874, p. 1031.
22. See Arnold S. Trebach, *The Heroin Solution* (New Haven, Conn.: Yale University Press, 1982), p. 39.
23. M. Manges, "A Second Report on the Therapeutics of Heroin," *New York Medical Journal*, 20 Jan. 1900, pp. 82–83.
24. James A. Inciardi, "Over-the-Counter Drugs: Epidemiology, Adverse Reactions, Overdose Deaths, and Mass Media Promotion," *Addictive Diseases: An International Journal*, 3 (1977), 253–272.
25. James Harvey Young, *The Medical Messiahs: A Social History of Health Quackery in Twentieth-Century America* (Princeton, N.J.: Princeton University Press, 1967), p. 29.

26. Cited in Young, p. 31.
27. Webb v. U.S., 249 U.S. 96 (1919).
28. U.S. v. Behrman, 258 U.S. 280 (1922).
29. Lindner v. U.S., 268 U.S. 5 (1925).
30. Rufus King, "The American System: Legal Sanctions to Repress Drug Abuse," in *Drugs and the Criminal Justice System,* ed. James A. Inciardi and Carl D. Chambers (Beverly Hills: Sage, 1974), p. 22.
31. See Morgan.
32. Perry M. Lichtenstein, "Narcotic Addiction," *New York Medical Journal,* 14 Nov. 1914, p. 962.
33. G. E. McPherson and J. Cohen, "Survey of 100 Cases of Drug Addiction Entering Camp Upton, New York," *Boston Medical and Surgical Journal,* 5 June 1919; Special Committee of Investigation, *Traffic in Narcotic Drugs* (Washington, D.C.: Department of Treasury, 1919); *Literary Digest,* 26 Apr. 1919, p. 32; *The Outlook,* 25 June 1919, p. 315; *The Survey,* 15 Mar. 1919, pp. 867–868; *American Review of Reviews,* July–Dec. 1919, pp. 331–332.
34. *Literary Digest,* 6 Mar. 1920, pp. 27–28; 16 Apr. 1921, pp. 19–20; 24 Feb. 1923, pp. 34–35; 25 Aug. 1923, pp. 22–23.
35. *Literary Digest,* 10 June 1922, p. 34.
36. *World's Work,* Nov. 1924, p. 17.
37. Lawrence Kolb and A. G. Du Mez, "The Prevalence and Trend of Drug Addiction in the United States and Factors Influencing It," *Public Health Reports,* 23 May 1924, pp. 1179–1204.
38. *Time,* 24 Aug. 1942, p. 52.
39. U.S. Treasury Department, Bureau of Narcotics, *Traffic in Opium and Other Dangerous Drugs* (Washington, D.C.: U.S. Government Printing Office, 1939), p. 14.
40. Larry Sloman, *Reefer Madness: A History of Marijuana in America* (Indianapolis: Bobbs-Merrill, 1979), p. 26. For a description of a late nineteenth-century hashish club, see H. H. Kane, "A Hashish-House in New York," *Harper's Monthly,* Nov. 1883, pp. 944–949, reprinted in Morgan, pp. 159–170.
41. *New York Times,* 6 July 1927, p. 10.
42. Sloman, pp. 30–31.
43. Sloman, p. 34.
44. Sloman, p. 63.
45. Sloman, pp. 58–59.
46. Max Lerner, *America as a Civilization: Life and Thought in the United States Today* (New York: Simon & Schuster, 1957), p. 666.
47. See *Newsweek,* 20 Nov. 1950, pp. 57–58; 29 Jan. 1951, pp. 23–24; 11 June 1951, pp. 26–27; 25 June 1951, pp. 19–29; 13 Aug. 1951, p. 50; 17 Sept. 1951, p. 60; *Life,* 11 June 1951, pp. 116, 119–122; *The Survey,* July 1951, pp. 328–329; *Time,* 26 Feb. 1951, p. 24; 7 May 1951, pp. 82, 85; *Reader's Digest,* Oct. 1951, pp. 137–140.
48. Isidor Chein, Donald L. Gerard, Robert S. Lee, and Eva Rosenfeld, *The Road to H: Narcotics, Juvenile Delinquency, and Social Policy* (New York: Basic Books, 1964), p. 14.

49. Richard A. Cloward and Lloyd E. Ohlin, *Delinquency and Opportunity* (New York: Free Press, 1960), pp. 178–186.
50. Edward Preble and John J. Casey, "Taking Care of Business: The Heroin User's Life on the Street," *International Journal of the Addictions,* 4 (1969), 2.
51. Kenneth Rexroth, "San Francisco Letter," *Evergreen Review,* Spring 1957, p. 11.
52. See Richard H. Blum and Associates, *Students and Drugs* (San Francisco: Jossey-Bass, 1970); Leslie Farber, "Ours Is the Addicted Society," *New York Times Magazine,* 11 Dec. 1966, p. 43; Joel Fort, *The Pleasure Seekers: The Drug Crisis, Youth, and Society* (New York: Grove Press, 1969); A. Geller and M. Boas, *The Drug Beat* (New York: McGraw-Hill, 1969); Helen H. Nowlis, *Drugs on the College Campus* (New York: Doubleday-Anchor, 1969); J. L. Simmons and B. Winograd, *It's Happening: A Portrait of the Youth Scene Today* (Santa Barbara, Calif.: Marc-Laired, 1966).
53. James A. Inciardi, "Drugs, Drug-Taking and Drug-Seeking: Notations on the Dynamics of Myth, Change, and Reality," in *Drugs and the Criminal Justice System,* ed. James A. Inciardi and Carl D. Chambers (Beverly Hills: Sage, 1974), pp. 203–222; George Johnson, *The Pill Conspiracy* (Los Angeles: Sherbourne, 1967).
54. Harry J. Anslinger and William F. Tompkins, *The Traffic in Narcotics* (New York: Funk & Wagnalls, 1953), pp. 37–38.
55. Cited in William Manchester, *The Glory and the Dream: A Narrative History of America, 1932–1972* (Boston: Little, Brown, 1974), p. 1362.
56. *The Realist,* Sept. 1966.
57. Timothy Leary, "Introduction," in *LSD: The Consciousness-Expanding Drug,* ed. David Solomon (New York: G. P. Putnam's, 1964), p. 17.
58. Cited in Manchester, p. 1366.
59. National Commission on Marihuana and Drug Abuse, *Drug Abuse in America: Problem in Perspective* (Washington, D.C.: U.S. Government Printing Office, 1973), p. 81.
60. Carl D. Chambers, Leon Brill, and James A. Inciardi, "Toward Understanding and Managing Nonnarcotic Drug Abusers," *Federal Probation,* Mar. 1972, pp. 50–55.
61. John C. Pollard, "Some Comments on Nonnarcotic Drug Abuse" (Paper presented at the Nonnarcotic Drug Institute, Southern Illinois University, Edwardsville, June 1967): John Griffith, "A Study of Illicit Amphetamine Drug Traffic in Oklahoma City," *American Journal of Psychiatry,* 123 (1966), 560–569.
62. U.S. Cong., Senate, Subcommittee to Investigate Juvenile Delinquency of the Committee on the Judiciary, *Legislative Hearings on S. 674, "To Amend the Controlled Substances Act to Move Amphetamines and Certain Other Stimulant Substances from Schedule III of Such Act to Schedule II, and for Other Purposes," July 15 and 16, 1971* (Washington, D.C.: U.S. Government Printing Office, 1972).
63. Carl D. Chambers, *An Assessment of Drug Use in the General Population* (Albany: New York State Narcotic Addiction Control Commission, 1970); James A. Inciardi and Carl D. Chambers, "The Epidemiology of Amphet-

amine Use in the General Population," *Canadian Journal of Criminology and Corrections,* Apr. 1972, pp. 166–172.

64. *Washington Post,* 12 Nov. 1972, p. B3.
65. For an overview of the history and clinical experiences related to methaqualone, see James A. Inciardi, David M. Petersen, and Carl D. Chambers, "Methaqualone Abuse Patterns, Diversion Paths, and Adverse Reactions," *Journal of the Florida Medical Association,* Apr. 1974.
66. AMA Department of Drugs, *AMA Drug Evaluations* (Acton, Mass.: Publishing Sciences Group, 1973), p. 313.
67. U.S. Cong., Senate, Subcommittee to Investigate Juvenile Delinquency of the Committee on the Judiciary, *Legislative Hearings on the Methaqualone Control Act of 1973, S.1252* (Washington, D.C.: U.S. Government Printing Office, 1973).
68. For a thorough analysis of Operation Intercept, see Lawrence A. Gooberman, *Operation Intercept: The Multiple Consequences of Public Policy* (New York: Pergamon Press, 1974).
69. Steven M. Greenberg, "Compounding a Felony: Drug Abuse and the American Legal System," in Inciardi and Chambers, *The Pill Conspiracy,* p. 186.
70. See Eric Josephson, "Marijuana Decriminalization: Assessment of Current Legislative Status" (Paper presented at the Technical Review on Methodology in Drug Policy Research, Decriminalization of Marijuana, National Institute on Drug Abuse, Rockville, Md., 20–21 Mar. 1980); James A. Inciardi, "Marijuana Decriminalization Research: A Perspective and Commentary," *Criminology,* May 1981, pp. 145–159.
71. The Domestic Council Drug Abuse Task Force, *White Paper on Drug Abuse* (Washington, D.C.: U.S. Government Printing Office, 1975), p. 25.
72. The White House, Drug Abuse Policy Office, Office of Policy Development, *National Strategy for Prevention of Drug Abuse and Drug Trafficking* (Washington, D.C.: U.S. Government Printing Office, 1984), p. 19.
73. Lloyd D. Johnston, Patrick M. O'Malley, and Jerald G. Bachman, *Use of Licit and Illicit Drugs by America's High School Students, 1975–1984* (Rockville, Md.: National Institute on Drug Abuse, 1985), p. 108.
74. See *War on Drugs,* June 1980.
75. *Business Week,* 24 June 1985, p. 104.
76. *USA Today,* 17 July 1985, p. 3A.
77. *Phencyclidine (PCP),* NCDAI Publication 18 (Rockville, Md.: National Clearinghouse for Drug Abuse Information, 1973).
78. A. Reed and A. W. Kane, "Phencyclidine (PCP)," *STASH Capsules,* Dec. 1970, pp. 1–2.
79. Sidney H. Schnoll and W. H. Vogel, "Analysis of 'Street Drugs,'" *New England Journal of Medicine,* 8 Apr. 1971, p. 791.
80. The author conducted both experiments.
81. *Personal Communication,* 7 Dec. 1969.
82. *Long Island Press,* 28 Nov. 1970.
83. E. F. Domino, "Neurobiology of Phencyclidine (Sernyl), A Drug with an Unusual Spectrum of Pharmacological Activity," *Internal Review of Neurobiology,* 6 (1964), 303–347.

84. *People,* 4 Sept. 1978, pp. 46–48. See also Ronald L. Linder, *PCP: The Devil's Dust* (Belmont, Calif.: Wadsworth, 1981).

85. Select Committee on Narcotics Abuse Control, *Executive Summary, Hearings on Phencyclidine, August 8* (Washington, D.C.: U.S. Government Printing Office, 1978).

86. *Cincinnati Post,* 2 June 1979, p. 23.

87. Harvey W. Feldman, "PCP Use in Four Cities: An Overview," in *Angel Dust,* ed. Harvey W. Feldman, Michael H. Agar, and George M. Beschner (Lexington, Mass.: Lexington, 1979), pp. 29–51.

88. National Institute on Drug Abuse, Division of Epidemiology and Statistical Analysis, *Annual Data, 1983, Data from the Drug Abuse Warning Network* (Rockville, Md.: National Institute on Drug Abuse, 1984), pp. 200–201.

89. Johnston, O'Malley, and Bachman, pp. 34–36.

90. *New York Times,* 9 Dec. 1984, p. 60.

91. *U.S. News & World Report,* 19 Nov. 1984, pp. 65–66.

92. R. K. Siegel, "PCP and Violent Crime: The People vs. Peace," *Journal of Psychedelic Drugs,* 12 (1980), 317–330; Eric D. Wish, "PCP and Crime: Just Another Illicit Drug?" Proceedings of the National Institute on Drug Abuse Technical Review on Phencyclidine, Rockville, Md., May 1985.

93. *Time,* 10 June 1985, p. 64. See also *New York Times,* 1 June 1985, p. 6; *USA Today,* 30 May 1985, p. D1.

CHAPTER TWO

SHIT, SMACK, AND SUPERFLY
Perspectives on the Nature of Heroin and Cocaine Use

English language usage is replete with any number of rather curious oddities. One of these is the *euphemism,* a delightfully ridiculous and roundabout word or phrase used to replace some other term or expression considered to be coarse, offensive, or otherwise painful. Among the most famous of American euphemisms are *affair* to communicate the idea of marital infidelity, *gay* for "homosexual," and *irregularity,* first posed by a 1930s' adman as a genial substitute for that abnormal condition of the bowels known as constipation. More recent examples, also products of the advertising industry, include *pre-owned vehicle* for "used car," *periodic pain* for "menstrual cramps," *BO* for "armpit odor," and *feminine hygiene* for the "vaginal douche" and "sanitary napkin." From the political–military complex there is *neutralization* or *executive action* (the murdering of some enemy agent), and death by *friendly fire* or *misadventure* (the accidental killing of American service personnel by their own comrades). Not to be forgotten is perhaps the most amusing euphemistic term of the Reagan administration—*revenue enhancement,* which means a tax increase.*

A second peculiarity of language is the redefinition of words, either through simple ignorance or deliberate intent. This variety of linguistic manipulation has been a particular problem in the drug field for quite some time. Few words in the English language, for example, have been as misdefined, misused, and misunderstood as *narcotic* and *addiction.* The consequences of these linguistic abuses have become apparent in the areas of drug-abuse legislation, prevention, education, and treatment.

---

*No doubt one of these days someone will invent a substitute term for *hemorrhoid,* a truly ugly word perhaps well in need of a euphemism. It would not be surprising if the new expression came from Parke-Davis, the makers of a hemorrhoid relief preparation that they have cleverly named *Anus*ol, and which they even more cleverly pronounce *An*-u-sol.

49

The wide and inconsistent usage of the term *narcotic* appears not only in the popular media but in legal and scientific circles as well. Sometimes *narcotic* is used to characterize any drug producing stupor, insensibility, or sleep, thus embracing a breadth of substances ranging from alcohol to heroin. It is used to classify compounds that are "addiction producing," a situation that creates even further confusion since *addiction* is defined so haphazardly. In legal matters, *narcotic* often designates *any* drug that is allegedly "dangerous," is widely abused, or has a high potential for abuse. As a result, such substances as marijuana, cocaine, PCP, and amphetamines have been considered, along with heroin and morphine in narcotics regulations, in spite of the fact that they have little in common with *true* narcotics. Cocaine, for example, has effects that are almost totally opposite those of heroin. In medicine, a field in which greater specificity would be expected, the terms *narcotics, opiates, dependence-producing drugs,* and *morphinelike drugs* are used interchangeably. Elsewhere, "narcotics" are simply "habit-forming" drugs.

In pharmacology, a science that focuses on the chemical nature, structure, and action of drugs, the designation of *narcotic* is quite specific.[1] It includes the natural derivatives of *Papavar somniferium*—the opium poppy—having both analgesic and sedative properties, and any synthetic derivatives of similar pharmacological structure and action. Thus, the range of substances that can be properly called narcotics is quite limited and encompasses four specific groups:

Natural narcotics
- opium, derived directly from *Papavar somniferium*
- morphine and codeine, derived from opium

Semisynthetic narcotics
- heroin
- Dilaudid

Synthetic narcotics with high potency
- methadone
- Demerol

Synthetic narcotics with low potency
- Darvon
- Talwin

Many other drugs are in the latter three categories, but the examples indicated are the best known and most widely abused.

A characteristic effect of narcotic drugs is "addiction," a phenomenon that has had many meanings over the years. The addiction label has been used interchangeably with "dependence producing," "habit forming," and "habituation." There are also the metaphors of "physical dependence" and "psychological dependence." If addiction truly meant all these things, almost anything could be addicting—from Coca-Cola to sex, watching TV—even eating, sleeping, playing chess, and breathing. This is why cocaine, marijuana, PCP, the amphetamines, and numerous other drugs have been called addicting, which they are not!

By contrast, *addiction* is a physiological phenomenon with a very specific meaning. Addiction is a craving for a particular drug, accompanied by physical dependence, which motivates continuing usage, resulting in tolerance to the drug's effects and a complex of identifiable symptoms appearing when it is suddenly withdrawn. Heroin is an addicting drug. Morphine is an addicting drug. The barbiturates are addicting drugs.*

Thus, although drugs and their actions should be designated in terms of their chemical structure and their effects on cellular biochemistry or physiological systems, there has been the tendency to classify most drugs according to the prevailing attitudes of the dominant cultural group and its most vocal representatives. Yet to be precise in the definitions of *narcotic* and *addiction* is not an attempt to engage in any semantic game (as has been the case with recent attempts to differentiate between illicit drug "use," "misuse," and "abuse"). *Narcotics* and *addiction* are based on objective pharmacological criteria, as opposed to the nominalist view that a narcotic is anything that someone may wish to call a narcotic. In the final analysis, however, with so many different applications and usages of *addiction* and *narcotics*, the terms have become relatively useless concepts. And in fact, many researchers in the drug field have abandoned them for this very reason, preferring such designations as *heroin users, cocaine users,* and *LSD users.*

HEROIN: "THE MOST DANGEROUS SUBSTANCE ON EARTH"

Known to its users as *shit, smack, horse, harry, henry, H, jones,* or simply *dope* or *junk,* to many in the law-enforcement community and the gen-

---

* Many people will argue that the physiological manifestations of amphetamine and cocaine dependence fall within this definition of addiction, a point that is commented on later in this chapter.

eral public heroin is "the most dangerous substance on earth."[2] Indeed, heroin is a powerful narcotic. Several times more potent than morphine, it suppresses both respiratory and cardiovascular activity, has strong analgesic effects and a high-addiction potential. At overdose levels heroin can produce coma, shock, and ultimately, respiratory arrest and death. For the better part of the twentieth century, heroin has been the most widely discussed drug of abuse, and the most feared. Yet for those involved in the production, distribution, sale, and use of this crystalline powder, heroin is something entirely different. It represents the cornerstone of several unique worlds with their own peculiar goals, values, rules, needs, and achievements.

Adventures on the Opium Express

The opium express is a world of production and trafficking networks that stretch around the world, from Asia to the United States. It is an enterprise that involves millions of peasant farmers and tens of thousands of corrupt government officials, disciplined criminal entrepreneurs, and street-level dealers.

A focal point in the trafficking complex of opium and heroin is the Golden Triangle, a vast area of Southeast Asia comprising the rugged Shan hills of Burma, the serpentine ridges of northern Thailand, and the upper highlands of Laos. This geographic area emerged during the late 1960s and early 1970s as the world's largest producer of illicit opium, providing yields of some 700 metric tons* annually.[3] For a time, the Golden Triangle also dominated the heroin-refining markets of Western Europe, and there is considerable agreement that the growing of opium in the region was introduced by Chinese political refugees. Using the Netherlands as their principal importation and distribution area, Chinese traffickers virtually controlled the heroin market—arranging for the purchase of raw opium, overseeing its conversion into heroin, and managing the international smuggling network. By 1978 to 1979, however, rivalries among the various Chinese drug syndicates, law-enforcement efforts against Oriental traffickers, and declining production due to poor crop yields served to reduce the importance of the region as a center of opium trade.

A second focal point in the opium–heroin trafficking complex is what has become known as the Golden Crescent, an arc of land stretching across Southwest Asia through sections of Pakistan, Iran, and Afghani-

---

* Both coca- and opium-production figures are typically expressed in metric tons—one metric ton equal to 1,000 kilograms or 2,204.6 pounds. In this example, 700 metric tons would be the equivalent of some 1.54 million pounds.

Table 2.1   Opium Production Estimates, 1984–1986 (in metric tons)

	1986	1985	1984
Southwest Asia			
Afghanistan	320–420	300–400	140–180
Iran	200–400	200–400	400–600
Pakistan	35–65	40–70	40–50
Southeast Asia			
Burma	532	424	534
Laos	50–100	100	30
Thailand	16–36	36	11
Mexico	21–45	21–45	21

SOURCE: Bureau of International Narcotics Matters, Department of State, *International Narcotics Control Strategy, 1986* (Washington, D.C.: Department of State, 21 Feb. 1986), p. 11.

stan. Emerging as the leading opium producer in the world during the late 1970s, the Golden Crescent successfully challenged its Southeast Asian counterpart by generating a raw material for heroin that was less expensive and generally more potent. By the mid-1980s, over half the heroin entering the United States originated as opium in the Golden Crescent. Iran was the key opium producer, and Pakistan and Afghanistan were the primary heroin refiners and shippers, having numerous illicit laboratories on both sides of the Khyber Pass.* By 1986, estimates suggested that the combined yield of Southeast and Southwest Asian opium production exceeded 1,500 metric tons (see Table 2.1).[4] Moreover, with illicit opium-poppy farming apparent in India, Colombia, and numerous other nations, the world production available for refining into heroin was probably more than 2,000 metric tons.

The actual process culminating in the use of heroin on the streets of rural and urban America begins in the remote sections of the Golden Triangle and Golden Crescent. There, hill-tribe farmers use the most basic agricultural techniques to cultivate the opium poppy.[5] The annual crop

---

* Despite the five-year presence of Soviet troops in Afghanistan and their skirmishes with Afghan rebels, the country has remained a major producer of opium and its derivatives. In fact, by the close of 1985 it was apparent that the widespread availability of opium and heroin in Afghan markets had begun to adversely affect the Soviet offensive. Reports indicated that many Soviet soldiers had become drug dependent and were raiding their own army supply rooms for guns, ammunition, and gasoline, with which they would barter for drugs. See the *New York Times,* 2 Nov. 1985, pp. 1, 6.

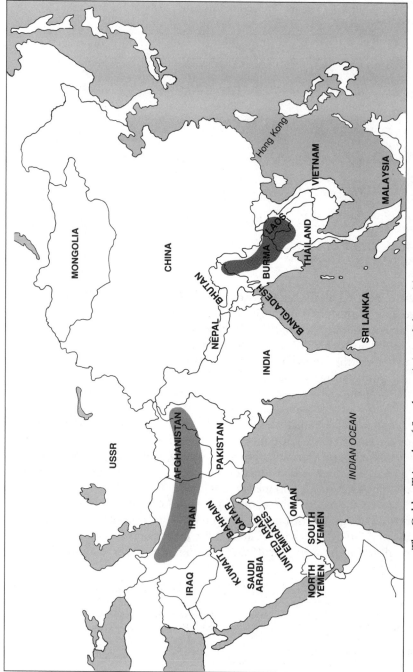

The Golden Triangle of Southeast Asia and the Golden Crescent of Southwest Asia

cycle begins in late summer as farmers scatter poppy seeds across the surface of their freshly hoed fields. Three months later, the plant is mature—a greenish stem topped by a brightly colored flower. Gradually the petals fall to the ground, exposing a seed pod about the size and shape of a small egg. Inside the pod is a milky white sap that is harvested by cutting a series of shallow parallel incisions across the surface of the pod. As the sap seeps from the incisions and congeals on the surface of the pod, it changes to a brownish-black color. This is raw opium, which the farmers collect by scraping the pod with a flat, dull knife.

The farmers then carry the raw opium on horseback to a local refinery, where it is immediately converted into morphine—a practice that traffickers prefer, since compact morphine "bricks" are easier and safer to smuggle than are bundles of sticky, pungent opium. The conversion of raw opium into pure morphine is an exercise in rudimentary chemistry. The opium is first dissolved in drums of hot water. Lime fertilizer is added to the steaming solution, precipitating out organic wastes and leaving the morphine suspended near the surface. Any residual waste matter is removed, and the morphine is transferred to another drum, where it is heated, stirred, and mixed with concentrated ammonia. The morphine solidifies and drops to the bottom of the container and is filtered out in the form of chunky white kernels. Once dried and packaged, the morphine weighs about 10% of the original raw opium from which it was extracted.

The process of transforming morphine into heroin is a bit more complex, and there was a time, from the end of World War II through the 1960s, when Hong Kong and Marseilles were the heroin-refining capitals of the world. More recently, this industry has become increasingly dispersed, with precision laboratories also in the opium-growing regions of Southeast and Southwest Asia, and in Turkey, Malaysia, and South America. The refining process occurs in five stages, to chemically bind acetic acid to the morphine molecule, thereby generating a substance that can be transformed into the powder known as heroin. Ten kilograms of morphine can produce an equivalent amount of heroin that ranges from 80% to 99% pure.

The trafficking of the refined heroin from the clandestine laboratories to United States ports involves an elaborate organizational web of transportation routes, couriers, and payoffs. Depending upon the particular trafficking organization, the drug may be transshipped by way of established routes through Indonesia, the Philippines, Syria, Eygpt, Kenya, Nigeria, Italy, France, England, West Germany, the Netherlands, Canada, or a combination thereof. If the circumstances demand it, an organization can quickly and ingeniously design alternate routes. In early 1983, for example, a Miami heroin trafficker indicated that, as the result of an arrest

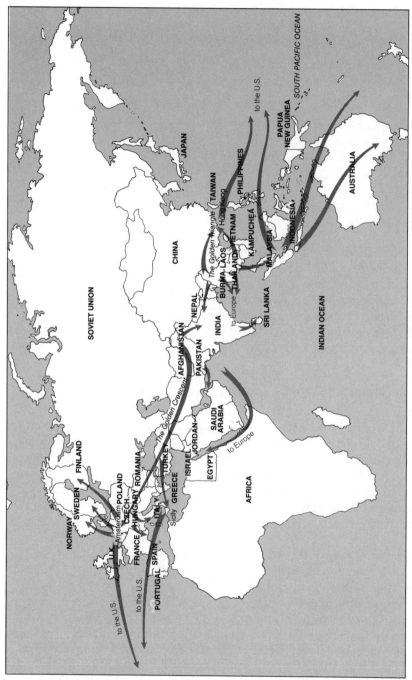

Heroin-Trafficking Routes

in Turkey, an assassination in Kuwait, and a plane crash in Corsica, one shipment of drugs had to be diverted through at least eight countries before it finally reached its final destination: *

> As the story got to me, which I'm sure is true knowing where it came from, the stuff [heroin] started out in a small lab near Ou Neua. That's a place in north Laos I think somewhere up near the Chinese border. It made its way to Bangkok okay where it was supposed to be flown to Athens, Amsterdam, New York, and then to Miami by car. But then things really got fucked up. The guy who's supposed to make the transfer in Athens gets picked up for somethin' or other, so they fly it to Singapore instead. They had someone there who could take it most of the way . . . but he decides to get himself killed in Kuwait before he even gets there. So get this: It goes back to Bangkok, to somewhere in India, then somewhere else in the Middle East, and then up the fucking Nile to Egypt. Then there's this mule in Corsica that's gonna take it, but he freaks out when his girlfriend finds out she don't know how to fly her plane too well and ends up cashing it in. . . . Somehow it finds its way to South Africa . . . it goes by ship to Uruguay, and then up through South America—Ecuador, Colombia, Peru and all that—to Panama, Mexico City, Chicago, Detroit, New York, and then Miami. . . . It's one for the Guinness book of fucking records.

The couriers who actually carry heroin across the world and into the United States are as diverse as the personalities who use the drug—members of the trafficking organizations traveling alone or with their families as tourists, corrupt diplomats, pilots and other airline personnel, professional athletes, students, ship captains, teachers, physicians, judges, and numerous others—even Playboy playmates. Recently, a number of heroin-smuggling operations have focused on attractive women. Lebanese traffickers, for example, are known to recruit svelte Scandinavian women who bypass the traditional heroin depots in New York's Harlem, flying directly to Arab communities in East Coast cities.[6]

Once in the United States, heroin may be *stepped on* (diluted) as many as 7 to 10 times. What started out in some remote Asian laboratory as 99% pure heroin is cut with lactose (milk sugar, a by-product of milk processing), quinine, cornstarch, or almost any other powdery substance

---

* As noted in Chapter 1, all undocumented quotations throughout this text are personal communications to the author.

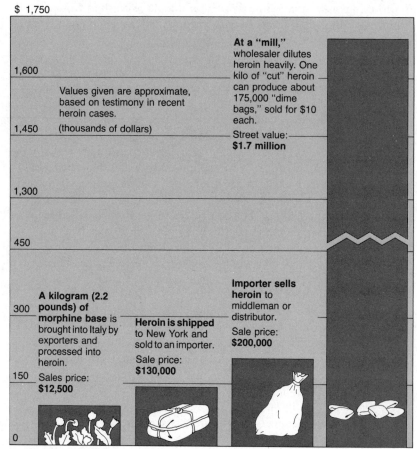

$ 1,750

1,600

Values given are approximate, based on testimony in recent heroin cases.

1,450   (thousands of dollars)

1,300

450

300

A kilogram (2.2 pounds) of morphine base is brought into Italy by exporters and processed into heroin.

150   Sales price: **$12,500**

0

Heroin is shipped to New York and sold to an importer.

Sale price: **$130,000**

Importer sells heroin to middleman or distributor.

Sale price: **$200,000**

At a "mill," wholesaler dilutes heroin heavily. One kilo of "cut" heroin can produce about 175,000 "dime bags," sold for $10 each.

Street value: **$1.7 million**

Transporting Heroin to the U.S.: From Poppy Field to "Dime Bag."
Source: *New York Times,* 21 May 1984, p. 84

that will dissolve when heated. Heroin is also mixed with cleansing powder and dirt, and even arsenic or strychnine if the user is singled out for a *hot shot* (fatal dose). Ultimately, the heroin sold on the street is less than 10% pure, and generally only 1% to 4% pure.

Concomitant with the trafficking and dealer dilution of heroin is the geometric increase in its price. In one trafficking operation, a kilogram of morphine base sold in Italy for $12,500; converted into heroin, that kilogram yielded an estimated $1.7 million in street sales.[7] Even more dramatically, although villagers in India's Siah Valley could earn the equivalent of $300 for 10 kilograms of raw opium in 1985, converted into heroin in New Delhi the price was $10,000,[8] with an escalation to $1.5 million on the streets of New York City—an overall increase of some 5,000%.

H Is for Heaven. H Is for Hell. H Is for Heroin. . . .

Why people use heroin, or any illicit drug for that matter, is not altogether understood. Theories are legion, so much so that one publication of the National Institute on Drug Abuse devoted its entire 488 pages to outlining the major views.[9] A number of investigators have described heroin users as maladjusted, hostile, immature, dependent, manipulative, and narcissistic individuals, suggesting that drug use is just one more symptom of their disordered personalities.[10] Others suggest that since drug use is an integral part of the general culture that surrounds the user, it is learned behavior.[11]

Sociologist Alfred R. Lindesmith's view, among the more often quoted, most simplistic, and least helpful theories of heroin use, explains addiction on the basis of the user's association of the drug with the distress accompanying the sudden cessation of its use.[12] *Using* heroin, he contends, is one thing, for people have various motivations for trying the drug. *Becoming addicted,* Lindesmith argues, is another. Users who fail to realize the connection between the withdrawal distress and the drug manage to escape addiction. Those who link the distress to the drug use, and thereafter use it to alleviate the distress symptoms, invariably become addicted.

There are other explanations: the bad-habit theory, disruptive-environment theory, cognitive-control theory, social-deviance theory, biological-rhythm theory, subcultural theory, social-neurobiological theory, and many more.[13] Among the more novel is Sandra Coleman's "incomplete mourning theory," an explanation holding that addictive behavior is a function of an unusual number of traumatic or premature deaths, separations, and losses that the drug user has not effectively resolved or mourned.[14]

Then there is the theory of the "addiction-prone personality," elucidated by Dr. Kenneth Chapman of the U.S. Public Health Service more than three decades ago:

> . . . the typical addict is emotionally unstable and immature, often seeking pleasure and excitement outside of the conventional realms. Unable to adapt comfortably to the pressures and tensions in today's speedy world, he may become either an

extremely dependent individual or turn into a hostile "lone wolf" incapable of attaching deep feelings toward anyone. In his discomfort, he may suffer pain—real or imaginary. The ordinary human being has normal defense machinery with which to meet life's disappointments, frustrations, and conflicts. But the potential addict lacks enough of this inner strength to conquer his emotional problems and the anxiety they create. In a moment of stress, he may be introduced to narcotics as a "sure-fire" answer to his needs. Experiencing relief from his pain, or an unreal flight from his problems, or a puffed-up sense of power and control regarding them, he is well on the road toward making narcotics his way of life.[15]

Stated differently, when "stable" people are introduced to drugs, they will discard them spontaneously before becoming dependent. Those who have "addiction-prone personalities," because of psychoses, psychopathic or psychoneurotic disorders, or predispositions toward mental disfunctioning, "become transformed into the typical addict."[16]

To the great misfortune of the heroin-using population, the concept of the addiction-prone personality has dominated thinking in the drug-abuse treatment industry for some five decades. Although the theory evolved from studies of addicts in psychiatric facilities during the early years of addiction treatment, it was applied universally and continues to be accepted by many.[17] Yet as researchers who have gone beyond the confines of their laboratories, hospitals, and university campuses to study addicts in their natural environments understand, and likely always did, users who come to the attention of psychiatric facilities are often quite different from those who remain active on the street for extended periods of time. Given this fact, it is no wonder that the field of addiction treatment has had so few successes over the years.

The difficulty with the concept of the addiction-prone personality, and all other theoretical explanations of heroin addiction, has been the assumption that one single theory will account for the entire spectrum of drug-using behaviors—a problem that has plagued discussions of deviant behavior in general. Unfortunately, this kind of thinking is not altogether that remote, at least in its logical structure, from the arguments of Dr. Benjamin Rush two centuries ago that there was *a* theory of disease rather than distinct theories of separate diseases. Yet in all likelihood, there are as many reasons for using drugs as there are individuals who use drugs. For some it may be a function of family disorganization, or cultural learning, or maladjusted personality, or an "addiction-prone" personality, or even "incomplete mourning." For others heroin use may be no more than a normal response to the world in which they live.

As the motivations for heroin use vary, so too do the patterns of initiation. Some careers in drug use are therapeutic in origin—through the chronic use of morphine, Demerol, Talwin, or another narcotic analgesic that was prescribed for the treatment of pain or some other ailment. For most, however, heroin is a later stage in a life-style of drug taking that began during early adolescence with the use of alcohol, codeine cough syrup, organic solvents, marijuana, and/or amphetamines. Whatever the pattern of initiation, *addiction* to heroin, if it occurs at all, is a lengthy process. Despite the "one shot and you're hooked" myth, to become addicted to heroin, one must work at it—particularly since most of the heroin currently available in the street community is less than 5% pure. Moreover, most people do not begin their heroin use by "mainlining" (intravenous injection). The recollections of David K., a New York City heroin user interviewed in 1984, illustrate a pattern of onset that is not altogether uncommon:

> One day my cousin comes over and he's using heroin, and he throws this 10-dollar bag of junk on the kitchen table and says, "Try some." I say, "Listen, Alfie, I ain't about to put any of your shit into my veins." He says, "No man, just snort some of it, it's great."
>
> So I decide to snort some of Alfie's shit. I close off one nostril and sniff the shit out of the shit. . . . It blew my fucking head off, really fucked me up. I got such a bad pain in my head that I thought I was fucking brain damaged. I puked my guts out. I was really sick. . . .
>
> A few weeks later I see Alfie again and ask him for some stuff, you know, just to try it again. You'd think that after that first time I might have learned something. But no. It's like when you try your first cigarette. You get dizzy and upset in your gut, but you do it again anyway because you want to be cool and since everybody else is doin' it there must be something to it. . . .
>
> So I snort again and *ho-ly fucking shit!* I felt like I died and went to heaven. My whole body was like one giant fucking incredible orgasm.

What David K. had experienced was his first *rush*. Or as described somewhat more vividly by former heroin addict Manuel J. Torres:

> . . . it's really something else. I mean, it's like the shit really hit the fan . . . you can't describe it. All the colors of Times Square tumble right over your forehead and explode in your

eyeballs like a million, jillion shooting stars. And then, each one of them goddamn stars novas in a cascade of brilliant Technicolor.

And the world levels out. You know what I mean? There's no right, no wrong. Everything's beautiful, and it's like nothing's happening baby but clear, crisp light. The mambo beat is like hot fuck notes bouncing off lukewarm street scenes. The drummer downstairs in the park is onto life's whole fucking secret, and the primitive urge of his swinging soul becomes a mellow sharpness in your ears. And you want to gather all of creation inside you; maybe for a minute you do. What a perfect Manny Torres you become for a moment![18]

After snorting on and off for several months, and still not addicted, David K. moved into the next stage of heroin use:

I ran into this lady that I used to fuck and hang out with a couple of years ago and she asks me if I want to come along with her while she *makes her connection* [buys heroin] and *fixes* [injects the drug]. After a while she asks me if I want to try the needle and I say no, but then I decide to go halfway and *skin-pop* [injecting into the muscle just beneath the skin]. Well, man, it was wonderful. Popping was just like snorting, only stronger, finer, better, and faster.

For David, skin-popping lasted for three months, although not on a daily basis. "I don't think I was addicted then," he said, "because sometimes I'd go for almost a whole week without popping and I didn't get sick." Then he began to *mainline* (inject the drug directly into the vein):

Travelin' along the mainline was like a grand slam home run fuck, like getting a blow job from Miss America. The rush hits you instantly, and all of a sudden you're up there on Mount Olympus talking to Zeus.

Two months later David decided that he was *hooked* (addicted). He was using heroin regularly, spending more than $200 daily on his habit, and getting sick when more than 6–8 hours would pass without fixing. And then, although he had no intentions of quitting his heroin use, he did admit that addiction had its drawbacks:

Any damn junkie that says that he doesn't like his shit is a fucking liar. They all love their dope. But your whole damn life revolves around your shit.

Or as Manny Torres described it:

> See, once you're hooked you're not your own boss any more. You belong to your habit. Plain and simple. You plan and scheme, and con, and lie, and hustle for your habit. Anybody and everybody becomes fair game. Look, you leave mother, brother, sister, father, friend for heroin. When you're hooked you gotta score. It ain't *maybe* I'll score, maybe I won't. It's, man, I'm *gonna* score and all hell ain't gonna stop me! And scoring can take time; it can be downright frustrating and uncomfortable. I've waited for over three hours on a street corner for a cat with a bag to surface. And you don't leave, 'cause he's the only one holding and if you miss him someone else will get the stuff and you'll be left holding air.[19]

Alfred R. Lindesmith and others have claimed that, once addicted, the rush, kick, and euphoria that heroin produces become of only minor importance in explaining continued usage; and that it is the fear of the withdrawal symptoms—the yawning, sneezing, crying, running nose, gooseflesh, rapid pulse, hot and cold flashes, nausea and vomiting, diarrhea, stomach cramps, and muscular spasms—that motivates further use.[20] Yet by contrast, Dr. David P. Ausubel once argued:

> The popular misconception that addicted individuals deprived of the drug suffer the tortures of the damned, and that once caught in the grip of physiological dependence the average person is powerless to help himself, are beliefs that have been touted on a credulous public by misinformed journalists and by addicts themselves.[21]

On this point, David K. commented:

> Listen, white brother, that's a crock of pure mule shit! Sure, you hurt, you hurt bad all over. But what you're really doin' is chasin' the rush and that wonderful feeling that you and the whole fucking world around you is cool. That's what you're really after, the high, the wonderful high. True, when you get busted and have to kick *cold* [without medication] in some dirty fucking stinking jail you raise hell and put on a show so maybe you'll get some medicine, but it's never as bad as you make it. . . . When it comes time to die, I want it to be an *OD* [overdose] on smack. That would be the greatest way to take the ride over the edge of the fucking world.

And, too, an ex-addict counselor in a Florida drug-treatment program added:

> When we are sure that the new resident has no concurrent ad-
> diction to some other drug, we just put him on the couch in
> the living room, give him a blanket, and ignore him. He'll
> start putting on his act, trying to get some sympathy. He'll
> look around the room and see some guy waxing the floor,
> somebody else at an ironing board, or somebody just reading
> a book. They're people who were shooting with him once out
> in the street and now they're all ignoring him. Pretty soon he
> settles down. He hurts, but it wears off in 24 to 48 hours.

The myth that heroin withdrawal is similar to the tortures of hell has a long history. As early as 1917 in a paper read before the California State Medical Association, Dr. A. S. Tuchler of San Francisco stated:

> When one is placed in confinement and deprived of the drug,
> the suffering, both physical and mental, endured by the ad-
> dict, is beyond comprehension and belief.[22]

More recently, the myth has been a product of the media, vividly presented in such films as *The Man with the Golden Arm* (1955), *Monkey
on My Back* (1957), and *French Connection II* (1975). But researchers
and clinicians in the drug field, and many heroin users as well, tend to
agree that withdrawal is no different, and no more severe, than the chills,
cramps, and muscle pains that are associated with a good dose of the
flu—something that almost everyone has experienced.*

Gambling with Death

Unlike the situation with many other drugs, chronic heroin use seems to
produce little direct or permanent physiological damage. Street heroin
users tend to neglect themselves, however, and commonly reported disorders include heart and lung abnormalities, *tracks* (scarred veins), malnutrition, weight loss, obstetrical problems in pregnant women, and
particularly hepatitis and local skin infections and abscesses.[23] Many heroin users live on the street, in alleys or abandoned buildings, and in gen-

---

* Remember that this is not necessarily the case with *all* addicting drugs. The unsupervised
withdrawal from barbiturates and other sedative drugs can bring on shock, coma, and
death.

eral ignore the standard practices that encourage good health. In 1985, a Philadelphia heroin user stated:

> When you spend most of your time hustling on the streets, scoring, fixing, scoring, fixing, hustling again, and living in some damp cellar that has dripping fungus on the walls you don't have time for such frills as fresh laundry, perfume baths, and gourmet food. . . .

And as David K. remarked:

> . . . once in a while I go home and I find that my sister has left me some clean clothes, but most of the time I wear the same fucking things from week to week. . . . I don't know how long it's been since I had a good shower, and for food it's either a taco, a Big Mac, or french fries and sour balls washed down with Coca-Cola and cheap wine.

For some women heroin users, there can be a number of additional problems. A heroin-using, part-time prostitute in Miami stated in 1984:

> . . . When you find yourself fucking for money, fucking for drugs, and sometimes fucking or sucking a hairy prick for something to eat or a place to sleep, you're not too careful about avoiding the cruds. What's more, since you're stoned most of the time you don't feel much in the way of pain, or either that your whole body hurts and you can't tell where the trouble is. . . . When some kind of mess starts leakin' from my crotch like toothpaste from a tube I know it's time to get my ass off to the clinic.

Even though the infections and malnutrition are the result of poor eating habits and lack of personal hygiene, hepatitis is the result of needle sharing. Associated with this in recent years is acquired immunodeficiency syndrome (AIDS). Since this invariably fatal disease was first described in June 1981, intravenous drug users have emerged as its second highest "at-risk" category. In late 1985, they represented some 17% of the 11,919 known cases. In New York City, heroin users accounted for some 33% of the reported AIDS victims.[24]

Next, there is the problem of heroin overdose, a phenomenon that is still not fully understood. Some users OD as the result of too much heroin or a too-potent heroin. In these instances, if death occurs, it is the result

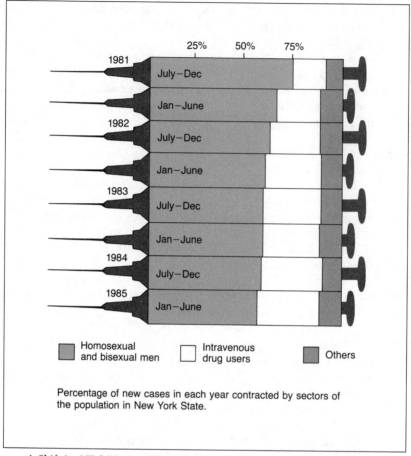

A Shift in AIDS Victims. SOURCE: *New York Times*, 20 Oct. 1985, p. 51

of respiratory depression, that is, suffocation. In other instances death is so rapid that the needle is often still in the user's arm when he or she is found. Such deaths are the result of asphyxiation caused by acute pulmonary edema (an accumulation of fluid in the lungs). Overdose deaths are more often the result of heroin intake combined with the concurrent use of alcohol and another sedative. There is also the difficulty posed by the adulterants used to "cut" heroin. Quinine is popular. An irritant, it can cause vascular damage, acute and potentially lethal disturbances in heartbeat, depressed respiration, coma, and respiratory arrest. Moreover, heroin plus quinine can have an unpredictable compounding effect.[25]

Overdose can also be a natural consequence of the very nature of the drug-taking and drug-seeking behaviors of heroin users. In their endless pursuit of the "high," users continually seek out "good stuff"—strong, potent heroin—and they have several alternatives. They can make their purchases from their regular dealer, one with whom they have been successful in the past. They can use the street "grapevine"—an informal, and often erroneous, communication network that lets them know where they can connect for "dynamite stuff." And finally, associated with the street grapevine are "brand names"—a phenomenon apparent in New York, Philadelphia, Miami, Chicago, St. Louis, Los Angeles, and other urban areas across the United States when heroin is in great supply.

The labeling of drugs, studied most extensively by ethnographer Paul J. Goldstein in New York City, has become a popular merchandising technique in the drug black market. The process occurs chiefly with heroin and involves distinctive packaging prior to sale. The bag containing the heroin is labeled with a name, symbol, or number, usually in a specific color. Among the "brand names" touted as "good stuff" in New York City have been such heroin labels as *Black Magic, Chako Fan, Death Row, 888, Fuck Me Please, Good Pussy, 90%, Kojak, The Beast, 32,* and *The Witch.*[26] In Miami, some highly sought-after names in 1985 included *Chain Saw, Savage Cunt, Mexican Satan, Hand Job, Golden Girl, Climax,* and *Rambo.* In 1986 the names included *Rocky IV, Slime, Jail Bait, Sweet Lucy's Tit,* and "Miami Vice." With respect to the functions of heroin labeling, Goldstein explained:

> Most [users] have limited capital to expend on heroin. There are a multitude of street dealers to choose from. Getting beat on a heroin purchase or buying inferior quality heroin is an omnipresent risk. The quality of heroin that is commonly available is poor. Heroin users have either experienced or heard reminiscences of the superior dope of yesteryear and may have occasionally encountered highly potent heroin themselves in more recent years. Heroin users always look to obtain the highest quality heroin in a confusing and uncontrolled marketplace. Most seem to feel that labeling bags of heroin assists them in their quest.[27]

Yet whether it is through brand names or grapevine rumor, the pursuit of the best heroin can have lethal consequences. During February 1975, for example, word quickly spread throughout the Miami drug community that a dealer in North Miami Beach had a supply of heroin so potent that he was hesitant to sell it. As one user put it: "It's supposed to be a gift

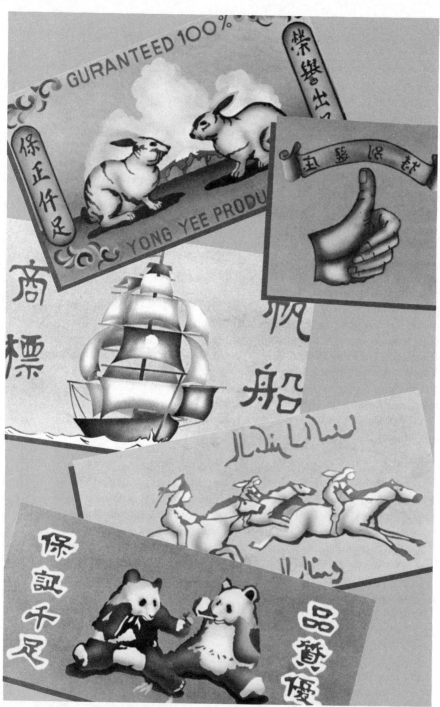

Throughout this century, packages of heroin trafficked into the United States have been trademarked with exotic and colorful labels. Those illustrated here are among the many accumulated in recent years by the Drug Enforcement Administration.

from God, a god by the name of Bentley." The dealer ultimately sold his supply but a sample was obtained for analysis. As it turned out, the drug was *Etorphine,* one of several compounds discovered by K. W. Bentley of Edinburgh during the early 1960s through a manipulation of the morphine molecule.[28] Bentley's compound had a potency several thousand times that of morphine. Before it finally disappeared from the streets, more than a score of heroin users in South Florida had tried it and fatally overdosed.*

Miami's Etorphine incident was not an isolated case, for the drug has periodically reappeared on the streets of South Florida in the years hence. Then there was *China White,* a pure, but rare and perhaps mythical strain of heroin from Southeast Asia that has been a fantasy among many West Coast users for more than a decade. "*Getting down* [shooting up] on it is a never-ending dream," said one user from Sacramento. In late 1980, the dream finally came true, or so it seemed. Word spread through southern California that "China White" had finally arrived on American shores. But the drug was not China White at all, and users began dying from it. It was a chemical similar in structure to *Fentanyl,* a synthetic narcotic analgesic 80 to 100 times more potent than morphine.[29] Moreover, the new synthetic was the first in a continuing series of what have become known as "designer drugs." So-named because they are new substances "designed" by slightly altering the chemical makeup of other illegal drugs, they are typically more potent and often contaminated versions of either Fentanyl or Demerol. One variety has been found to destroy brain cells; another produces the symptoms of Parkinson's disease and accelerated aging; a third paralyzes its users; and a fourth has a potency 6,000 times that of heroin—producing instantaneous death.[30] These new drugs have posed such a threat to heroin users seeking a fix that one recently testified: "I don't know if the next dose will kill me."[31]

The precise number of overdoses from heroin (and other illicit narcotics) use is probably impossible to estimate. Users, unless their conditions appear especially life threatening, are rarely brought to hospital emergency rooms for treatment. In the case of lethal overdoses, it is not always possible to classify the exact cause of death. On the basis of data that the Drug Abuse Warning Network collected, some 11,000 to 13,000 heroin overdoses result in emergency room treatment each year, with at least an additional 1,000 resulting in a visit to the county morgue.[32]

---

* Under the Controlled Substances Act of 1971, *Etorphine* is classified as a Schedule I drug, which means that, like heroin and LSD, it has no accepted medical use in the United States and its mere possession is a violation of federal law. *Etorphine hydrochloride,* a less potent variety, is used occasionally by veterinarians to immobilize wild animals. In fact, even this milder form is so strong that a 2-cc dose is capable of immobilizing a 4-ton elephant.

The Heroin Epidemics

Although opiate use, in its various forms, has been common throughout United States history, its current manifestation—the intravenous use of heroin—apparently developed during the 1930s and became widespread after 1945.[33] Between 1950 and the early 1960s, most major cities experienced a low-level spread of heroin use, particularly among the black and other minority populations. Thereafter, use began to grow rapidly, rising to peaks in the late 1960s and then falling sharply. The pattern was so ubiquitous that it came to be regarded as "epidemic" heroin use.[34] More recent "epidemics" occurred in 1973–1974, 1977–1978, and 1982–1983, defined as such on the basis of the numbers of new admissions to heroin-treatment facilities. Yet interestingly, no one really knew how widespread heroin use was during those years, and even today the estimates are often no more than scientific guesses.

Throughout the 1960s, the Treasury Department's Bureau of Narcotics would periodically announce the number of active narcotics addicts in the United States. As of December 31, 1967, for example, it set the number at 62,045.[35] This figure—not 60,000 or 65,000, but 62,045—suggested considerable precision. New York City's many drug-abuse researchers, clinicians, and members of law-enforcement groups found the estimate suspect, however, since from their experiences the heroin problem was much greater. In fact, a heroin user from New York's Harlem area jokingly stated that " . . . there are more junkies than that just on my street."

The suspicions were justified, of course, for the bureau's figure was based almost exclusively on reports from local police departments. Moreover, New York had its own such file at the time, one that reported almost twice the national bureau's number of new cases for the same year.[36] In an attempt to foist some scientific rationality into the estimates of heroin prevalence, in 1969 John C. Ball of Temple University and Carl D. Chambers of the New York State Narcotic Addiction Control Commission combined data from the New York and national Bureau of Narcotics files with figures provided by the federal drug-treatment facilities in Lexington, Kentucky, and Fort Worth, Texas. Through a complex series of ratios and correction factors, they came up with a figure of 108,424 heroin addicts for the year 1967.[37] Even Ball and Chambers, however, were not altogether confident with their estimate, for they were acutely aware of the potentially vast number of unreported cases.

In 1970, using scientific survey methodology, cross-sectional studies of the general population finally reached the drug field.[38] As indicators of heroin use, however, the data were disappointing. It was known at the outset that general population surveys could access only the more stable "at-home" populations, thus excluding residents of jails and penitentiaries, mental institutions, migrant workers, those on skid rows, and others living on the street.[39]

As the drug field moved through the 1970s, the National Institute on Drug Abuse developed what it called "heroin trend indicators," relative estimates generated from a composite of reported heroin-related deaths, hospital emergency room visits, heroin-treatment admissions, and high school and household surveys. On the basis of these data, the estimated number of heroin users in the United States for 1977 ranged from 396,000 to 510,000.[40] There were other figures, also. During the same year, for example, sociologist William J. Chambliss of the University of Delaware argued that the official estimates were no more than political ploys designed to downplay the scope of heroin addiction in the United States. He offered the number of 1 million. As it turned out, however, the Chambliss figure was no more than an imaginative guess, perhaps tempered by an ideological position that was unbiased by the rigors of scientific survey methodology.[41]

By the mid-1980s, government reports were maintaining that the number of heroin users was somewhere in the vicinity of 500,000, having been at that level for about a decade.[42] Personal interviews with drug-abuse researchers and government officials during late 1985 tended to confirm the 500,000 estimate, "give or take 50,000 or so," as several suggested.

COCAINE: "THE MOST DANGEROUS SUBSTANCE ON EARTH"

Cocaine is known to its users as *shit, coke, bernice, big C, corrine, lady snow, toot, nose candy,* and in some circles as *Super Fly* (from the 1972 Warner Brothers movie of the same name). When TV's Mike Hammer, actor Stacy Keach, appeared before a government committee in 1985 to confess his problems with cocaine, some observers referred to the drug as "the most dangerous substance on earth." But wait, there seems to be a contradiction here. Earlier, heroin was reportedly the "most dangerous" of all. But then, at different times and in various media such drugs as marijuana, LSD, PCP, the amphetamines, Quaalude, and Ecstasy have each been designated as the world's most dangerous substance.

Regardless of the epithets, the aura surrounding today's "coke" is quite different from that of Angelo Mariani's Vin Coca, John Pemberton's French

Wine Coca, or even Sigmund Freud's cocaine. Cocaine use in contemporary America is considered a major health problem, with estimates of the number of regular users ranging as high as 10 to 20 million, with an additional 5,000 each day trying the drug for the first time.[43]

Adventures Along the Cocaine Highway

At the end of the 1880s when Sigmund Freud and his colleagues discovered that cocaine was not the all-purpose wonder drug that they had hoped for, they quickly withdrew their support for its applications in medical therapy. Aside from the drug's use by the patent-medicine industry until the passage of the Pure Food and Drug Act in 1906, cocaine moved underground, and remained there for the better part of a century. Its major devotees included prostitutes, jazz musicians, fortune-tellers, criminals, and blacks. Its relegation to the netherworlds of crime and the bizarre should not suggest, however, that people in this country were unconcerned with the use of cocaine by "alien" subcultures. Quite the contrary. During the early decades of the twentieth century, commentaries about cocaine took on racial overtones, precipitated by white fears of the blacks' sexual and criminal impulses. In 1910, for example, testimony before a committee of the House of Representatives referenced these fears and also included almost every white stereotype of blacks:

> The colored people seem to have a weakness for it [cocaine]. It is a very seductive drug, and it produces extreme exhilaration. Persons under the influences of it believe they are millionaires. They have an exaggerated ego. They imagine they can lift this building, if they want to, or can do anything they want to. They have no regard for right or wrong. It produces a kind of temporary insanity. They would just as leave rape a woman as anything else and a great many of the southern rape cases have been traced to cocaine.[44]

In later decades cocaine use was associated with such exotic groups as the "beatniks" of New York's Greenwich Village and San Francisco's North Beach, the movie colony of Hollywood, and to such an extent with the urban "smart set" that *coke* became known as "the rich man's drug."

During the late 1960s and early 1970s, cocaine use began to move from the underground to mainstream society, to a great extent the result of a series of decisions made at the time in Washington, D.C. *First,* the U.S. Senate and the federal drug-enforcement bureaucracy sponsored legislation that served to reduce the legal production of amphetamine-type drugs in the United States and to place strict controls on Quaaludes and other abused sedatives. *Second,* and most importantly, the World Bank allocated funds for the construction of the Pan American Highway through the Huallaga River valley in the high jungles of Peru. These two factors combined to usher in the cocaine era.

The growing of coca leaves had always been popular on the slopes of the Peruvian Andes, but cultivation was for the most part limited for local consumption in tea or for chewing. Only relatively small amounts of the leaves were available for processing into cocaine. Travel throughout the rugged Andes terrain was difficult, and the coca leaves had to be carried out by mule pack. The World Bank's construction of a paved thoroughfare through the Huallaga valley opened up transportation routes for the shipping of coca, and the reduced availability of amphetamines and sedatives in the United States helped to provide a ready market for the new intoxicant. With the North Americans' increasing usage of cocaine, South American growers and entrepreneurs responded by opening vast new areas for the cultivation of coca.

The cocaine highway begins in the Andes Mountains of South America where the coca leaves are grown. There are the Chapare, Beni, and Yungas regions of northern and central Bolivia—areas characterized by spectacular mountain peaks with lofty snowcapped passes and thundering waterfalls that roller coaster down into subtropical valleys and moist tumbling lowlands. In Peru there are remote high jungles surrounding the Upper Huallaga River, a tributary of the mighty Amazon. In Ecuador there are highlands on both sides of the equator and areas adjacent to Guayaquil, that nation's largest city. In southeastern Colombia, there is the vast and virtually uninhabited Amazonas territory; and there are plantations in East Asia, Bali, and the Caribbean. In these regions, on some 350,000 acres of scattered fields, peasant farmers cultivate coca. More than 100,000 metric tons of leaf are produced annually, the majority of production occurring in Bolivia and Peru.[45]

The production of cocaine begins with the coca leaf. In the natural greenhouses of the Chapare, the Upper Huallaga, and similar forsaken tropical slopes and lowlands, rows of *Erythroxylan coca* are neatly planted. At harvest time, the leaves are carefully picked, dried, and bundled for pack carriers who transport them to the clandestine processing laboratories. In Peru's Upper Huallaga, the labs are usually nearby, but in the Bolivian Chapare, often the carriers must bear their loads across hundreds of miles of footpaths to the Beni, a jungle and savanna province the size of Kansas with no paved highways and few roads of any kind.

At the jungle refineries the leaves are sold for $8 to $12 a kilo. The leaves are then pulverized, soaked in alcohol mixed with benzol (a petroleum derivative used in the manufacture of motor fuels, detergents, and insecticides), and shaken. The alcohol–benzol mixture is then drained, sulfuric acid is added, and the solution is shaken again. Next, a precipitate is formed when sodium carbonate is added to the solution. When this is washed with kerosene and chilled, crystals of crude cocaine are left behind. These crystals are known as *coca paste*. The cocaine content of leaves is relatively low—0.5% to 1% by weight as opposed to the paste, which has a cocaine concentration ranging up to 90% but more commonly only about 40%.

From the coca fields and refineries, the cocaine highway leads to Amazonia—a land of superlatives and the largest single geographical feature of the South American continent. Amazonia, known to the world as "the Amazon," is a river, a valley, and a tropical rain forest. The river begins high in the Peruvian Andes and runs more than 4,000 miles along the equator to the Atlantic Ocean. Drawing its initial strength from hundreds of small mountain streams, it tumbles through steep gorges and eventually opens out into a mile-wide flow in northern Peru. The Amazon is also fed by 200 major tributaries, 17 of which are more than 1,000 miles long. At points along its course in Brazil, the river is several hundred feet deep and often more than 7 miles across. When it finally reaches the Atlantic Ocean, the river discharges 3.4 million gallons of water each minute, staining the sea brown with silt for 150 miles. The river valley and tropical rain forest cover 2.5 million square miles of Brazil, Peru, Colombia, Ecuador, Bolivia, Venezuela, Suriname, and Guyana. If it were a country, Amazonia would be the ninth largest in the world, more than half the size of the United States.[46] Impossible to patrol, yet near cities closely linked to the outside world, Amazonia offers almost limitless potential as a drug base.

At the edge of Amazonia in eastern Bolivia is Santa Cruz. Two decades ago the city looked much like a small town on the Texas panhandle. Horses roamed its dusty streets, few people could be seen, and about the only sound that could be heard was the howling wind. Then came the discovery of oil and natural gas, and finally the trafficking in cocaine. The once-pathetic outpost suddenly became a boom town. Still hot and dusty, Santa Cruz is now Bolivia's second largest city. It has a university, an international airport, golf and tennis clubs, and several hotels, including a Holiday Inn. As a key point along the cocaine highway, the city is a gathering place for Colombian and American buyers of coca paste. Often amidst the coca merchants is a collection of military personnel who provide smugglers with protection and secure contraband routes.

In the paradise of lush, subtropical vegetation of western Amazonia is Tingo Maria, Peru. It is a jungle town of 20,000 and one of the few places in the world where jet aircraft land on a grass runway. Tingo Maria is also an architectural nightmare. Most of the buildings appear hastily built of cinder blocks, with little paint or other finishing work. In a few places the streets are paved, but only haphazardly. Tingo Maria has one hotel, built during World War II for U.S. military officers and mining engineers. Described as already run-down in the 1950s,[47] it is now the State Tourist Hotel—still run-down but in a more-or-less state of arrested decay. The primary business enterprise of Tingo Maria is coca leaves and coca paste, which are sometimes openly bartered on its dusty streets. While traders deal in their coca products, a garrison of the Peruvian Army is often present, its efforts directed exclusively against local bandits and anti-government guerillas.

Some 400 miles north of Tingo Maria is Iquitos, deep in Peruvian Amazonia. It is a relatively modern city of 80,000 and is located directly on the great river. As a port 2,300 miles upriver from the Atlantic that can be reached by oceangoing freighters, it is a pivotal point in the cocaine commerce. To understand this, one need only visit a few of the many bars in Iquitos. Populated by picturesque adventurers and other characters seemingly from grade B movies, deals in coca paste can be readily overheard.

A few hundred miles downriver on the Amazon is Leticia, Colombia, a town of only a few thousand. Overpowered outboards as well as *Magnums, Cigarettes, Excaliburs, Scarab Sports,* and other high-performance racing boats of a vintage that might be seen on TV's "Miami Vice," fill the small marinas that dot the riverbank. Fairly common, too, are rows of small seaplanes docked incongruously among the muddy decay that is characteristic of almost every jungle river town. It would appear that Leticia exists for no reason but smuggling. The thousands of surrounding small tributaries and inlets make it impossible to control boat and seaplane traffic. Moreover, located just west of Brazil and east of the Peruvian frontier, Leticia is an ideal haven for anyone attempting to move goods from one country to another. The traffic, by the way, is not only in coca products but in stolen art and jewelry, guns, and rare animals—alive and skinned.

From Santa Cruz, Tingo Maria, Iquitos, Leticia, and other remote outposts, the coca paste works its way through Peru, Ecuador, and Brazil to Colombia. The principal destinations in Colombia where the paste is refined into cocaine include the areas surrounding the cities of Bogotá, Medellín, Barranquilla, and Cartagena. There the paste is treated with ether, acetone, and hydrochloric acid, resulting in a cocaine that is typically 85% to 97% pure, with no toxic adulterants.

The final segment of the cocaine highway extends by air through a series of refueling and transshipping stops in the Bahamas, Central America, Cuba, and Mexico to Miami, New Orleans, Dallas, New York, Atlanta, Boston, or one of many small Atlantic or Gulf Coast ports. The

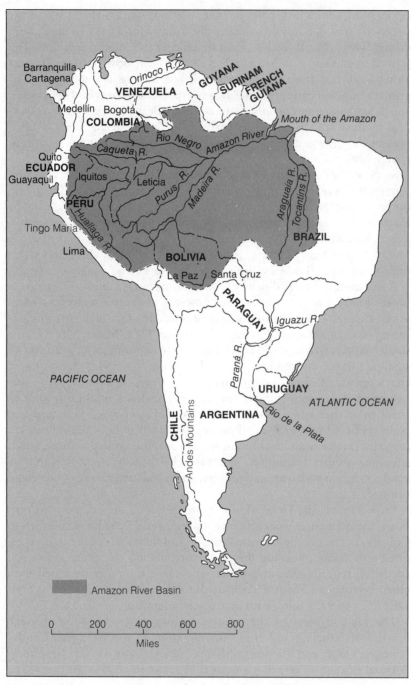

Amazonia

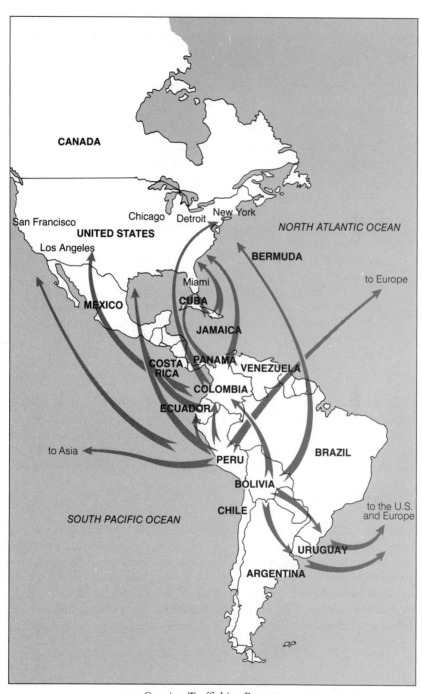

Cocaine-Trafficking Routes

penetration of U.S. borders occurs at major airports, deserted airstrips, and through a variety of obscure air–sea routes chosen because of their impossibility to control. A small-time Miami trafficker explained in 1983:

> With the combination of good coordination, good connections, good navigation equipment, good navigation skills, plus a few payoffs here and there, coke can be safely brought in at any time. . . . In one operation we had, we had a guy fly out of Cartagena with refueling stops in Jamaica and Nassau. After a little money changed hands there with the right officials, then he headed towards Miami and dropped the 10-kilo watertight package out the window into the water, to a prearranged spot just a few miles offshore just the other side of the reefs. Then he landed at Miami International and went through customs like everyone else and came out perfectly clean. That was on a Saturday night. The next afternoon, when the water was full of Sunday boaters, another guy went out with a good set of Loran numbers.* He located the exact spot, went over the side with fins, mask, and snorkel and found the thing in 40 feet of water. Then he did some fishing and came back late in the afternoon with all the other boaters. He had his girlfriend and her kid with him, so everything looked ordinary and nobody looked suspicious. It's a clean arrangement. . . .

By the time cocaine has been cut several times—with lactose, baking soda, caffeine, quinine, lidocaine, powdered laxatives, or even borax—to an average of 12% purity, it ranges in street price from $50 to $120 a gram. What started out as 500 kilograms of coca leaves worth $4,000 to the grower ultimately yields 8 kilos of street cocaine valued at $500,000.

Fire in the Brain

Lured by the Lorelei of orgasmic pleasure, millions of Americans use cocaine each year—a snort in each nostril and the user is up and away for 20 minutes or so. Alert, witty, and with it, the user has no hangover, no physical addiction, no lung cancer, and no holes in the arms or burned-out cells in the brain. The cocaine high is an immediate, intensely vivid, and sensation-enhancing experience. Moreover, it has the reputation for being a spectacular aphrodisiac: it is believed to create sexual desire,

---

* *Loran* is a navigational device that provides boaters with lines of positions derived from signals emitted from coastal-transmitting stations. Any given location offshore, described in terms of its Loran "numbers," can be found with almost pinpoint accuracy.

to heighten it, to increase sexual endurance, and to cure frigidity and impotence.

Given all these positives, no wonder cocaine has become the "all-American drug" and a $30 to $50 billion-a-year industry. It permeates all levels of society, from Park Avenue to the ghetto: lawyers and executives use cocaine; baby boomers and yuppies use cocaine; police officers, prosecutors, and prisoners use cocaine; politicians use cocaine; housewives and pensioners use cocaine; Democrats, Republicans, and Socialists use cocaine; students and stockbrokers and children and athletes use cocaine; even some priests and members of Congress use cocaine.[48]

Yet, the pleasure and feelings of power that cocaine engenders make its use a problematic recreational pursuit. In very small and occasional doses it is no more harmful than equally moderate doses of alcohol or marijuana, and infinitely less so than heroin, but there is a side to cocaine that can be very destructive. That euphoric lift, with its feelings of confidence and being on top of things, that comes from but a few brief snorts is short-lived and invariably followed by a letdown.

Since the body does not develop any significant tolerance to cocaine, and since physical dependence similar to that on heroin never develops, the drug can be said to be nonaddicting. Yet some will argue this position, pointing to the many chronic users who compulsively indulge in cocaine. Sidney Cohen of the Neuropsychiatric Institute at the Los Angeles School of Medicine, for example, suggests that the notion that cocaine does not produce addiction comes from the early professional literature, written at a time when the quantities of the drug used were smaller than those taken by contemporary users.[49] He adds that the high doses of cocaine currently used, combined with the frequency with which they are taken, produce a withdrawal syndrome characterized primarily by psychological depression. Yet in counterpoint, what seems to be happening in these cases is only strong *psychic dependence.* * Compulsive users seek the extreme mood elevation, elation, and grandiose feelings of heightened mental and physical prowess induced by the drug. When these begin to wane, a corresponding deep depression is felt, which is in such marked contrast to the users' previous states that they are strongly motivated to repeat the dose and restore their euphoria. Thus, when chronic users try to stop using cocaine, they are often plunged into a severe depression from which only

---

* A good bit of the confusion about the nature of cocaine dependence comes from well-meaning, but nevertheless irresponsible, statements. In *The All-American Cocaine Story* (Minneapolis: CompCare Publications, 1984), author David R. Britt states:

> Yes, cocaine is extremely addicting. Anyone who tells you that cocaine is not an addictive drug is misinformed and self-deluding. Those "experts" who make a big distinction between physical addiction and "psychological dependence" epitomize mental masturbation.

the drug can arouse them. For those who insist on calling cocaine an addicting drug, perhaps they could be persuaded to use the term *psychogenic addiction*. Users experiencing the sudden emotional letdown after the cessation of cocaine's effects *think* they have a physical need for the drug. Hence, the addiction is "psychogenic"—emanating from the mind. *

In addition to the strong psychic dependence, chronic cocaine use typically causes hyperstimulation, digestive disorders, nausea, loss of appetite, weight loss, occasional convulsions, and sometimes paranoid psychoses and delusions of persecution. Moreover, repeated inhalation can result in erosions of the mucous membranes, including perforations of the nasal septum. A chronic "runny nose" is often a mark of the regular cocaine user. The reasons for these effects on the nose are well understood. Cocaine totally numbs the nasal membranes, which then shrink as their blood supply diminishes. When the drug wears off, the mucous membranes demand the blood supply that was withheld, and the nose becomes congested, with the symptoms of a head cold likely to follow. Moreover, any cocaine that remains undissolved in the nose can cause burns and sores, which can eventually lead to degeneration of the nasal mucous membranes or eat through the cartilage itself.

These are the effects of "snorting" cocaine, the most common method of ingestion, but there are other ways of taking the drug, each of which can bring on an added spectrum of complications. One of these methods is *freebasing*, a phenomenon that has been known in the drug community for at least a decade but that moved into the mainstream of cocaine use only recently. Freebase cocaine is actually a different chemical product from cocaine itself. In the process of freebasing, street cocaine, which is usually in the form of a hydrochloride salt, is treated with a liquid base to remove the hydrochloric acid. The free cocaine is then dissolved in a solvent such as ether, from which the purified cocaine is crystallized. These crystals are then crushed and used in a special heated glass pipe. Smoking freebase cocaine provides a more potent *rush* and a more powerful high than regular cocaine, and as such, its use is that much more seductive. Moreover, the freebasing process involves the use of ether, a highly volatile petroleum product that has exploded in the face of many a user.

Cocaine has also been used as a sex aid, a practice that has brought

---

* At the annual meeting of the Society for Neuroscience in 1985, researchers reported that the craving typically associated with cocaine cessation can be eased by drugs that stimulate dopamine production in the brain. Whether this finding will ultimately shed some light on the "cocaine addiction" debate is difficult to tell. (See the *New York Times*, 22 Oct. 1985, p. C5.)

both pleasurable and disastrous results. A sprinkle of cocaine on the clitoris or just below the head of the penis will anesthetize the tissues and retard a sexual climax. But with persistent stimulation, the drug will ultimately promote an explosive orgasm. However, the urethra (the tube inside the penis or the vulva through which urine is eliminated) is very sensitive to cocaine. At a minimum, the drug will dry out the urethral membranes, which must remain moist to function properly. At a maximum, since the absorption rate of cocaine through the walls of the urethra is quite rapid, overdoses have been known to happen.

Common in the drug-using communities of Colombia, Bolivia, Ecuador, Peru, and other South American nations is the use of "basuco," or coca paste.[50] It is typically smoked, in cigarettes mixed with either tobacco or marijuana. Laboratory analyses have demonstrated that the cocaine content of paste ranges from 40% to 91%. In addition, in coca paste there are traces of all the chemicals used to initially process the coca leaves—kerosene, sulfuric acid, methanol, benzoic acid, and oxidized products of these solvents, plus any number of other alkaloids that are present in the coca leaf.[51] The smoking of paste was first noted in South America during the early 1970s and seemed to be restricted to that part of the world, appealing primarily to low-income groups because it is inexpensive when compared to refined cocaine.[52] By 1985, however, the practice had finally made its way to the United States, first in Miami where it was imported, and then elsewhere. Interestingly, the paste quickly became known to young North American users as "bubble gum," probably because of the phonetic association of the South American "basuco" with the American Bazooka bubble gum.

Among chronic users of cocaine, the intravenous use of the drug has become more noticeable in recent years. This route of administration produces an extremely rapid onset of the drug's effects, usually within 15 to 20 seconds, along with a rather powerful high. It also produces the more debilitating effects of psychoses and paranoid delusions, similar to those of the amphetamine "speed freak." These occur more rapidly than when cocaine is chronically snorted.* One related phenomenon is the increasing intravenous use of cocaine in combination with another drug. Known as "speedballing," the practice is not at all new. The classic *speedball* is a mixture of heroin and cocaine. It was referred to as such by the heroin-using community as early as the 1930s, and as *whizbang* as far back as 1918.[53] Whether the user's primary drug of choice is cocaine or

---

* When cocaine was first introduced during the latter part of the nineteenth century, intramuscular injections were frequently employed. This mechanism, however, has never been reported among contemporary users.

heroin, the speedball intensifies the euphoric effect. It can also be quite dangerous: speedballing killed actor–comedian John Belushi in 1982.

The most recent entry to the arena of cocaine use is the cocaine "rock," a pebble-sized crystalline form of cocaine base. The new product came from a Los Angeles basement chemist who discovered a way to transform a gram of cocaine into a half dozen "rocks" that could be sold and smoked for as little as $25 each.[54] The rocks are produced by cutting cocaine with baking soda and then cooking the mixture in a test tube. The process is simple and quick, and the resulting product is relatively pure, inexpensive, and easily hidden, passed, or disposed of. Already common in southern California at the close of 1984, by the middle of 1985 cocaine "rocks" could be found in the classrooms and on the streets of Miami, New York, New Orleans, and Philadelphia.

Finally, some substitute drugs have effects similar to cocaine, but they are actually other stimulants marketed as the genuine article. Known to some users as "crack" or "crank,"* their contents are often a mystery. They can contain freebase residue, concentrated caffeine, amphetamines, prescription stimulants, or any combination thereof. A recent entry to this substitute market is *pemoline,* a potent central nervous system stimulant used for the treatment of attention-deficit disorders.[55]

Whether the pattern of use involves snorting, freebasing, shooting, speedballing, or smoking paste or rocks, the hazards of cocaine use can go well beyond those already noted. Some individuals, likely few in number, are hypersensitive to cocaine, and as little as 20 milligrams can be fatal. Since cocaine is a potent stimulant that rapidly increases the blood pressure, sudden death can also occur from only small amounts among users suffering from coronary artery disease or weak cerebral blood vessels. Cocaine is also a convulsant that can induce major seizures and cause fatalities if emergency treatment is not immediately at hand. Post-cocaine depression, if intense, can lead to suicide. If the dose is large enough, cocaine can be toxic and result in an overdose. For the majority

---

* "Crank" and "crack" are often used here as street names for many different drugs. These are not errors. Rather, street names tend to vary by geographic location, by drug-using group, and by time. In 1985 on the East Coast, no less than four different substances were being referred to as *crank*—cocaine, cocaine substitutes, amphetamines, and the drug extracted from the cotton plug found in nasal inhalers. On this latter point, many decongestant inhalers contain *propylexedrine,* a substance that is less potent than cocaine or the amphetamines but nevertheless stimulates the central nervous system. The drug is extracted and taken intravenously, and has been known to cause complications such as convulsions, strokes, respiratory and kidney failures, and death. (See the *New York Times,* 22 Sept. 1985, p. 34.) *Crack* sometimes refers to cocaine substitutes, and on the East Coast, it is what Californians call cocaine "rocks." (See the *New York Times,* 29 Nov. 1985, pp. A1, B6.)

of users, this can occur with as little as 1 gram, taken intravenously. When injected, cocaine has been known to cause all those diseases that result from the use of unsterile needles—hepatitis, infections, and even AIDS.*,[56]

Many different mechanisms have been used to classify cocaine users into different groups. Some classifications have been based on frequency and amount of use, whereas others have focused on motivations, routes of administration, or context of use.[57] Perhaps the most practical way of differentiating types of cocaine users is the simple fourfold classification of *experimenters, social–recreational users, involved users,* and *dysfunctional abusers*—a general classification that has been widely applied in the drug field for quite some time.[58]

The *experimenters* are by far the largest group of cocaine users. They most frequently try cocaine a time or two in a social setting, but the drug does not play a significant role in their lives. They use cocaine experimentally because their social group relates the drug's effects as being pleasurable. Experimenters do not seek out cocaine but may use it when someone presents it to them in an appropriate setting. In this situation, they may "snort" the drug once or twice because it does something *to* them. As a University of Delaware senior commented in 1985:

> I generally don't use drugs, except maybe a little grass now and then. My only experience with coke was a few weeks ago in the dormitory. My roommate came in with a couple of other guys and started getting high on it. They kept trying to get me to do some, and finally I snorted some just for the heck of it. When I did, it was quite a blast at first, from my head all the way down, and then I felt like I was floating. After, I felt a little weird. . . . It was good. . . .

Social–recreational users differ from experimenters primarily in terms of frequency and continuity of consumption. For example, they may use cocaine when they are at a party and someone presents the opportunity. Cocaine still does not play a significant role in these users' lives. They still do not actively seek out the drug but use it only because it does some-

---

* Numerous cocaine-related deaths have resulted from "body packing," a smuggling rather than an ingestion method. Small amounts of cocaine are packed into condoms, which are then swallowed or secreted in the rectum or vagina. Unless the carrier is a suspected cocaine courier or "mule," the drug's detection by Customs agents is difficult. On many occasions one or more of these condoms have ruptured, releasing lethal amounts of pure cocaine into the carrier's body. In one case, more than five dozen cocaine-packed condoms were found in the stomach of a smuggler. See the *Wall Street Journal,* 5 Aug. 1982, pp. 1, 8.

thing *to* them—it makes them feel good. A 28-year-old Miami woman related:

> Partying can be even more fun with a few lines of coke. I never have any of my own, but usually I'll tie in with some guy who does. We'll get a little stoned, and maybe go to bed. It's all in good fun. . . .
>
> Another time I was on a double date and this guy had some good *toot*. We drove up to Orlando and went into Disney World. Do you know what it's like goin' through the haunted mansion stoned like that? It's a whole different trip. . . .

For *involved users*, a major transition has taken place since the social–recreational use. As users become "involved" with cocaine, they also become drug seekers, and cocaine becomes significant to their lives. Although they are still quite able to function—in school, on the job, or as a parent or spouse—their proficiency in many areas begins to decline markedly. Personal and social functioning tends to be inversely related to the amount of time involved users spend with cocaine. They still have control over their behavior, but their use of the drug occurs with increasing frequency for some adaptive reason; cocaine does something *for* them.

Involved cocaine users are of many types. Some use the drug to deal with an unbearable work situation, indulging in controlled amounts several times a day. Others use cocaine to enhance performance or bolster their self-esteem. And still a third group regularly uses cocaine to deal with stress, anxiety, or nagging boredom. As one involved user, a self-employed accountant, put it:

> I seem to be always uptight these days with almost everything I do. Everybody seems to always want something—my clients, my wife, the bank, the world. . . . A few *lines* [of cocaine] every two–three hours gets me through the day—through the tax returns, the tension at home, the bills, sex, whatever. . . . Without the coke I'd probably have to be put away somewhere. . . .

The *dysfunctional abusers* are what have become known as the "coke-heads" and "cokeaholics." For them, cocaine has become *the* significant part of their lives. They are personally and socially dysfunctional and spend all of their time in cocaine seeking, cocaine taking, and other related activities. Moreover, they no longer have control over their cocaine use.

Although dysfunctional cocaine use is the least common pattern, it is nevertheless widespread. The list of those acknowledging such dysfunctional use to the media tends to sound like an excerpt from the Who's Who in entertainment and sports. A number of these have squandered as much as $1,000 a day on the drug—John Phillips, founder of The Mamas and the Papas singing group; his daughter Mackenzie Phillips, who once starred in TV's "One Day at a Time"; guitarist Keith Richards of the Rolling Stones; John Lucas of the Washington Bullets; Carl Eller of the Minnesota Vikings; Thomas "Hollywood" Henderson of the Dallas Cowboys; and Stacy Keach, TV's Mike Hammer. Also, Academy Award winner Julia Phillips, producer of *The Sting* and *Close Encounters of the Third Kind*, spent more than $1 million on cocaine over a 10-year period. Phillips became a dedicated cocaine user during the 18-hour days of filming *Close Encounters;* in a *Time* magazine interview, she commented:

> It didn't do much for personal relationships, and a lot of this business is personal relationships. I could stay up all night thinking up ideas, but I wasn't likely to present them in the nicest fashion possible. I mean tact goes out the window. . . .
>
> I looked like someone out of Dachau. I had terrible hallucinations, particularly when night fell. There was always a prowler outside my front door with evil in his heart and a gun in his hand. I thought I had bugs coming out of my skin. . . .
>
> My little girl used to follow me around the house with a deodorant can spraying behind me because she hated the smell from freebasing. . . .[59]

POSTSCRIPT

How many more years pervasive heroin and cocaine use will persist in the United States is difficult to predict. In all likelihood, it will be for quite some time. Heroin use has been around for more than a century, and cocaine use for an even longer period. Neither treatment nor law-enforcement efforts have had significant accomplishments with either problem. The legalization of heroin and cocaine would not appear to be the answer, for both drugs are far too seductive to place uncontrolled on the open market.

Looking toward the future, one scenario might be plausible. The research, treatment, education, prevention, and law-enforcement efforts with respect to heroin use have not solved that problem, although to a great extent they seem to have contained it. As noted earlier, the number of estimated heroin users hit a level of 500,000 during the mid-1970s and has remained there ever since—more or less. The education and prevention initiatives targeting marijuana seem to have had some impact, and its use has declined somewhat in the 1980s. It, too, may level off and remain at a plateau at some point in the near future. Perhaps the same situation will occur with cocaine. One must not forget, however, that the stabilization of heroin use and the current declines of marijuana use are in part an outgrowth of the appearance of cocaine as a new drug fad. As such, perhaps a decline in cocaine use will come only as the result of the emergence of some new intoxicant, or the reemergence of some other drug that was discarded in years past.

Notes

1. Ruth R. Levine, *Pharmacology: Drug Actions and Reactions* (Boston: Little, Brown, 1973), p. 336.
2. *New York Times*, 17 Aug. 1972, p. 16.
3. See Alfred W. McCoy, *The Politics of Heroin in Southeast Asia* (New York: Harper & Row, 1972); Editors of Newsday, *The Heroin Trail* (New York: New American Library, 1974).
4. Department of State, Bureau of International Narcotics Matters, *International Narcotics Control Strategy Report, 1985* (Washington, D.C.: Department of State, 1 Feb. 1985), pp. 4, 11–13.
5. For perspectives on the history of opium, the opium culture, and the processing of opium into heroin, see Dean Latimer and Jeff Goldberg, *Flowers in the Blood: The Story of Opium* (New York: Franklin Watts, 1981); Joseph Westermeyer, *Poppies, Pipes, and People: Opium and Its Use in Laos* (Berkeley: University of California Press, 1982); Peter W. White, "The Poppy," *National Geographic*, Feb. 1985, pp. 142–189.
6. *Newsweek*, 10 Oct. 1984, p. 29.
7. *New York Times*, 21 May 1984, p. B4.
8. *U.S. News & World Report*, 11 Mar. 1985, p. 47; and White, p. 155.
9. Dan J. Lettieri, Mollie Sayers, and Helen Wallenstein, eds., *Theories on Drug Abuse: Selected Contemporary Perspectives* (Rockville, Md.: National Institute on Drug Abuse, 1980).
10. David P. Ausubel, "Causes and Types of Drug Addiction: A Psychosocial View," *Psychiatric Quarterly*, 35 (1961), 523–531; Jonathan D. Cowan, David C. Kay, Gary L. Neidert, Frances E. Ross, and Susan Belmore, "Drug Abusers: Defeated and Joyless," in *Problems of Drug Dependence*, ed. Louis S. Harris (Rockville, Md.: National Institute on Drug Abuse, 1979), pp. 170–176.
11. Calvin J. Frederick, "Drug Abuse: A Self-Destructive Enigma," *Maryland State Medical Journal*, 22 (1973), 19–21.

12. Alfred R. Lindesmith, *Opiate Addiction* (Bloomington, Ind.: Principia Press, 1947); reprinted edition, *Addiction and Opiates* (New York: Aldine, 1968).

13. Lettieri, Sayers, and Wallenstein.

14. Sandra B. Coleman, "The Family Trajectory: A Circular Journey to Drug Abuse," *Family Factors in Substance Abuse,* ed. B. Ellis (Rockville, Md.: National Institute on Drug Abuse, 1978).

15. Kenneth Chapman, "A Typical Drug Addict," *New York State Health News,* 28 Aug. 1951.

16. Orin Ross Yost, *The Bane of Drug Addiction* (New York: Macmillan, 1964), pp. 68–69, 82.

17. See Harvey B. Milkman and Howard J. Shaffer, eds., *The Addictions: Multidisciplinary Perspectives and Treatments* (Lexington, Mass.: Lexington Books, 1985).

18. Richard P. Rettig, Manuel J. Torres, and Gerald R. Garrett, *Manny: A Criminal Addict's Story* (Boston: Houghton Mifflin, 1977), pp. 33–34.

19. Rettig, Torres, and Garrett, p. 35.

20. Lindesmith, pp. 28–31.

21. David P. Ausubel, *Drug Addiction* (New York: Random House, 1958), p. 26; see also Isidor Chein, Donald L. Gerard, Robert S. Lee, and Eva Rosenfeld, *The Road to H: Narcotics, Delinquency, and Social Policy* (New York: Basic Books, 1964), pp. 113, 248.

22. A. S. Tuchler, "The Narcotic Habit: Further Observations on the Ambulatory Method of Treatment," *California Eclectic Medical Journal,* 38 (1917), 261–264.

23. See Alex W. Young, "Skin Complications of Heroin Addiction: Bullous Impetigo," *New York State Journal of Medicine,* 15 June 1973, pp. 1681–1684; B. W. Pace, W. Doscher, and I. B. Margolis, "The Femoral Triangle: A Potential Death Trap for the Drug Abuser," *New York State Journal of Medicine,* Dec. 1984, pp. 596–598; Wayne Tuckson and Bernard B. Anderson, "Mycotic Aneurysms in Intravenous Drug Abuse: Diagnosis and Management," *Journal of the National Medical Association,* 77 (1985), 99–102; Glenn W. Geelhoed, "The Addict's Angioaccess: Complications of Exotic Vascular Injection Sites," *New York State Journal of Medicine,* Dec. 1984, pp. 585–586.

24. *Clinical Research Notes* (Rockville, Md.: National Institute on Drug Abuse, Feb. 1984), p. 2; *Newsweek,* 12 Aug. 1985, p. 22; *New York Times,* 20 Oct. 1985, p. 51.

25. For a discussion of the causes of heroin overdose, see Peter G. Bourne, ed., *Acute Drug Emergencies: A Treatment Manual* (New York: Academic Press, 1976); David M. Petersen and Earl L. Mahfuz, "Heroin Overdose Deaths: A Critical Examination of Deaths Attributed to Acute Reaction to Dosage," *Sandoz Psychiatric Spectator,* 10 (1977), 5–8.

26. Paul J. Goldstein, Douglas S. Lipton, Edward Preble, Ira Sobel, Tom Miller, William Abbott, William Paige, and Franklin Soto, "The Marketing of Street Heroin in New York City," *Journal of Drug Issues,* Summer 1984, pp. 553–566.

27. Goldstein et al., p. 559.

28. K. W. Bentley and D. G. Hardy, "New Potential Analgesics in the Morphine Series," *Chemical Society Proceedings*, 1963, p. 220. See also B. T. Alford, R. L. Burkhart, and W. P. Johnson, "Etorphine and Diprenorphine as Immobilizing and Reversing Agents in Captive and Free-Ranging Mammals," *Journal of the American Veterinary Medical Association*, 164 (1974), pp. 702–705; Jerry McAdams, "Elephant Juice," *Quarter Horse Track*, Aug. 1981, pp. 6–9.

29. *Newsweek*, 5 Jan. 1981, p. 21.

30. *USA Today*, 15 Feb. 1985, p. 1A; *New York Times*, 24 Mar. 1985, p. 22; *Time*, 8 Apr. 1985, p. 61; *Business Week*, 24 June 1985, pp. 101–102.

31. *U.S. News & World Report*, 5 Aug. 1985, p. 14.

32. National Institute on Drug Abuse, Division of Epidemiology and Statistical Analysis, *Drug Abuse Warning Network, Semiannual Report* (Rockville, Md.: National Institute on Drug Abuse, 1985), pp. 4–5.

33. John C. Ball and Carl D. Chambers, *The Epidemiology of Opiate Addiction in the United States* (Springfield, Ill.: Chas. C. Thomas, 1970), p. 147.

34. Leon Gibson Hunt, *Recent Spread of Heroin Use in the United States: Unanswered Questions* (Washington, D.C.: Drug Abuse Council, 1974). See also Joan D. Rittenhouse, ed., *The Epidemiology of Heroin and Other Narcotics* (Rockville, Md.: National Institute on Drug Abuse, 1977).

35. *Active Narcotic Addicts as of December 31, 1967, Annual Report* (Washington, D.C.: Bureau of Narcotics, 1968).

36. Zili Amstel, Carl L. Erhardt, Donald C. Krug, and Donald P. Conwell, "The Narcotics Register: Development of a Case Register" (Paper presented at the Thirty-first Annual Meeting of the Committee on Problems of Drug Dependence, National Academy of Sciences, National Research Council, Palo Alto, Calif., 25 Feb. 1969).

37. Ball and Chambers, pp. 71–73.

38. For the first of these surveys, see Carl D. Chambers, *An Assessment of Drug Use in the General Population* (Albany, N.Y.: State Narcotic Addiction Control Commission, 1970). Whereas this first survey focused exclusively on New York, subsequent efforts conducted by the National Institute on Drug Abuse have examined the nation as a whole.

39. Carl D. Chambers, James A. Inciardi, and Harvey A. Siegal, *Chemical Coping: A Report on Legal Drug Use in the United States* (New York: Spectrum Publications, 1975), p. 2.

40. Heroin Indicators Task Force, *Heroin Indicators Trend Report, 1976–1978—An Update* (Rockville, Md.: National Institute on Drug Abuse, 1979), p. 16.

41. William J. Chambliss, "Markets, Profits, Labor and Smack," *Contemporary Crises*, 1 (1977), 53–76.

42. The White House, Drug Abuse Policy Office, Office of Policy Development, *National Strategy for Prevention of Drug Abuse and Drug Trafficking* (Washington, D.C.: U.S. Government Printing Office, 1984), p. 24.

43. *Newsweek*, 25 Feb. 1985, p. 23.

44. Cited by H. Wayne Morgan, *Drugs in America: A Social History, 1800–1920* (Syracuse, N.Y.: Syracuse University Press, 1981), p. 93.

45. Bureau of International Narcotics Matters.
46. For more complete descriptions of Amazonia, see Brian Kelly and Mark London, *Amazon* (San Diego: Harcourt Brace Jovanovich, 1983); Roger D. Stone, *Dreams of Amazonia* (New York: Viking, 1985).
47. See Ronald Wright, *Cut Stones and Crossroads: A Journey into the Two Worlds of Peru* (New York: Viking, 1984), p. 42.
48. See *U.S. News & World Report*, 22 Mar. 1982, pp. 27–29; *Wall Street Journal*, 22 Sept. 1983, pp. 1, 22; *Time*, 2 Apr. 1984, p. 87; *USA Today*, 3 July 1984, p. 3A; *New York Times*, 28 Nov. 1984, p. A18; *Miami Herald*, 14 Mar. 1985, p. 7A; *Psychology Today*, Jan. 1985, p. 20.
49. Sidney Cohen, "Recent Developments in the Use of Cocaine," *Bulletin on Narcotics*, Apr.–June 1984, p. 9.
50. F. Raul Jeri, "Coca-Paste Smoking in Some Latin American Countries: A Severe and Unabated Form of Addiction," *Bulletin on Narcotics*, Apr.–June 1984, pp. 15–31.
51. M. Almeida, "Contrabucion al Estudio de la Historia Natural de la Dependencia a la Pasta Basica de Cocaina," *Revista de Neuro-Psiquiatría*, 41 (1978), 44–45.
52. F. R. Jeri, C. Sanchez, and T. Del Pozo, "Consumo de Drogas Peligrosas por Miembros Familiares de la Fuerza Armada y Fuerza Policial Peruana," *Revista de la Sanidad de las Fuerzas Policiales*, 37 (1976), 104–112.
53. See Eric Partridge, *A Dictionary of the Underworld* (New York: Bonanza Books, 1961), pp. 665, 770; Harold Wentworth and Stuart Berg Flexner, *Dictionary of American Slang* (New York: Thomas Y. Crowell, 1975), p. 507; Richard A. Spears, *Slang and Euphemism* (Middle Village, N.Y.: Jonathan David, 1981), p. 369.
54. *Newsweek*, 11 Feb. 1985, p. 33.
55. Susan E. Polchert and Robert M. Morse, "Pemoline Abuse," *Journal of the American Medical Association*, 16 Aug. 1985, pp. 946–947.
56. Cohen, p. 8.
57. See, for example, Nannette Stone, Marlene Fromme, and Daniel Kogan, *Cocaine: Seduction and Solution* (New York: Pinnacle, 1984).
58. This classification was originally developed by Carl D. Chambers in 1970 as a way of categorizing prescription drug abusers.
59. *Time*, 6 July 1981, p. 63.

CHAPTER THREE

THE VILIFICATION OF EUPHORIA
An Inquiry into the Creation of the American "Dope Fiend"

Myth is a body of lore regarded as roughly true. It implies collective fantasy, drawing its fabulous plots from notions based more on traditions and convenience than on fact. Myth guides conduct by orienting, sustaining, or suppressing aspects of social behavior.

The chronicle of the American nation, from its earliest pages, reflects a noticeable dependence on myth in its perception and understanding of the use of drugs for the enhancement of pleasure or performance. Remarkably, this phenomenon seems to persist despite any contradictions by science and logic. For indeed, people typically seem to ignore the treasuries of evidence descriptive of drugs, drug users, and drug taking that the fields of pharmacology, medicine, and the social sciences have provided, in favor of many prevailing mythical systems.

It is generally believed, for example, that all drug users are degenerate and dependent people, that heroin and cocaine are the most dangerous substances on earth, that PCP is a Jekyll and Hyde drug that immediately changes mild-mannered users into raving maniacs, that drug users are responsible for the vast majority of urban street crimes, that the use of marijuana invariably leads to heroin addiction, that more effective policing can eliminate drug use and drug-related crime, that severe punishment of drug users will prevent others from using drugs, that life sentences for drug dealers will curtail drug selling, that heroin addicts are enslaved to their drugs and are forced to commit crimes in order to support their habits, and that establishing the "British system" of heroin maintenance in the United States will eliminate street crime by drug users.

This brief listing reflects but a sampling of the mythical images that characterize popular drug awareness. Yet even these few have managed to galvanize the perceptions and responses of the legislature, the media, systems of law enforcement, the public at large, and to some extent, even the

91

scientific community. The curiosity, however, is the way in which the drug myths came into being, managing to persist for years hence.

RELIGIOUS ALCHEMY, D. B. COOPER, AND THE GENESIS OF THE DRUG MYTHS

Myth descends from a process—a series of actions and responses. It passes directly from both literary and folk traditions into belief. The art form of myth is drama, with plot, characters, and dialogue. The performance displays a collection of themes and events, and their interpretation invariably becomes understood as "real." Many myths are the result of simple misunderstanding, reinterpretations of fact or deliberate misdirection to suit one's own needs or beliefs, and erroneous or quasi-scientific methods of inquiry. This spirit of mythmaking is apparent, for example, in the journalistic sensationalism of the nineteenth-century American "dime novelists," the approximations of fact by armchair historians, and the religious alchemy of generations of Christian writers and contemporary television evangelists.

Among the more curious myths that endured for centuries in much of the world was that of the unicorn, a product of the Holy Bible.[1] The books of the Old Testament were first written in Hebrew and Aramaic, but circa 250 B.C. a group of Hellenistic Jews translated the Scriptures into Greek, producing a version of the Bible known as the *Septuagint*. In the original Scriptures, the Hebrew writers had mentioned with some awe an animal they called *Re'em*. In Job 39:9–12 and Num. 23:22, the Re'em was noted as having great strength. It was characterized as fleet, fierce, indomitable, and especially distinguished by the armor of its brow, but it was never actually described. Later studies discovered that Re'em was *Bos Primigenius,* or the urus, a wild ox that is believed to be the ancestor of European domestic cattle. But the urus, now extinct, had never been seen by the translators since it no longer existed where they lived. Yet the traits of the Re'em awakened dim recollections of another beast that was believed to be as fierce, mysterious, strange, and remote. They used the Greek word μονόκερως or *monokeros*.

The monokeros of the ancient Greeks came from the writings of Ctesias, the historian and one-time physician of the Persian King Artaxerxes II. In 398 B.C. he had produced a volume on India, based primarily on the tales and hearsay of travelers. In it he described a "wild ass of India" that had all the characteristics of the mythical unicorn. Zoologists have determined that Ctesias' monokeros or "wild ass of India" was actually the Indian rhinoceros, with admixtures of features of some other animal. But in English, monokeros means unicorn. Re'em was translated into monokeros with one main result: for many centuries to come, the existence of the unicorn would be reiterated, and it could not be doubted, for it was repeatedly mentioned in the Holy Bible.

More entertaining is the myth of D. B. Cooper, the skyjacker who jumped from a Northwest Orient Airlines jetliner in 1971 with a $200,000 ransom that he had demanded from airline officials. After he parachuted from the plane over Ariel, Washington, the FBI launched a massive manhunt. Cooper was never found, and almost immediately he became a modern-day folk hero—a twentieth-century Robin Hood. Popular mythology holds that he got away, that he beat the system. Every year on the Saturday after Thanksgiving in Ariel the festivities of D. B. Cooper Day are held. Hundreds of people, some from as far away as England, clog the town's only street to pay tribute to the perpetrator of America's only unsolved skyjacking. It is an article of faith among them that somehow, somewhere, Cooper is managing to live a discreetly decadent life on his marked money.[2] What the cultists do not understand is that when Cooper jumped from the 10,000-foot altitude into 200-mph freezing rain and air, dressed only in a light business suit and raincoat, it is likely that his body was thrown into immediate shock and that he did not stay conscious long enough even to open his parachute.

By contrast to the tales of the unicorn and D. B. Cooper, the genesis of the drug myths is considerably more complex, having come from numerous medical, political, legislative, scientific, and moral postures of American society. They emerged, in part, from

- The rural creeds of nineteenth-century Methodism, Baptism, Presbyterianism, and Congregationalism that emphasized individual human toil and self-sufficiency, while designating the use of intoxicants as an unwholesome surrender to the evils of an urban morality;
- The medical literature of the late 1800s that arbitrarily designated the use of opium, morphine, and cocaine as a vice, a habit, an appetite, and a disease;
- The early association of opium smoking with the Chinese—a cultural and racial group that had been legally defined as "alien," a designation that endured until around 1943;
- The effects of American narcotics legislation that served to define all heroin users as criminal offenders;

- Nineteenth- and twentieth-century police literature that stressed the involvement of professional and other habitual criminals with the use of drugs;

- The initiatives of moral crusaders who defined drug use as "evil" and, in so doing, influenced national opinion makers and rule creators;

- The publicized findings of misguided research efforts, those contaminated by the use of biased samples, impressionistic data, and methodological errors; and

- Cultural and intellectual lag—that vast and ecumenical gap that stretches between the publication of new discoveries and the ultimate dismissal of earlier proclamations.

And, too, the drug myths are a product of the mass media, where sentimentalized melodramas and irresponsible reporting—*The Man with the Golden Arm, Valley of the Dolls,* "Miami Vice," "Hill Street Blues," "60 Minutes," *Reader's Digest*—provide uninformed audiences with misshapen portraits of the worlds of drug use.

THE TALE OF THE TERRIBLE VICE

Although opium and its derivatives had been available as general remedies in patent medicines well before the Revolutionary War, it was not until the mid-nineteenth century that concern over their "evil effects" began to surface. Among the earliest to focus on opiate use as a growing social problem was physician George B. Wood in 1856.[3] Although Wood noted the range of physical impairments that could be attributed to chronic opium intoxication, his treatise focused on *evil*. Opiate use led to a loss of self-respect, Wood argued; it was a yielding to seductive pleasure, a form of moral depravity, and a *vice* that led "to the lowest depths of evil." Many of Wood's colleagues quickly agreed, and much of the medical literature that examined the opium problem during the next three decades more often stressed the moral rather than the medical issues.[4] As one commentator put it: "the morbid craving of morphia ranks amongst the category of other human passions, such as smoking, gambling, greediness for profit, and sexual excesses."[5]

To this collection of testimonials ascribing varying levels of stigma to the opiate user, a number of other medical commentators borrowed ideas suggested by the recently introduced theories of biological determinism and criminal anthropology. At the time, the writings of Charles Darwin had become prominent, and Italian physician Cesare Lombroso had just presented his thesis of "criminal man."[6] Lombroso argued that there is a "born criminal type;" that the criminal is an "atavism"—a throwback to an earlier stage in human evolution, a more apelike evolutionary ancestor. There was also Richard L. Dugdale's publication of *The Jukes*, a study which held that crime is caused by "bad heredity," and that criminality, degeneracy, and feeblemindedness are biologically transmitted through poor germ plasm.[7] Applying such notions to the drug-using population, it was claimed that addiction is the result of inherited predispositions: therefore, morphine takers will likely also indulge excessively in alcohol, absinthe drinking, and cocaine use.[8]

Public concern was also mounting over opium smoking in American cities. When gold was discovered in California in 1848, migrants from the Atlantic states as well as from Europe, Australia, and Asia contributed to the gold-seeking population. Among them were some 27,000 Chinese. With the lure of work in the mines and in the construction of railroads across the trans-Mississippi West, by the 1870s the Chinese population had expanded to more than 70,000. With them, the new Asian immigrants had imported their cultural tradition of opium smoking, and they quickly established smoking parlors that were frequented by Orientals and Americans alike.[9]

With a Chinatown beginning in 1872 in New York City, a city at the very center of the nation's publishing capitals, knowledge of the Chinese way of life and the practice of opium smoking became readily disseminated. Common in mass-market publishing during that time were anti-urban exposés, lurid guidebooks describing the many "evils" of the "great metropolis."[10] Chinatown was a popular subject, and the customs of Orientals as well as the "evil" nature of the opium "joints" were often highlighted. In one volume, published in 1892 under the title *Darkness and Daylight; or, Lights and Shadows of New York Life*, the descriptions of the opium dens offered clear reflections of the Victorian moral climate of the era. For example:

> Near the farther end of the room was a bunk occupied by four white women, three of them apparently being adept in the vice, and the fourth a novice. Four persons crowd a bunk very closely; two recline their heads upon pillows or headrests, and the other two make use of their companions for the same purpose. A party may consist of either men or women, or it may be made up of both sexes; opium smokers do not stand on ceremony with each other, and strangers will recline on the

same bunk and draw intoxication from the same pipe without the least hesitation. The old adage says "Misery loves company"; this is certainly the case with debauchery, and especially of debauchery with opium.[11]

Although the use of opium was not a crime during those years, it was illegal in New York City to operate an opium-smoking parlor. Police efforts to close the establishments were vividly presented in the urban "guidebooks." Moreover, descriptions of the opium habit and its consequences were dramatized as evil in the police literature of the day, directly associating drug-taking behavior with criminality. In 1884, for example, in a lengthy volume written and published by A. E. Costello, New York's chief of police, the dynamics of opium smoking were related with numerous vivid illustrations. In the commentary, Costello stated:

> A comparatively new criminal agency has been at work in certain sections of the city, spreading the fruitful seeds of contamination, and throwing additional responsibilities on the already overburdened shoulders of the police. The agency in question is what is known as "the opium habit." In a remarkably short space of time this terrible vice has taken deep root, and it is very much to be feared that it will not down, but that it has come to stay. . . . Unfortunately, this pernicious habit is not confined to the children of the flowery kingdom; a legion of opium smokers to the manner born, and many of them people of respectability and refinement, are slaves of the habit. . . . The most debased and wretched practice of the habit is smoking, which is now engaged in in scores of "joints" in New York.[12]

And finally, by 1896, the term *dope fiend* had made its way into popular slang usage, implying that drug taking *was,* or at least resulted in, an evil obsession.[13]

MRS. VANDERBILT, CAPTAIN HOBSON, AND "THE LEGEND OF THE LIVING DEAD"

To suggest that during the late nineteenth century a fully committed effort was underway to criminalize the drug user would be an overstatement. Commentaries *were* in the medical and police literature. Also, occasional writers linked drug use with sexual license. Some authorities reported that "old smokers" of opium used the drug to seduce innocent girls;[14] that "female smokers, if not already lost in the point of virtue, soon become so";[15] and that "rapes, seductions, and other criminal acts occur, sometimes boldly, or with secretiveness and cunning."[16] These sordid links of drug taking with vice and crime did have their impact on the shaping of public attitudes. In the main, however, people had many ambivalent views about drug abuse.

Experts knew that opium and morphine did not create sexual psychotics, and they were quite vocal about it.[17] Medical, pharmaceutical, and other organizations understood what they considered to be the threats that addiction posed for women and youth. Yet while loathing and fearing addiction, at the same time they had sympathy for addicts. They condemned the use of drugs for escape or sensual pleasure, but they also felt that morphinism was a form of physiological slavery that ought to be treated with pragmatic therapy rather than moralism. A growing body of confessional literature also revealed that addicts led lives of despair, that they sought freedom from the superhuman forces of addiction and repeatedly underwent rigorous cures.[18]

After the passage of the Harrison Act in 1914, however, the criminalization process began in earnest. By that time, concerned people viewed heroin use with increasing alarm. Heroin was considered the most threatening drug in history, appealing to a new youthful generation that seemed indifferent to the standards of conduct of the wider society. Moreover, as more and more users were arrested for the illegal possession of the drug, the association of heroin with crime became more firmly entrenched.

Chronologically first among the post-Harrison Act crusaders was Mrs. William K. Vanderbilt of New York society's elite "Four Hundred." Jousting for prominence in the society pages of the New York press, the ladies of Gotham's "best families" pursued causes in the name of social reform. To keep up with her rivals who had become famous as suffragettes during these pre-World War I years, Mrs. Vanderbilt set out on a campaign against heroin. She wanted to prevent the drug from adding to its already engorged prison of "lost souls." She organized antinarcotics committees, led marches down Fifth Avenue, and warned New Yorkers of the armies of dangerous "fiends" roaming Harlem and the Bronx. Her endeavors resulted in a series of newspaper accounts that described an epidemic of heavy addiction within the youth culture and more than 1.5 million violent and dangerous addicts at large in the streets. The propaganda also included rumors of fiendish enemy agents prowling through the school yards of urban America with candy laced with heroin, seducing innocent children and teenagers into lives of addiction, vice, crime, and despair.[19] The reports quickly spread from the New York dailies to popular national magazines, and the *Literary Digest* offered commentaries on "American enslavement to drugs";[20] *The Outlook* described how drugs were being trafficked by gamblers, cabdrivers, domestics, vagrants, lunchroom helpers, poolroom employees, porters, and laundrymen;[21] and the *American Review of Reviews* stated that there were 5 million addicts nationwide, that the trafficker was a criminal of the worst type, and that the "drug menace" *had* to be stamped out.[22] All of that was only the beginning. In the 1920s, Captain Richmond Pearson Hobson entered the crusade.

Described by one of his biographers as a man of "virtually unlimited moral indignation,"[23] Hobson was one of the most celebrated heroes of the Spanish-American War. He was also an adept temperance lecturer, but when national Prohibition went into effect he became a reformer without a cause. Hobson soon realized the potential of the addiction issue and began an unprecedented campaign of sensationalism. Through newspaper columns, magazine articles, and national radio broadcasts, he popularized the notion that addicts are "beasts" and "monsters" who spread their disease like medieval vampires.

Hobson launched his effort by forming the International Narcotic Education Association, and almost immediately, his views were seen in popular magazines and press reports all across the nation. In the May 24, 1924, issue of the *Literary Digest*, he was quoted as saying:

> Every heroin addict, because of the drug's action on his brain, has a mania to spread his addiction to others, the drug is four times as powerful as morphine and comes in a convenient deceptive form of a white powder called "snow," which is generally "whiffed" into the nostrils.
>
> One "snow party" a day for a week makes a youth an addict. Organized efforts are directed at the young. Besides the professional peddlers we have a million young recruiting agents in our midst insanely trapping our youth into addiction. A sure symptom of the activities of this organization is seen in the rising tide of crime.[24]

The problem of "1 million heroin addicts" was an idea that Hobson pushed heavily, incorporating it into a pamphlet he entitled *The Peril of Narcotics—A Warning to the People of America*. He urged Congress to publish 50 million copies of the little booklet so that every home in the nation would have one on hand. Even government antidrug forces, well aware of Hobson's sensationalism and exaggeration, opposed the request. The Federal Narcotics Control Board found the warnings in *The Peril of Narcotics* . . . fantastic: that 1 ounce of heroin will cause 2,000 addicts;

that "in using any brand of face powder regularly, it is a wise precaution to have a sample analyzed for heroin." [25]

Undaunted, Hobson continued his drive. He managed to have *The Peril of Narcotics . . .* read into the *Congressional Record,* and he sent copies under a congressional frank to 5,000 superintendents of education, and hundreds of college and university presidents, officials of parent-teacher associations, and distinguished citizens listed in *Who's Who in America.* [26]

Captain Hobson ultimately achieved his greatest visibility in 1928, when NBC donated time for the radio broadcast of an emotionally charged address in which addicts were depicted as an army of the "living dead." In part:

> To get his heroin supply the addict will not only advocate public policies against the public welfare, but will lie, steal, rob, and if necessary, commit murder. Heroin addiction can be likened to a contagion. Suppose it were announced that there were more than a million lepers among our people. Think what a shock the announcement would produce! Yet drug addiction is far more incurable than leprosy, far more tragic to its victims, and is spreading like a moral and physical scourge.
>
> There are symptoms breaking out all over the country and now breaking out in many parts of Europe which show that individual nations and the whole world is menaced [sic] by this appalling foe . . . marching . . . to the capture and destruction of the whole world.
>
> Most of the daylight robberies, daring holdups, cruel murders, and similar crimes of violence are now known to be committed chiefly by drug addicts, who constitute the primary cause of our alarming crime wave.
>
> Drug addiction is more communicable and less curable than leprosy. Drug addicts are the principal carriers of vice diseases, and with their lowered resistance are incubators and carriers of the streptococcus, pneumococcus, the germ of flu, of tuberculosis, and other diseases.
>
> *Upon the issue hangs the perpetuation of civilization, the destiny of the whole world and the future of the human race!* [27]

Hobson's descriptions of addicts suggested to his readers and listeners images of wicked-looking denizens of the urban slime—ugly, scarred, and having all the stereotypic characteristics of the mugger and rapist. Yet the typical heroin user was hardly that. Most were young white males from the slums of eastern cities. They were citizens by birth, although their parents were typically immigrants. Moreover, they were poorly educated, and if they were employed they worked at unskilled or semiskilled jobs. Most addicts spent much of their time on the city streets, running with juvenile gangs.[28] In short, the heroin users of Hobson's time were indistinguishable from most of urban America's second-generation immigrant children—almost all were poor, uneducated, unemployed, and running in the streets. The only differentiating characteristic—if at all observable— was their narcotics use, which usually began with opium smoking within the context of their gang activities. They were indeed vagabonds and petty thieves, but so too were their nondrug-using peers in the Irish, Italian, Jewish, German, and Polish ghettos of the cities. Some heroin users were indeed gamblers and professional criminals, but these generally represented a small minority.

By the middle of the 1930s, Captain Hobson had shifted his energies. He moved to the forefront with Harry J. Anslinger's fight against the evil weed of the fields. As for heroin, Hobson's dementia was no longer needed. There were others who carried on the crusade. He died in 1937, but by then the image of the addict had been well established. "Dope fiends," as they were called, were sex-crazed maniacs, degenerate street criminals, and members of the "living dead." "Narcotics," including marijuana and cocaine, reportedly ravaged the human body; they destroyed morality; addicts were sexually violent and criminally aggressive; they were weak and ineffective members of society; addiction was contagious since users had a mania for perpetuating the social anathema of drug taking; and finally, once addicted, the user entered into a lifetime of slavery to drugs.[29] Then came the war years and more pressing concerns. The problems of addiction were set aside, at least temporarily, not to be resurrected for almost a decade.

JAILBAIT STREET, ROCK 'N' ROLL, AND WHITE AMERICAN RESPECTABILITY

The United States entered the mid-century as the most powerful nation on earth. World War II had ended the Great Depression and unleashed a prosperous postwar era; unemployment had stabilized at a uniquely low level, and most Americans reveled in a new economic privilege. The period has been called the Fabulous Fifties, for retrospective glances have characterized it as a golden age of simplicity and innocence—the thrilling days of bobby socks and soda fountains, of hot rods and Elvis Presley. There were no real wars, no riots, and no protests. But *all* was not well.

Along with the postwar prosperity, heroin addiction once more became visible. Having seemingly diminished when the draft sent the young white users off to war, it moved underground into the black ghetto, where it began to spread. The 1950s were also a time of youthful rebellion, and many adults in mainstream America feared that heroin use would become epidemic among the children of white society.

Of the many forms of youth rebellion, however, it appeared that juvenile delinquency, not heroin addiction, became the most visible. Education reporter Benjamin Fine of the *New York Times* predicted in the early 1950s that by the middle of the decade the number of youths being processed by the police would exceed 1 million. His estimates were quickly realized, and property crimes and car theft were the major juvenile offenses. The young were also committing acts of inexplicable and pointless violence—beatings, rape, and murder. Although statistically few of America's teenage groups were involved in violent crime, those that were had seemingly terrorized entire cities.[30] These were the fighting gangs of the 1950s—the Roman Lords, Young Stars, Pigtown, Scorpions, and other urban street gangs as portrayed in Irving Shulman's *The Amboy Dukes* and Hal Ellson's *Jailbait Street.**

Curiously, however, although street crime was heavily tied to delinquency, at least as far as the media were concerned, juvenile drug use seemed to be absent from the gang culture. Isidor Chein's *The Road to H,* a pioneering, although theoretically problematic, study of narcotics use among juveniles, reflected what most other informed efforts had found.

---

* Throughout New York City during the 1950s, rumor had it that up in the far reaches of the East Bronx was the most fearsome gang of all, the "Fordham Baldies." So terrible were they, with shaved heads as a mark of their membership, that the mere mentioning of their presence in a local neighborhood would clear the streets of youths—both gang members and nongang members alike. But no one ever seemed actually to encounter the Baldies face to face—ever. In the years hence, many concluded that they were a myth, and in all of the literature descriptive of the New York ganglands of the 1950s, the Baldies are never mentioned. Even in the 3,652 issues of the rigorously indexed *New York Times* their name never appears. Yet in an autobiography of a heroin addict, written during the 1970s, its author makes one brief mention of the Baldies, and his remarks suggest how the myth may have started:

> The gangs we used to rumble with mostly were the Hoods, of course, and then the Seven Crowns, the Scorpions, occasionally the Mau Maus, and then the Fordham Baldies. The Baldies were a group of guys made up of the sons of racketeers from the Fordham Road area. The Godfather up Fordham way used to be known as Baldie. So naturally the kids took that name. They were a pretty tough group so we mostly left them alone.

See Richard P. Rettig, Manuel J. Torres, and Gerald R. Garrett, *Manny: A Criminal Addict's Story* (Boston: Houghton Mifflin, 1977), p. 27.

Adolescent drug use was concentrated in the ghetto, most widespread where income and education were lowest. Drug use, was *not,* however, intrinsically tied to gang activities. Some drug users were in organized juvenile gangs, yet these were less often involved in gang fighting.[31]

Extensive gang involvement or not, drug use, and particularly heroin addiction in the central cities, was indeed spreading at an unprecedented rate. Although the media may have over-sensationalized their reporting,[32] researchers, clinicians, and law-enforcement groups working in the drug field were well aware of the growing problem. There were, after all, many indicators of the new trend. At New York's Bellevue Hospital during the years 1940–1948, no adolescents had been admitted for treatment with a diagnosis of drug addiction: in 1949 there was one, followed by 6 in 1950, and 84 during the first two months of 1951.[33] In port cities around the nation, the number of heroin seizures had dramatically increased.[34] At the federal drug-treatment centers in Lexington, Kentucky, and Fort Worth, Texas, the proportion of youths being admitted was expanding at a geometric rate.[35] In New York and other major cities, the number of youths coming to the attention of the police, the courts, and social-work and other human-service agencies on drug-related matters was also advancing. Finally, although it could be effectively argued that public pressure to do something about the "heroin problem" had encouraged selective enforcement of the narcotics laws, drug-related arrests were up in most large American cities.

In terms of the reasons for the new heroin epidemic, *Life* magazine felt it had the answer:

> What had come over today's 15-year-olds? One answer was the brazen pusher, who, needing customers, was now cynically making them among naive youngsters, usually, but not always, from poor homes. Another answer was marijuana, widely available and publicized as nonaddictive—which is scientifically true but tragically misleading since it is usually the first step toward ultimate enslavement by heroin.[36]

Harry J. Anslinger of the Bureau of Narcotics had a different answer. He blamed parents. In the October 1951 issue of the *Reader's Digest* he argued that most juvenile addicts come from families in which there is no proper parental control or training in decent personal habits. "Rarely," he added, "does a boy or girl from a normally balanced family in any income bracket become an addict."[37] In other words, Anslinger was suggesting that *decent people just don't use drugs!* Finally, the Crime Investigating Committee of the U.S. Senate had the solution to the problem: stiffer penalties for narcotics violators, "for no penalty is too severe for a criminal of such character"; increase the number of agents assigned to narcotics work; cancel the sailing papers of any seaman convicted of a narcotics violation; and initiate a worldwide ban on the growing of the opium poppy.[38]

Although it seemed clear from both media and scientific reports that heroin use was almost exclusively a problem of the central-city ghetto, there was considerable concern within the white middle class as to "contaminating factors" that might induce drug using and other undesirable behaviors among the more socially privileged youth. A prime target of the parental establishment was the new *rock 'n' roll* music.

When Alan Freed, a disk jockey for Cleveland radio station WJW, introduced the term in 1951, little did he imagine what the impact of rock 'n' roll would be on American life and world social patterns. The new music had elements of the country-and-western sounds of the rural white working class, but it was primarily made up of the "rhythm and blues" of an urbanizing black America. As a product principally of the black community, it clearly had a racial stigma attached to it.[39] American racism condemned black tastes in general and "black records" in particular. When Freed presented rock 'n' roll—a ghetto euphemism for both dancing and sex—to white youth, it was an immediate success. Some whites had already been listening to the all-black rhythm and blues radio shows, but it was not a taste that the majority cultivated. Freed, a white DJ, put the music in a more familiar and acceptable format, reassuring the majority of repressed and nervous white kids. His framework encouraged them to make the effort to overcome their bland, stereotyped musical background.[40]

The acceptance of rock 'n' roll was part of the new youth rebellion. At the same time it served to threaten every phobia of white American respectability—particularly when children were heard chanting, "Rock 'n' roll is here to stay!" Parents, congresspeople, and social commentators of the period claimed that it had infected white teenagers all across the country. It introduced them to their sexuality, to interracial contacts, to bizarre dance rituals, and most seriously, *to drugs*. As authors Jack Lait and Lee Mortimer articulated in their 1952 best-seller *U.S.A. Confidential:*

> Like a heathen religion, it is all tied up with tom-toms and hot jive and ritualistic orgies of erotic dancing, weed smoking and mass mania, with African jungle background. Many music shops purvey dope. White girls are recruited for colored lovers. Another cog in the giant delinquency machine is the radio disc jockey. . . . We know that many platter spinners are hopheads. Many others are Reds, left-wingers, or hecklers of

> social convention. . . . Through disc jocks, kids get to know colored and other hip musicians; they frequent places the radio oracles plug, which is done with design . . . to hook jives and guarantee a new generation subservient to the Mafia.* ,41

Lait and Mortimer went on to describe how marijuana use leads to addiction, how it generates orgies of interracial sex, and how "Negroes" are a "decidedly anti-Semitic" group involved in "Jew baiting." See Lee Mortimer and Jack Lait, *New York Confidential* (New York: Viking, 1948), pp. 117–120.

Yet regardless of the white phobias of the 1950s, rock 'n' roll endured, and its relationship to drugs was never established.† In spite of media contentions about a connection between drug use and middle-class delinquency, throughout the decade heroin addiction appeared to remain at a relatively low level in white neighborhoods. Yet narcotics use continued to grow at an alarming rate in the ghetto, particularly among the youths of black America and other minority populations. For many of them, drug use had become a way of life, and street crime was typically a part of their drug-taking and drug-seeking activities.42

---

* For more widely read observers, what appeared in *U.S.A. Confidential* was no surprise, for authors Lait and Mortimer had already established their general ignorance and prejudice. In *New York Confidential,* a piece of popular reportorial carrion they had written a few years earlier stated:

> . . . from the days of earliest slavery in the United States and West Indies, Negroes have swept away their heavy inhibitions, forgotten the burn of the lash and the clank of the shackles with an age-old drug, hashish.
> Hashish was used among the ancients to stimulate armies for killing. . . .
> There are about 500 apartments in Harlem, known as "tea pads," set up exclusively for marijuana addicts.

† Although rock 'n' roll survived and evolved, Alan Freed did not. As depicted in *American Hot Wax,* a 1978 Paramount Pictures release, he was destroyed by the violence of the 1950s mainstream. At a show promoted by Freed in Boston, police interrupted the performance by turning on the house lights. Later, members of the audience spread through the city, fighting. One person was killed, several were beaten, and Freed was charged with anarchy and inciting to riot. It took him many years and a considerable sum of money before the charges were finally dismissed. Then he was charged in investigations of *payola*—a standard practice in the record industry where bribes were given to disk jockeys to secure air time for certain records. Only the rock 'n' roll industry was targeted, and Freed received only a $300 fine, but his career was ruined. He moved from station to station, drinking heavily and continually pursued by harassing indictments. He died in 1965 at the age of 43. Contemporary rock has also received some parental repression. Concerned over the many lyrical references to sex in rock songs, in 1985 the Parents' Music Resource Center influenced a measure of voluntary compliance by the recording industry to place warning labels on albums and cassettes that contain sexually explicit lyrics. (See *U.S. News and World Report,* 26 Aug. 1985, p. 52; *Christian Science Monitor,* 23 Aug. 1985, pp. 1, 36.)

The Riddle of the Sphinx

The Sphinx was a monster of Greek mythology that had the face of a woman, the body of a lion, and the wings of a bird. For years she perched on Mount Phicium, near the ancient city of Thebes, posing a riddle to all passersby. "What goes on four feet," she would ask, "on two feet, and three, but the more feet it goes on the weaker it be?" Those who could not answer her riddle were promptly devoured—which were all, save one. Oedipus answered her directly. "It is *man*," he stated, "for he crawls as an infant, walks upright as an adult, and totters with a staff in old age." Upon hearing this, the Sphinx slew herself. Oedipus was made king of Thebes, and went on to other adventures.

In the drug field, for as long as commentators were sensationalizing crimes allegedly the maniacal handiwork of heroin, cocaine, and marijuana users, researchers argued a corresponding riddle. Is criminal behavior antecedent to addiction; or, does criminality emerge subsequent to addiction? More specifically, is crime the result of or a response to a special set of life circumstances brought about by the addiction to narcotic drugs? Or conversely, is addiction per se a deviant tendency characteristic of individuals already prone to offense behavior? Moreover, and assuming that criminality may indeed be a pre-addiction phenomenon, does the onset of chronic narcotics use bring about a change in the nature, intensity, and frequency of deviant and criminal acts? Does criminal involvement tend to increase or decrease subsequent to addiction? There were also related questions. What kinds of criminal offenses do addicts engage in? Do they tend toward violent acts of aggression? Or are their crimes strictly profit oriented and geared toward the violation of the sanctity of private property? Or is it both?

As early as the 1920s, researchers had been conducting studies—many studies—seeking answers to these very questions. Particularly, Edouard Sandoz at the Municipal Court of Boston and Lawrence Kolb at the U.S. Public Health Service examined the backgrounds of hundreds of heroin users, focusing on the drugs–crime relationship.[43] Their conclusions were relatively informed ones, however ignored. Basically, what they found within criminal justice and treatment populations were several different types of cases. Some drug users were habitual criminals, and likely always had been; others were simply violators of the Harrison Act, having been arrested for no more than the illegal possession of narcotics. Moreover, with both types a record of violent crimes was absent.

The analyses provided by Sandoz, Kolb, and others established the parameters of several points of view:

- Addicts ought to be the object of vigorous law-enforcement activity, since the majority are members of a criminal element and drug addiction is simply one of the later phases of their deviant careers.

- Addicts prey upon legitimate society, and the effects of their drugs do indeed predispose them to serious criminal transgressions.

- Addicts are essentially law-abiding citizens who are forced to steal to adequately support their drug habits.

- Addicts are not necessarily criminals but are forced to associate with an underworld element that tends to maintain control over the distribution of illicit drugs.[44]

The notion that addicts ought to be the objects of vigorous police activity, a posture that later became known as the *criminal model of drug abuse,* was actively and relentlessly pursued by the Federal Bureau of Narcotics and other law-enforcement groups. Their argument was fixed on the notion of criminality, for on the basis of their own observations, the vast majority of heroin users encountered were members of criminal groups. To support this view, the Bureau of Narcotics pointed to several studies that demonstrated that most addicts were already criminals before they began using heroin.[45] Addicts, the bureau emphasized, represent a destructive force confronting the people of America. Whatever the sources of their addiction might be, they are members of a highly subversive and antisocial group. For the bureau, this position did indeed have some basis in reality. Having been charged with the enforcement of a law that prohibited the possession, sale, and distribution of narcotics, what bureau agents were confronted with were *criminal* addicts, often under the most dangerous of circumstances. It was not uncommon for agents to be wounded or even killed in arrest situations, and analyses of the careers of many addicts demonstrated that their criminal records were lengthy. Moreover, there was the matter of "professional" underworld involvement with narcotics, a point that Commissioner Anslinger himself commented on in 1951:

> It is well established that a larger proportion of the pickpocket artists, the shoplifters, the professional gamblers and card sharks, the confidence men operating fake horse race or fake stock sale schemes, the "short con" men such as the "short-change artists" or the coin matchers, are addicted to the use of narcotic drugs.[46]

Anslinger was referring to the world of *professional thieves,* and studies have demonstrated that predators of this kind are involved not only in the use of narcotics but in trafficking as well.[47] Anslinger was *wrong*, however, in his belief that all heroin users are from the same mold. Studies of drug-using populations of his time have referenced the existence of numerous and alternative patterns of narcotic addiction. The professional thieves about which Anslinger spoke were a group of highly skilled yet essentially nonviolent criminals who made a regular business of stealing. Crime was their occupation and means of livelihood, and as such, they devoted their entire time and energy to stealing. They operated with proficiency; they had a body of skills and knowledge that was utilized in the execution and planning of their work; and they were graduates of an informal developmental process that included the acquisition of specialized skills, knowledge, attitudes, and experience. Finally, in identifying themselves with the world of crime, professional thieves were members of an exclusive fraternity that extended friendship, understanding, sympathy, security, safety, recognition, and respect.[48] Their pattern of addiction revolved around the use of heroin or morphine by needle, or the smoking of opium. Spree use of drugs was also common, generally to reduce the boredom associated with incarceration, or as part of pleasure-seeking activities.

By contrast, during the years between 1900 and 1960, there was a pattern of addiction characteristic of a core of *middle-aged white southerners*. Identified through patient records at federal drug-treatment facilities, they were usually addicted to morphine or paregoric, and their drugs had been obtained from physicians through legal or quasi-legal means. As "patients" under treatment for some illness, these addicts were not members of any deviant subcultures and did not have contacts with other addicts.[49]

There were also groups of *hidden addicts* who, because of sufficient income and/or access to a legitimate source of drugs, had no need to make contacts with visibly criminal cultures to obtain drugs. Among these were musicians, physicians, and members of other segments of the health professions.[50]

Finally, there was the stereotyped *heroin street addict*—the narcotics user of the American ghetto of whom the mass media spoke. Heroin street addicts were typically from the socially and economically deprived segments of the urban population. They began their careers with drug experimentation as adolescents for the sake of excitement or thrills, to conform with peer-group activities and expectations, and/or to strike back at the authority structures which they opposed. The use of alcohol, marijuana, codeine, or pills generally initiated them into substance abuse, and later drug intake focused primarily on heroin. Their status of addiction was often said to have emerged as a result of an addiction-prone personality, and they supported their habits through illegal means. Also among this group were *poly-drug users*—those who concurrently abused a variety of drugs.*

Most law-enforcement agencies focused their attention and their commentary on those who manifested the pattern of heroin street addiction. In what may be one of the most scientifically prejudiced and ignorant studies targeting this group, FBI agent James P. Morgan, a former detective in the narcotics bureau of the New York City Police Department, compiled data in 1965 to prove conclusively that addiction *was indeed* a criminal problem.[51] His population included 135 narcotics users he had personally arrested during preceding years. Playing the roles of both police officer and "scientific" researcher, Morgan extensively questioned his quarries regarding their careers in crime and addiction. In terms of the validity and reliability of the responses received, Morgan was quite confident that his information was accurate. In fact, he said so himself: "I do not believe that any false answers were given to the questions." Morgan's analysis indicated that "only 15 of the addicts studied were able to prove that they were lacking a criminal background." So "logically," and with apparent confidence, he concluded:

> The statistical results of this study revealed that those addicts studied become what they are, not by accident, but as a result of criminal tendencies which they had already exhibited.

Reading on in Morgan's essay, and in more serious works that address the issue of "criminal tendencies," one could not avoid recalling Cesare Lombroso's thoughts on "born criminals" and "atavisms" and "inherited predispositions to crime" of a century earlier. Aside from Morgan's problems with sample bias and misguided interpretation, perhaps if given more time he might have resurrected Lombroso's ideas. After all, if his addicts did indeed have criminal tendencies, maybe their head shapes and sizes could have been significant in understanding their behaviors.

What Agent Morgan & Co. were responding to in their commentaries were the clinicians and social scientists of the 1950s and early 1960s who had put forth the notion of a *medical model of addiction*, as opposed to the *criminal* view of law enforcement. The medical model, which physicians first proposed in the late nineteenth century, held that addiction was a chronic and relapsing disease. The addict, it was argued, should be dealt with as any patient suffering from some physiological or medical disorder. At the same time, numerous proponents of the view sought to

---

* This listing of patterns of addiction is by no means exhaustive; there were, and still are, many more types.

mitigate addict criminality by putting forth the "enslavement theory of addiction." The idea here was that the monopolistic controls over the heroin black market forced "sick" and otherwise law-abiding drug users into lives of crime to support their habits.

POSTSCRIPT

From the 1920s through the close of the 1960s, hundreds of studies of the relationship between crime and addiction were conducted.[52] Invariably, when one analysis would appear to support the medical model of addiction, the next would affirm the criminal model. Given these repeated contradictions, something had to be wrong—and indeed there was. The theories, hypotheses, conclusions, and other findings generated by almost the entire spectrum of research were actually of little value, for there were awesome biases and deficiencies in the very nature of their designs. Data-gathering enterprises on criminal activity had usually restricted themselves to drug-users' arrest histories, and there can be little argument about the inadequacy of official criminal statistics as measures of the incidence and prevalence of offense behavior. Those studies that did manage to go beyond arrest figures to probe self-reported criminal activity were invariably limited to either incarcerated heroin users or addicts in treatment settings. The few efforts that did manage to locate active heroin users in the street community typically examined the samples' drug-taking behaviors to the exclusion of their drug-seeking behaviors. Given the many methodological difficulties, it was impossible to draw many reliable conclusions about the nature of drug-related crime—about its magnitude, shape, scope, or direction. Not until the 1970s and 1980s were more sophisticated studies of drug use finally undertaken.

Notes

1. For a more complete analysis of the unicorn myth, see James A. Inciardi, Alan A. Block, and Lyle A. Hallowell, *Historical Approaches to Crime: Research Strategies and Issues* (Beverly Hills: Sage, 1977), pp. 11–13.
2. *New York Times,* 25 Nov. 1979, p. 45; *People,* 3 Mar. 1980, pp. 45–46; *Newsweek,* 26 Dec. 1983, p. 12.
3. George B. Wood, *A Treatise on Therapeutics and Pharmacology of Materia Medica* (Philadelphia: J. B. Lippincott, 1856).
4. See, for example, F. E. Oliver, "The Use and Abuse of Opium," in *Third Annual Report,* Massachusetts State Board of Health (Boston: Wright and Potter, 1872), pp. 162–177; J. M. Hull, "The Opium Habit," in *Third Bien-*

nial Report, Iowa State Board of Health (Des Moines: George E. Roberts, 1885), pp. 535–545.

5. E. Levinstein, "The Morbid Craving of Morphia," cited in Charles E. Terry and Mildred Pellens, *The Opium Problem* (New York: Bureau of Social Hygiene, 1928), p. 139.

6. Cesare Lombroso, *Crime, Its Causes and Remedies* (Boston: Little, Brown, 1911).

7. Richard L. Dugdale, *The Jukes* (New York: Putnam, 1911).

8. W. G. Thompson, *Textbook of Practical Medicine* (Philadelphia: Lea Brothers, 1902).

9. See Frank Soule, John H. Gilran, and James Nisbet, *The Annals of San Francisco* (San Francisco: A. L. Bancroft, 1878); Herbert Asbury, *The Barbery Coast* (Garden City, N. Y.: Garden City, 1933).

10. J. W. Buel, *Sunlight and Shadow of America's Great Cities* (Philadelphia: West Philadelphia Publishing Co., 1891); Edward Crapsey, *The Nether Side of New York* (New York: Sheldon, 1872); Gustav Lening, *The Dark Side of New York Life and Its Criminal Classes* (New York: Fred'k Gerhard, 1873); Edward Winslow Martin, *Sins of the Great City* (Philadelphia: National, 1868).

11. Helen Campbell, Thomas Knox, and Thomas Byrnes, *Darkness and Daylight; or, Lights and Shadows of New York Life* (Hartford, Conn.: A. D. Worthington, 1892), p. 570.

12. A. E. Costello, *Our Police Protectors* (New York: Author's Edition, 1884), pp. 516–524. See also Thomas Byrnes, *Professional Criminals of America* (New York: G. W. Dillingham, 1895), pp. 39–40.

13. Harold Wentworth and Stuart Berg Flexner, *Dictionary of American Slang* (New York: Thomas Y. Crowell, 1960), p. 161.

14. Alonzo Calkins, *Opium and the Opium Appetite* (Philadelphia: J. B. Lippincott, 1871), pp. 324–330.

15. H. H. Kane, *Opium Smoking in America and China* (New York: G. P. Putnam's, 1881), p. 81.

16. Thomas D. Crothers, *Morphinism and Narcomaniacs from Other Drugs* (Philadelphia: W. B. Saunders, 1902), pp. 88, 112–113.

17. For example, see J. B. Mattison, "The Impending Danger," *Medical Record,* 22 Jan. 1876, pp. 69–71.

18. H. Wayne Morgan, *Yesterday's Addicts: American Society and Drug Abuse: 1865–1920* (Norman: University of Oklahoma Press, 1974), p. 28.

19. See Rufus King, *The Drug Hang-Up: America's Fifty-Year Folly* (New York: W. W. Norton, 1972), pp. 23–27.

20. *Literary Digest,* 26 Apr. 1919, p. 32.

21. *The Outlook,* 25 June 1919, p. 315.

22. *American Review of Reviews,* July 1919, pp. 331–332.

23. Cited in David T. Courtwright, *Dark Paradise: Opiate Addiction in America before 1940* (Cambridge, Mass.: Harvard University Press, 1982), p. 33.

24. *Literary Digest,* 24 May 1924, p. 32.

25. Committee on Education of the House of Representatives, Conference on

Narcotic Education, *Hearings on HJR 65,* 69th Cong.,1st sess. 16 Dec. 1925, pp. 2–3.

26. David F. Musto, *The American Disease: Origins of Narcotic Control* (New Haven, Conn.: Yale University Press, 1973), p. 322.

27. National Broadcasting Company, "The Struggle of Mankind Against Its Deadliest Foe," radio broadcast, 1 Mar. 1928.

28. Courtwright, p. 91.

29. James A. Inciardi, "Youth, Drugs, and Street Crime," in *Drugs and the Youth Culture,* ed. Frank R. Scarpitti and Susan K. Datesman (Beverly Hills: Sage, 1980), p. 176.

30. Douglas T. Miller and Marion Nowak, *The Fifties: The Way We Really Were* (Garden City, N. Y.: Doubleday, 1977), pp. 279–287.

31. Isidor Chein, Donald L. Gerard, Robert S. Lee, and Eva Rosenfeld, *The Road to H: Narcotics, Delinquency, and Social Policy* (New York: Basic Books, 1964). See also Harold Alksne, *A Follow-up Study of Treated Adolescent Narcotics Users* (New York: Columbia University School of Public Health and Administrative Medicine, 1959); Isidor Chein and Eva Rosenfeld, "Juvenile Narcotic Use," *Law and Contemporary Problems,* Winter 1957, pp. 52–68; A. S. Meyer, *Social and Psychological Factors in Opiate Addiction* (New York: Columbia University Bureau of Applied Social Research, 1952).

32. *Newsweek,* 25 June 1951, pp. 19–20; 11 June 1951, pp. 26–27; 17 Sept. 1951, p. 60; *Life,* 25 June 1951, pp. 21–24; *The Survey,* July 1951, p. 328; *Time,* 26 Feb. 1951, p. 24; 7 May 1951, pp. 82, 85; 3 Oct. 1955, pp. 63–64; *Reader's Digest,* Dec. 1957, pp. 55–58; *The Nation,* 31 Aug. 1957, pp. 92–93; *Ladies' Home Journal,* Mar. 1958, pp. 173–175.

33. *Newsweek,* 13 Aug. 1951, p. 50.

34. *Newsweek,* 11 June 1951, p. 26.

35. *Newsweek,* 20 Nov. 1950, pp. 57–58.

36. *Life,* 11 June 1951, p. 116.

37. *Reader's Digest,* Oct. 1951, pp. 137–140.

38. *Time,* 10 Sept. 1951, p. 27.

39. Ian Whitcomb, *After the Ball: Pop Music from Rag to Rock* (New York: Viking, 1974), pp. 219–241.

40. Miller and Nowak, p. 295.

41. Jack Lait and Lee Mortimer, *U.S.A. Confidential* (New York: Crown, 1952), pp. 37–38.

42. David M. Wilner, Eva Rosenfeld, Donald L. Gerard, and Isidor Chein, "Heroin Use and Street Gangs," *Journal of Criminal Law, Criminology and Police Science,* Nov.–Dec. 1957, pp. 399–409.

43. Edouard C. Sandoz, "Report on Morphinism to the Municipal Court of Boston," *Journal of Criminal Law and Criminology,* 13 (1922), 10–55; Lawrence Kolb, "Drug Addiction and its Relation to Crime," *Mental Hygiene,* 9 (1925), 74–89.

44. James A. Inciardi, "The Villification of Euphoria: Some Perspectives on an Elusive Issue," *Addictive Diseases: An International Journal,* 1 (1974), 245.

45. U.S. Treasury Department, Bureau of Narcotics, *Traffic in Opium and Dan-*

gerous Drugs for the Year Ended December 31, 1939 (Washington, D.C.: U.S. Government Printing Office, 1940).

46. Harry J. Anslinger, "Relationship Between Addiction to Narcotic Drugs and Crime," *Bulletin on Narcotics*, 3 (1951), 1–3.
47. James A. Inciardi and Brian R. Russe, "Professional Thieves and Drugs," *International Journal of the Addictions*, 12 (1977), 1087–1095.
48. For detailed descriptions and analyses of the history, social organization, occupational structure, and criminal activities of professional thieves, see Edwin H. Sutherland, *The Professional Thief* (Chicago: University of Chicago Press, 1937); James A. Inciardi, *Careers in Crime* (Chicago: Rand McNally, 1975).
49. John C. Ball, "Two Patterns of Narcotic Addiction in the United States," *Journal of Criminal Law, Criminology and Police Science*, 52 (1965), 203–211; John A. O'Donnell, "The Rise and Decline of a Subculture," *Social Problems*, Summer 1967, pp. 73–84.
50. Charles Winick, "Physician Narcotic Addicts," *Social Problems*, Fall 1961, pp. 174–186; Charles Winick, "The Use of Drugs by Jazz Musicians," *Social Problems*, Winter 1961, pp. 240–253.
51. James P. Morgan, "Drug Addiction: Criminal or Medical Problem," *Police*, July–Aug. 1966, pp. 6–9.
52. For bibliographies and analyses of the literature on drug use and crime, see Harold Finestone, "Narcotics and Criminality," *Law and Contemporary Problems*, Winter 1957, pp. 72–85; Florence Kavaler, Donald C. Krug, Zili Amsel, and Rosemary Robbins, "A Commentary and Annotated Bibliography on the Relationship between Narcotics Addiction and Criminality," *Municipal Reference Library Notes*, 42 (1968), 45–63; Jared R. Tinklenberg, "Drugs and Crime," in *Drug Use in America: Problem in Perspective*, Appendix, vol. I, National Commission on Marihuana and Drug Abuse (Washington, D.C.: U.S. Government Printing Office, 1973), pp. 242–267; Gregory A. Austin and Dan J. Lettieri, *Drugs and Crime: The Relationship of Drug Use and Concomitant Criminal Behavior* (Rockville, Md.: National Institute on Drug Abuse, 1976); Research Triangle Institute, *Drug Use and Crime: Report of the Panel on Drug Use and Criminal Behavior* (Springfield, Va.: National Technical Information Service, 1976); Stephanie W. Greenberg and Freda Adler, "Crime and Addiction: An Empirical Analysis of the Literature, 1920–1973," *Contemporary Drug Problems*, 3 (1974), 221–270; Robert P. Gandossy, Jay R. Williams, Jo Cohen, and Henrick J. Harwood, *Drugs and Crime: A Survey and Analysis of the Literature* (Washington, D.C.: United States Department of Justice, National Institute of Justice, 1980); David N. Nurco, John C. Ball, John W. Shaffer, and Thomas Hanlon, "The Criminality of Narcotic Addicts," *The Journal of Nervous and Mental Disease*, 173 (1985), 94–102.

CHAPTER FOUR

THE DRUGS–CRIME CONNECTION

A Journey into the Street Worlds of Heroin, Cocaine, and Crime

In 1956, while mainstream America was persecuting Alan Freed and the Fordham Baldies were terrorizing the imaginations of New York youth, Senator Price Daniels of Texas was quoted as saying:

> Addiction is bad enough in itself. But with it goes crime, committed to pay for the habit. This combination of addiction and crime is a very communicable disease.[1]

If one had not known otherwise, one might have thought the words had come from the ghost of Captain Richmond Hobson, echoing lines from his enthusiastic "living dead" sermon of almost three decades earlier. Senator Daniels, however, did Hobson one better. He claimed that he had established a startling fact: that narcotic addiction was directly responsible for one-fourth of *all* the crimes committed in the United States. His declaration was an interesting one, for not only was the nature and extent of drug-related crime virtually unknown but, further, absolutely no one had even the vaguest idea of how much crime of *any* kind there was in the nation.

Then came the 1960s, a decade that occupies an individual summit in Americans' jagged images of the crime and violence in their midst. It began with the assassination of John Fitzgerald Kennedy, the fourth president of the United States to die by such violent means. But Kennedy's death was only the beginning. His alleged assassin, Lee Harvey Oswald, was shot to death within 36 hours of the president. In 1965 Black Muslim leader Malcolm X died violently in New York City. In 1967 American Nazi leader George Lincoln Rockwell was murdered by one of his followers. The next year the lives of civil-rights leader Dr. Martin Luther

115

King, Jr., and Senator Robert Kennedy were taken by assassination. Of less political renown, the 1960s also saw the cold-blooded murders of three young civil-rights workers by members of the Ku Klux Klan in Mississippi, with the connivance of local law-enforcement officers; the firebombing of the "freedom riders" in Alabama; the bloody battles at Kent State, "Ole Miss," and other campuses across the nation spurred by America's involvement in the Vietnam War; the ghetto riots in Los Angeles, Newark, Detroit, and numerous other densely populated urban areas; and the police riot at the 1968 Democratic Convention when Chicago's Mayor Richard Daley unleashed a force of 18,000 law-enforcement officers, Illinois National Guardsmen, and regular Army troops armed with rifles, flamethrowers and bazookas against peace marchers demonstrating their opposition to the Vietnam War. There was also street crime.

During the first half of the decade alone, reported crimes of violence had increased by one-half, property crimes by two-thirds, and the overall crime rate by almost one-half. In response, newly elected President Lyndon Johnson announced a "war on crime" during an address to the Eighty-ninth Congress on March 8, 1965. The visible army in his "war" was the President's Commission on Law Enforcement and Administration of Justice, established by Johnson to study the problems of crime and justice.[2] A major task of the commission, at a time when politicians, parents, and the press were claiming that addiction was responsible for up to *half* the crime in the nation, was to examine the drug problem and its relation to crime.

When the commission's work was complete, the task force assigned to study narcotics and drug abuse made the following embarrassing, however honest, announcement:

> The simple truth is that the extent of the addict's or drug abuser's responsibility for all nondrug offenses is unknown. Obviously it is great, particularly in New York City, with its heavy concentration of users; but there is no reliable data to assess properly the common assertion that drug users or addicts are responsible for 50 percent of all crime.[3]

Professionals in the drug field applauded the announcement, hoping that, finally, resources would be made available to measure the phenomenon in question. To their chagrin, however, no federal funds were earmarked for focused studies of the drugs—crime nexus, and on into the next decade the issue remained unresolved. By that time, common assertions had pushed the amount of crime presumed to have been committed by addicts up to 90%.

A WONDERFULLY WICKED WEEVIL AND NIXON'S WORLDWIDE WAR ON DRUGS

When Richard M. Nixon assumed the presidency of the United States he spoke of a "war on drugs" and a "war on heroin." He established a Special Action Office for Drug Abuse Prevention, but according to investigative reporter Edward Jay Epstein, the real purpose of the "war" was to increase the power of the White House bureaucracy. Epstein maintained that under the aegis of a "war on heroin," Nixon had established two new agencies—the Office of Drug Abuse Law Enforcement and the Office of National Narcotics Intelligence—created for the purpose of investigating his political enemies.[4] Whether or not this was really so, Nixon's "war" seemed to accomplish little.

Yet there *was* Nixon's "screwworm" project.[5] This was an effort by the White House, the Department of Agriculture, and NASA to create a wonderfully wicked weevil that, when released in Turkey and the Golden Triangle, would eat the plants that produced the pod that gave the opium that supplied the drug that obsessed poor Richard Nixon. A "screwworm" as such was actually created, but its developers feared that if released, it might start eating rice, wheat, and other plants once it had devoured the world's poppy crop. That, combined with the possibility of its crossing international boundaries to attack Soviet poppies, ultimately led to the little bug's demise.

In 1972, the "fear of crime" climbed to new heights. According to a Gallup Poll in that year, almost half of those surveyed were afraid to walk in their neighborhoods at night, and drug addiction was cited among the major reasons for the high crime rate.[6] By January 1973, crime was ranked highest among the nation's urban problems, with drug use ranking third.[7] President Nixon, by that time in his second term and all too busy denying his complicity in the Watergate "cover-up," nevertheless responded with a statement reemphasizing his "war on drugs":

> No single law-enforcement problem has occupied more time, effort, and money in the past four years than that of drug abuse and drug addiction. We have regarded drugs as "public enemy number one," destroying the most precious resource we have—our young people—and breeding lawlessness, violence and death.[8]

Although often accused of exaggeration, this time many of the president's claims were quite accurate. Estimated federal expenditures for drug-abuse prevention and law enforcement were indeed staggering—increasing from $150.2 million in 1971 to $654.8 million just two years later.[9] But Nixon's descriptions of the drug problem and its relation to crime often went beyond the parameters of reasonable estimate. He referred to heroin use as a plague that threatened every man, woman, and child in the nation with the "hell of addiction," and maintained that addict crime—largely in the form of "crime in the streets"—cost the nation roughly $18 billion a year. Yet the billions of dollars of losses from thefts and robberies that Nixon claimed addicts were committing to buy their heroin supplies was actually over 25 times greater than the value of all property stolen and unrecovered throughout the United States in 1971.[10]

EXPERTS, PANELS, AND CRIME IN THE STREETS

In the aftermath of Watergate and Nixon's resignation, the Steelers' victory over the Vikings in Super Bowl IX and Evel Knievel's unsuccessful attempt to leap across Idaho's 1,600-foot-wide Snake River Canyon on a motorcycle, and five decades of banter about the nature and extent of drug-related crime, the National Institute on Drug Abuse (NIDA) convened a one-day workshop in 1975 for the purpose of establishing a federal drugs—crime research agenda. Subsequently, a panel of experts was assembled to examine any available data and prior research on the topic, to determine what questions could be readily addressed, and to recommend research approaches for studying questions that remained unanswered.

The ultimate conclusion of the panel was politically disturbing, to at least a few government drug officials at any rate. Many studies had heretofore demonstrated a statistical correlation between drug use and crime. From such data, policymakers had drawn an inference of causality—that is, that *drug use causes crime*. Yet the panel, on the basis of existing data and prior research, called the inference of causality into question, suggesting that the "drug use causes crime" conclusion could not be drawn from what was known. Moreover, in holding that any such linkage could not be demonstrated, the panel was questioning the fundamental assumption of American drug-control policy—that by reducing the demand for drugs through drug-treatment initiatives, the criminality of the addict could be eliminated.[11] Nevertheless, NIDA established a federal drugs—crime research agenda. In the years hence, both NIDA and the National Institute of Justice funded a series of studies, principally in New York, Baltimore, and Miami, that began the building of a more meaningful data base on the elusive drugs—crime connection.

On the basis of extensive follow-up studies of addict careers in Baltimore, John C. Ball of Temple University and David N. Nurco of the University of Maryland School of Medicine found that there were high rates of criminality among heroin users during those periods that they were addicted and markedly lower rates during times of nonaddiction.[12] This finding was based on the concept of the "crime-days per year at risk." The "crime-day" was defined as a 24-hour period during which an individual committed one or more crimes. Thus, "crime-days per year at risk" was a rate of crime commission that could vary anywhere from 0 to 365. Over the addiction careers of the Baltimore addicts studied, the average crime-days per year at risk was 230, suggesting that their rates of criminality were not only persistent on a day-to-day basis but also tended to continue over an extended number of years and periods of addiction.[13]

In the New York studies, the investigators operated from a storefront. During their six-year project, they conducted interviews with hundreds of criminally active drug users recruited from the streets of east and central Harlem. The findings on drug-related criminality tended to confirm what was being learned elsewhere and provided insights as to how addicts functioned on the streets—how they purchased, sold, and used drugs; the roles that drugs played in their lives; and how the street-level drug business was structured.[14]

The studies in Miami demonstrated that the amount of crime drug users committed was far greater than anyone had heretofore imagined, that drug-related crime could at times be exceedingly violent, and that the criminality of heroin and cocaine users was far beyond the control of law enforcement.[15]

APPROACHING THE FRONT LINES OF DRUG USE AND CRIME

In an effort to generate a substantial data base descriptive of the nature and extent of crime among drug users, a series of interview studies were conducted in Dade County, Florida, from 1977 through 1985. For the sake of comparative data, interviews with smaller groups of informants were also conducted in New York City; San Antonio; Dayton, Ohio; and Wilmington, Delaware. In all, more than 3,000 face-to-face interviews were conducted. Although a number of these interviews involved drug users in treatment programs and detention centers, almost two-thirds were contacted at a time when they were actively using drugs and committing crimes in the street community.

Locating and interviewing people on the street who are active in the worlds of both drug use and crime is not as difficult as it might seem. The investigators had been conducting drug studies in both Miami and New York for a period of years, and a number of contacts had been built up with users, dealers, and treatment people. These individuals represented "starting points." That is, they went to the streets with one or more interviewers who were familiar with the local street scene and introduced them to an active drug user. It was explained to the user that it was a research project, that names would not be collected, that the identity of the respondents would be kept confidential, and that none of the information would be turned over to law-enforcement authorities. As one of these contacts, a counselor at a Miami drug-treatment program, commented to a drug user about to be interviewed:

> Listen brother, all this man wants to know is what you're doin' and what's goin' on. He's okay. He ain't gonna jive ya and he ain't gonna fuck ya in the ass. . . . It's cool. . . . Just be honest for 20–30 minutes and he'll give ya 10 bucks for your time.

And the contact person added:

> . . . and now listen to the most important part. I don't want you or none of ya friends fuckin' with him. If it gets back ta me that anyone was ripped off or fucked over in any way, I'm gonna come out here and personally cut your balls off—one at a time!

There were added safeguards. *First,* in research of this type, the Drug Enforcement Administration and the National Institute on Drug Abuse provide investigators with a grant of confidentiality. The grant is a signed document that guarantees that the investigator cannot be forced to divulge the identity of his or her informants to any law-enforcement authority, court, or grand jury. All informants were made aware of the grant and were given copies if they requested it. *Second,* to eliminate any hesitation by informants, questions about their criminal activities were asked in a way that would be deemed no more than "hearsay" in a court of law. In other words, the dates and places of specific crimes were not asked. Rather, it was a matter of asking how many burglaries or how many robberies the informant had committed during the last year. *Third,* questions about any rapes or homicides committed were simply not asked, although a number of the informants volunteered such information.

During or after each interview, at a time when the rapport between interviewer and respondent was felt to be at its highest level, each respondent was asked to identify other drug users with whom he or she was acquainted. These individuals, in turn, were located and interviewed, and the process was repeated until the social network surrounding each user was exhausted. As described, the method restricted the pool of users interviewed to those who were currently active in the street subculture. In addition, it eliminated former users as well as those who were only peripheral to the mainstream community of street drug users. Although the plan did not guarantee a totally unbiased sample, the use of several "starting points" within the same locale eliminated the problem of drawing all respondents from only one social network.

A major question that might be posed regarding this type of research relates to the validity of the information gathered. Do drug users tend to distort or cover up the less desirable aspects of their lives on the street? The answer to this question is *no!* A variety of controlled studies have been undertaken in this behalf over the years. Addict self-reports of arrests have been compared with official records; information on drug use has been compared with urinalysis results; and intraquestionnaire safeguards and interview–reinterview procedures have been tested. In all instances, it would appear that drug users tend to tell the truth *to the best of their ability.*[16]

This latter phrase, "to the best of their ability," has been italicized because in a variety of situations drug-using criminals simply cannot accurately remember what they may have been doing. Researchers in the drug field have long since realized the futility of collecting useful data on heroin users' daily drug intake. Most regular heroin users living on the streets use as much heroin as they can get their hands on. Depending on their funds, their ability to "score," and the availability of heroin, some days they get a lot, some days just a little, and on a few occasions none at all. These kinds of fluctuations, combined with the fact that users do not maintain a daily record of their heroin intake, tend to make accurate recall difficult. Moreover, many heroin users, depending on whom they are talking to, may deliberately lie about heroin intake. A woman heroin user in Miami indicated in 1979:

> When my parole officer picked me up I told her I was using only a dime bag a day. She saw the fresh tracks on my arms so she knew I was usin' so I didn't want to lie about that. But I didn't want her to know I was usin' heavy 'cause she might take me in. But she took me in anyway. The next thing I know she's got me talkin' to a hospital social worker, tryin' to find out what I was doin' and how I was feelin' and how much I

was usin'. I told her I was clean and that my P.O. [parole offi-cer] was just tryin' to fuck me over. I thought maybe she could talk my P.O. out of violatin' me. But I end up gettin' my black ass locked up anyway and when I got to detention I started screamin' that I was sick and had a $200-a-day habit and I needed medication. . . . By the time the day was over I had told so many fucking stories that I had no idea of how much the fuck I was usin' that day, or any other day.

As such, should a heroin user say that he or she shoots up six times a day or has a $300-a-day habit, the information is probably incorrect. A more reliable indicator is simply to determine whether use is daily, several times a week, or once a week.

A second problem is accurately recalling criminal activity, particularly for those who commit crimes with great frequency. To cite an example, when a Miami heroin user was asked how many burglaries he had com-mitted during the previous 12 months, his response was: "Oh man, it must have been thousands." To a researcher, such an answer is of abso-lutely no empirical value. To aid the user in providing a more accurate estimate, the interviewer helped him to reconstruct his life events and ac-tivities for the preceding year. Several dates were found to be prominent in his mind—his birthday, Christmas, April 17 when his mother died, July 15 when he was stabbed in a fight with a connection, April 19 when he retaliated and shot his connection to death, December 14 when he was arrested for possession of heroin, and other dates. For each, he was asked what he did on those dates, and then the week before and the week after. In time, a clearer picture of his criminality was put together, and what was originally "thousands" of burglaries was only 40 to 50.

NARCOTICS, COCAINE, AND THE MIAMI STREET SCENE

Of the more than 3,000 people interviewed, one cohort included 573 Miami narcotics users contacted during 1978 through 1981.* Although a

---

*Although more than 3,000 interviews were conducted in all, only a portion of the data is reported here. The analysis that follows reviews some findings on 1,002 heroin and other drug users contacted during the 1978–1981 period, combined with ethnographic anecdotes collected since then. In Chapter 5, data from interviews collected through 1985 are intro-duced. For analyses of segments of the other data, see footnote 15 in Chapter 4.

few of them were recent admissions to local drug-treatment programs or the county stockade, the overwhelming majority—476, or 83%—were active in the street community at the time of interview. *All* were current users of narcotics. That is, they had used heroin or illegal *methadone** on one or more occasions during the 90-day period before the interview. Furthermore, like other populations of street-drug users that have been studied, most were males (68%), the median age was 26.9 years, and 52% were white, 36% were black, and 12% were Hispanic.

Without question, these narcotics users had long histories of multiple-drug use with identifiable patterns of onset and progression. Using median age as an indicator, they had begun their careers in substance abuse with alcohol at an age of 13.7 years, followed by their first other drug experimentation about a year later. Marijuana use began at a median age of 15 years, followed by the use of sedatives at 17.1 years, heroin at 18.9 years, and cocaine at 19.4 years. Any differences between the men and women in the cohort were only minor.

All these narcotics users were heavily involved with drugs, using an average of five different substances. As indicated in Table 4.1, *all* had used narcotics during the 90-day period prior to interview, and in excess of 90% were using narcotics either daily or several times a week. In addition, most were current users of sedatives, cocaine, alcohol, and marijuana. With regard to the high levels of multiple drug use, a 19-year-old woman who had started her drug career with alcohol at age 11 commented:

> Part of the reason [for multiple drug use] is just for the hell of it and part is because you're just so used to stickin' something in your arm or up your nose or into your mouth. In the morning I'll use a little *shit* [heroin] to get the cobwebs out of my brain and get the blood movin' around. Then when you're waitin' downtown with a few others for the *man* [the connection] maybe someone will pass around a little wine and reefer. Some of us will shoot a little coke to beef up the *shit* they deal in 'round here. They try to tell ya it's "good stuff" and that's all they got. What a bunch a shit! What shit that is.

Early involvement in criminal activity was characteristic of the great majority of the narcotics users interviewed. Virtually all reported having committed crimes at some time in their lives, with the median age of the

---

* Methadone is a synthetic narcotic drug used in the treatment of heroin addiction. The dynamics of "methadone maintenance," as the treatment regimen is called, are discussed at length in Chapter 5.

Table 4.1 Current Drug Use and Cumulative Frequency of Use Among 573 Narcotics Users, Miami, Florida, 1978–1981

Current Drug Use	Male, % (*n* = 387)	Female, % (*n* = 186)	Totals, % (*n* = 573)
Heroin/illegal methadone			
Daily	69.5	67.7	68.9
Several times a week or more	92.8	95.7	93.7
Weekly or more	96.4	98.4	97.0
Any use in last 90 days	100.0	100.0	100.0
Other sedatives			
Several times a week or more	42.6	52.7	45.9
Every two weeks or more	64.1	72.0	66.7
Any use in last 90 days	70.3	74.2	71.6
Cocaine			
Weekly or more	43.9	47.8	45.2
Any use in last 90 days	61.8	61.8	61.8
Amphetamines			
Several times a week or more	8.5	11.8	9.6
Every two weeks or more	15.8	18.8	16.8
Any use in last 90 days	21.2	22.0	21.5
Hallucinogens/solvents–inhalants			
Weekly or more	3.4	4.8	3.8
Any use in last 90 days	11.1	12.9	11.7
Marijuana			
Daily	42.1	39.8	41.4
Several times a week or more	76.0	65.1	72.4
Weekly or more	84.5	76.3	81.8
Any use in last 90 days	88.1	79.0	85.2
Alcohol			
Several times a week or more	52.7	44.6	50.1
Every two weeks or more	71.6	66.1	69.8
Any use in last 90 days	78.0	75.8	77.3

first criminal act just short of 15 years. As suggested by Table 4.2, a property offense—burglary, shoplifting, vehicle theft, or some other larceny—was usually the first crime committed. Interestingly, however, almost all

Table 4.2   Criminal Histories of 573 Heroin Users, Miami, Florida, 1978–1981

Criminal Characteristics	Male, % (n = 387)	Female, % (n = 186)	Totals, % (n = 573)
Ever committed offense	99.7	98.9	99.5
Age of first crime (median)	14.4	15.3	14.7
First crime committed			
Robbery	6.2	3.2	5.2
Assault	7.0	5.4	6.5
Burglary	27.1	6.5	20.4
Vehicle theft	7.0	1.1	5.1
Shoplifting	18.3	37.6	24.6
Other theft/larceny	16.0	10.2	14.1
Prostitution	0.0	12.9	4.2
Drug sales	3.6	2.7	3.3
Other/no data	14.5	19.4	16.1
No crime	0.3	1.1	0.5
Have arrest history	94.3	88.7	92.5
Age at first arrest (median)	16.6	17.3	16.8
Total arrests (median)	4.4	4.9	4.5
Ever incarcerated	80.9	71.5	77.8

these users differentiated between simple pilfering and more serious property crimes. A 23-year-old respondent recalled:

> I used to rip off the supermarket and the 7/11 store ever since I can remember. My aunt would be goin' up and down the aisles puttin' stuff in the basket and I'd be right behind her eatin' cookies 'n candy off the shelves. . . . That doesn't count, it was just kid stuff and nobody cared. The first time—the first real score—I remember like it was today. I was real young—maybe 10 years old—and I was runnin' with these guys from Grand Avenue—a real tough area back in the sixties. We were in this big tool shop on the corner and this guy, I just couldn't be-fucking-lieve it. He rips open this display thing and takes out this fancy electric drill and hands it to me and puts it in my school bag and says git! I was scared shitless that we'd be caught. . . . I thought we'd really hit the big time then.

A total of 24 of the women narcotics users in the cohort had started their criminal careers with prostitution, and they too seemed to have different ways of defining whether or not their behavior was "criminal." One woman who stated that her first crime was prostitution at the age of 13, also indicated:

> I had sex for the first time when I was 10, somewhere 'round there. I remember I wanted to see some Steve McQueen movie real bad. I thought I was in love with the guy [McQueen] an' I would've done anything to see that show. . . . This jerk in my class said he'd take me if I'd play around with him a little afterwards, you know. So I did. . . . But that ain't prostitution. It was just fuckin' around. We all used to do that. What about all these *fine ladies* who are taken to a *fine restaurant* and a show and after let their man put it to 'em. That's the same thing. It's just gettin' laid. It wasn't prostitution 'til I started takin' money for it and doin' it regular.

Almost all of the 573 narcotics users had been arrested at least once, usually by age 17. Most had fewer than five arrests, and the majority had been to jail or prison at least once.

The number of crimes committed by these narcotics users was extensive. As illustrated in Table 4.3, the 573 users reportedly committed 215,105 offenses during the 12-month period prior to interview—an average of 375 crimes per subject during the course of a year. At first glance, this figure—more than 215,000 criminal offenses—would appear astronomical, thus requiring careful analysis. For example, of the total offenses, some 38%—over 82,000—involved drug sales, and an additional 22% included other "victimless crimes" such as prostitution, procuring, gambling, and alcohol violations. As such, more than 60% of the total offenses involved crimes against the public health, order, and safety. This, however, should not be interpreted as a minimizing of their criminal patterns. On the contrary. As the data indicate, the same 573 narcotics users were also responsible for almost 6,000 robberies and assaults, almost 6,700 burglaries, almost 900 stolen vehicles, more than 25,000 instances of shoplifting, and more than 46,000 other events of larceny and fraud.

The data in Table 4.3 address a number of other significant issues as well. *First,* there was great diversity in the range of the users' criminal events: 38% were robbers; 21% were assaulters; 53% were burglars; 19% stole automobiles; 38% were forgers; 24% engaged in confidence games; 53% dealt in stolen goods; 22% were prostitutes; 84% were drug sellers; and almost all were thieves. *Second,* the incidence of arrest among these narcotics users was extremely low. Of the 215,105 offenses, only

Table 4.3 Criminal Activity During the One-Year Period Prior to Interview of 573 Narcotics Users, Miami, Florida, 1978–1981

Crime	Total Offenses	Type as % of Total Offenses	Type as % of Sample Involved	Type as % of Offenses Resulting in Arrest
Robbery	5,300	2.5	37.7	0.8 ($n = 44$)
Assault	636	0.3	20.9	5.5 ($n = 35$)
Burglary	6,669	3.1	52.7	0.8 ($n = 52$)
Vehicle theft	841	0.4	19.4	0.8 ($n = 7$)
Theft from vehicle	3,708	1.7	28.1	0.4 ($n = 15$)
Shoplifting	25,045	11.6	62.1	0.4 ($n = 104$)
Pickpocketing	2,445	1.1	4.5	<0.1 ($n = 2$)
Prostitute theft	4,093	1.9	15.9	<0.1 ($n = 4$)
Other theft	6,668	3.1	31.1	0.6 ($n = 39$)
Forgery/counterfeiting	7,504	3.5	37.5	0.8 ($n = 59$)
Con games	3,162	1.5	23.9	<0.1 ($n = 1$)
Stolen goods	17,240	8.0	53.4	0.1 ($n = 22$)
Prostitution	26,045	12.1	22.2	0.3 ($n = 89$)
Procuring	7,107	3.3	24.1	<0.1 ($n = 3$)
Drug sales	82,449	38.3	83.9	0.1 ($n = 86$)
Arson	17	<0.1	1.7	0.0 ($n = 0$)
Vandalism	322	0.1	7.2	0.9 ($n = 3$)
Fraud	1,165	0.5	10.5	0.5 ($n = 6$)
Gambling	12,939	6.0	36.1	<0.1 ($n = 4$)
Extortion	240	0.1	7.5	0.0 ($n = 0$)
Loan-sharking	795	0.4	7.0	0.0 ($n = 0$)
Alcohol Offenses	296	0.1	6.6	7.1 ($n = 21$)
All other	419	0.2	2.3	3.1 ($n = 13$)
Totals	215,105	100.0	—	0.3 ($n = 609$)

609 resulted in an arrest. Stated differently, only three-tenths of 1 percent of the crimes resulted in arrest—that is, one arrest for every 353 crimes committed. More specifically, consider the following ratios of crimes committed to ensuing arrests:

robberies and assaults	75:1
forgery and counterfeiting	127:1
burglary and other theft	219:1
drug sales	959:1
confidence games	3,162:1

Furthermore, these narcotics users reported 17 crimes of arson, 240 incidents of extortion, and 795 cases of loan-sharking. *None* of these resulted in arrest. This would certainly suggest that narcotics users, at least those studied in Miami but likely most others, are highly successful criminals that systems of urban law enforcement are unable to control. As one heroin user who specialized in residential burglary explained it:

> It is so fucking easy to take down a house, or two or three, just in one morning and there's almost no risk. At 8 o'clock in the morning mommy and daddy go off to work and the kids go off to school. By 9:30 A.M. the whole fucking neighborhood is fucking dead. Now, this is important. You go to some neighborhood like Coral Gables, South Miami, Kendall or the other places where there's lots'a bushes and trees. There's so much cover that sometimes you can practically walk right up to the back door without even lookin' around. . . . And the real funny thing is that the jerk-offs will put bars and dead bolts on the front door but'll have just a flimsy lock in the back that lets you almost dance right in. . . . There was this one place that I hit three times in the same year and they still didn't learn nothin' about locks. . . . Jerk-offs.

In addition to the 573 narcotics users, another 429 were interviewed whose current drug use did not include narcotics. In many ways they were similar to the narcotics users in terms of their patterns of onset and progression into drug use and crime. Some had experimented with heroin and other narcotics early in their careers, and a few had even used narcotics regularly for short periods. Primarily, however, their drug use focused on alcohol, sedatives, marijuana, and/or cocaine. Both their drug-using and criminal careers had begun at about age 15.

As indicated in Table 4.4, like the users of narcotics, these individuals were heavily involved in crime. The 429 nonnarcotic drug users reported the commission of some 137,076 criminal offenses during the 12-month period prior to interview—an average of 320 crimes per respondent. Also, as was the case among the narcotics-using criminals, there were proportionately few crimes that resulted in arrest—one-half of 1% of the total.

Comparing the two groups in other ways, however, there seem to be some significant differences. The nonnarcotics users did indeed commit fewer crimes on a per capita basis. Moreover, almost two-thirds of their offenses were focused on shoplifting, prostitution, and drug sales, with

Table 4.4 Criminal Activity During the 12-Month Period Prior to Interview Among 429 Nonnarcotic Drug Users, Miami, Florida, 1978–1981

Crime	Total Offenses	Type as % of Total Offenses	Type as % of Sample Involved	Type as % of Offenses Resulting in Arrest
Robbery	1,698	1.2	29.4	2.7 ($n = 46$)
Assault	407	0.3	28.2	22.1 ($n = 90$)
Burglary	3,944	2.9	40.6	4.7 ($n = 185$)
Vehicle theft	618	0.5	16.3	4.4 ($n = 27$)
Theft from vehicle	2,536	1.9	11.9	0.4 ($n = 11$)
Shoplifting	21,247	15.5	33.6	0.3 ($n = 66$)
Pickpocketing	2,354	1.7	6.3	0.1 ($n = 3$)
Prostitute theft	2,245	1.6	6.1	0.1 ($n = 3$)
Other theft	4,548	3.3	17.2	0.5 ($n = 23$)
Forgery/counterfeiting	1,936	1.4	15.2	1.5 ($n = 30$)
Con games	2,103	1.5	9.8	0.2 ($n = 4$)
Stolen goods	11,960	8.7	25.9	0.2 ($n = 23$)
Prostitution	24,966	18.2	10.5	0.2 ($n = 49$)
Procuring	4,363	3.2	5.8	0.1 ($n = 5$)
Drug sales	38,378	28.0	30.5	0.2 ($n = 66$)
Arson	391	0.3	2.6	0.5 ($n = 2$)
Vandalism	259	0.2	5.3	0.0 ($n = 0$)
Fraud	1,409	1.0	7.5	0.3 ($n = 4$)
Gambling	8,819	6.4	17.5	0.1 ($n = 10$)
Extortion	50	<0.1	4.4	0.0 ($n = 0$)
Loan-sharking	1,506	1.1	4.4	<0.1 ($n = 1$)
Alcohol Offenses	1,319	1.0	7.5	3.4 ($n = 45$)
All other	20	<0.1	1.6	75.0 ($n = 15$)
Totals	137,076	100.0	—	0.5 ($n = 708$)

the balance scattered in very small proportions throughout all the remaining crime categories. The two groups are contrasted empirically in Table 4.5.

Thus, it would appear that in general, the narcotics-using group were more criminally involved. They committed more crimes, engaged in a greater diversity of offenses, and significantly larger proportions committed the more serious crimes of robbery and burglary.

Without getting more deeply into the complexities of empirical data,

Table 4.5 Criminal Involvement of Narcotic and Nonnarcotic Drug Users, Miami, Florida, 1978–1981

	Narcotic	Nonnarcotic
Mean offenses per user	375	320
Mean violent crimes per user (robberies/assaults)	10.4	5.1
Violent crimes (% of total)	2.8	1.5
Property crimes (% of total)	36.0	39.0
Drug sales (% of total)	38.3	28.0
% robbers	37.7	29.4
% assaulters	20.9	28.2
% drug sellers	83.9	30.5
% burglars	52.7	40.6
% shoplifters	62.1	33.6

how can these findings be initially interpreted with respect to the enduring questions about drug use and crime? Does drug use, and specifically heroin use, cause crime? Or are narcotics users already criminals in the first place, with drug use occurring later in their deviant careers? The answers to these questions are still not easy; the inference of causality and the age-old "enslavement theory" of addiction are issues not addressed directly until Chapter 5, but some preliminary notions can be drawn from the data.

First, it would appear that although the members of both cohorts studied were already substance abusers by the time they began regular criminal activity, it cannot be said that there is an inference of causality between drug use and street crime. For the nonnarcotics users, drugs and crime seemed to emerge hand in hand. For the narcotics users, drug use did indeed occur first, but heroin use did not appear until after they were well into their criminal careers.

Second, and in a contrasting direction, it can be said that *narcotics drive crime.*[17] When comparing the two groups, the narcotics users were involved with greater frequency, intensity, diversity, and severity than the nonnarcotics users. This conclusion tends to be supported by the Baltimore studies that observed the same phenomenon when comparing heroin users during alternative periods when they were addicted and were not addicted.[18]

Third, it has been argued widely in recent years that a small number of habitual "career criminals" are responsible for a relatively great proportion of the crime in the United States.[19] These data would tend to argue against that position. It has been estimated in recent years that there are no less than 500,000 heroin addicts in the nation. What proportion of these are "on the street" at any given time is not known, but unquestionably the number is substantial. The heroin users in this study, and the hundreds of thousands of others elsewhere in Miami, New York, Chicago, and other cities represent a rather substantial cohort of habitual offenders. As shown in the statistics presented in Table 4.3, some 216 heroin users were responsible for over 5,000 robberies during a one-year period, and some 302 users committed almost 7,000 burglaries during the same period of time. A number of the sampled cases were among both the robbery and burglary groups. At such rates of crime commission, it would be logical to infer that a great number of heroin users are career offenders.

In certain sectors of the political sphere it might be a great temptation to do some simple multiplication with the above figures. Given that there are an estimated 500,000 heroin users in the United States and that each user, as in Miami, commits an average of 375 crimes during a one-year period, would it not be logical to conclude that addict crime comes to 187.5 million offenses each year? Given that, would it not then be logical to incarcerate all heroin addicts and thus have an almost crime-free society? Yet reasonable people, if they were seriously to ponder such conclusions, would quickly realize the absurdity of it all. If there were indeed 187.5 million crimes being committed each year by the addict population, not to mention all the crimes perpetrated by others, American society would have long since fallen into a state of anarchy. Rather than the organized and relatively stable social system that now exists, America would appear more like the apocalyptic nightmare world of *Mad Max* and *The Road Warrior*. Going beyond simple-minded reasoning, there are some very good justifications for not venturing into such mathematical absurdities. As has been pointed out by many drug-abuse researchers and most recently by Bruce D. Johnson and his associates at the New York State Division of Substance Abuse Services, there are many different kinds of heroin users, and perhaps an even greater variety of nonheroin types. By cross classifying the type and frequency of criminal activities with the varying regularity of heroin intake, the Johnson/New York studies identified at least 27 distinct heroin-user types. At one end of the spectrum were highly predatory and dangerous armed robbers, and at the other end were innocuous low-level street drug dealers. There were also some whose only crime was the illegal possession of heroin.[20]

Fourth, it can be readily concluded that drug-related crime is out of control, with law enforcement and the administration of justice incapable of managing it. Since less than 1% of the crimes committed result in arrest, it would appear that the efficient control of drug-related crime is well beyond the scope of contemporary policing. As a Miami police officer reflected:

> I'm sure the police can do better, much better. But to bring it under complete control would be impossible. The citizen would simply not tolerate what would have to be done. If we increased the force 100-fold, and put a cop on every corner, in every doorway, on every roof, and in every house, then Miami could be crime-free. But then it would be like Soviet Russia.

SHOOT-OUT AT DADELAND MALL

It has been a recurring theme over the years that drugs instigate users to acts of wanton violence. Richmond Pearson Hobson and many others before and after him said it about heroin; Harry J. Anslinger and members of other antimarijuana contingents made a similar proclamation about the evil weed of the fields; and at various times the same has been said about cocaine, the amphetamines, and PCP. Moreover, there is a lengthy literature on the issue, with inconsistencies and contradictions on both sides of the argument.

During the 1920s, after Captain Hobson had launched his ravings against the quagmire of heroin use, Dr. Lawrence Kolb of the U.S. Public Health Service responded with what turned out to be one of the most often-quoted statements in the literature on drugs and violence:

> There is probably no more absurd fallacy prevalent than the notion that murders are committed and daylight robberies and holdups are carried out by men stimulated by cocaine or heroin which has temporarily distorted them into self-imagined heroes incapable of fear. . . . Violent crime would be much more prevalent if all habitual criminals were addicts who could obtain sufficient morphine or heroin to keep themselves fully charged with one of these drugs at all times.[21]

Kolb's argument was based on his belief that all preparations of opium capable of producing addiction tend to inhibit aggressive impulses and, furthermore, that the soothing narcotic properties of the opiates have the effect of making psychopaths less likely to commit crimes of violence.

From a strictly pharmacological point of view Kolb was correct, for the opiates do indeed depress the central nervous system. He went on to document his position empirically by comparing homicide rates in Chicago and New York for the period 1912 through 1923. His argument was that the incidence of heroin and morphine use had increased in those cities during that 12-year period, but that a corresponding increase in homicide rates was not apparent.[22] Yet Kolb's conclusion from the data was an exercise in self-deception for several reasons. The homicide rate in New York *had* remained constant over the period in question, but in Chicago it had shifted from 9.5 homicides per 100,000 population in 1912 to 12.7 in 1923—a 25% increase. Even more importantly, Kolb's attempt to correlate rates of homicide *within cities* with rates of addiction among individuals *living within those cities* was a basic methodological blunder that has become known in the social sciences as the "ecological fallacy."[23] Any attempt to employ a cause-and-effect relationship, or in Kolb's case the lack of such, must also account for the possibility of intervening variables. This was especially the case for early twentieth-century Chicago, a time when that city was experiencing explosive growth. As the result of international migrations and the rural–urban drift associated with the Industrial Revolution, the population of Chicago had increased by 500,000 per decade for three consecutive decades: from 1.7 million in 1910 to 3.4 million by 1930—the same general period that Kolb was referencing. The stability of communities and basic social processes had been altered to a degree that simplistic analyses such as Kolb's were impossible. There was a manifest absence of established institutional patterns in many regions of Chicago, and neighborhoods grew and changed hands so rapidly that sometimes the only constant feature appeared to be mobility.

Despite Kolb's basic errors, his conclusion seemed to be a logical one. In the decades hence, others reiterated his position. In 1957, for example, the Council on Mental Health of the American Medical Association clearly stated that the belief that opiates per se directly incite otherwise normal people to violent assaultive criminal acts, including sexual crimes, is not tenable.[24] During the 1960s the President's Commission on Law Enforcement and Administration of Justice reached the same conclusion.[25] What the American Medical Association and the president's commission were reacting to was the growing body of studies that were empirically documenting that drug users were *not* coming to the attention of the criminal justice system for the commission of violent crimes. In 1957, for example, sociologist Harold Finestone's study of a jail population found that heroin users engaged primarily in nonviolent property crimes.[26] The perspective that developed from the work of Finestone and others was that narcotics users tended toward burglary and prostitution—low-risk activities that generated the income necessary to purchase drugs. Thus, noneconomically productive crimes, such as assault, were avoided. Other studies have argued that individuals who are involved in violent crime become less so after initiation into drug use.[27] Perhaps all of that was so in the 1920s through the 1960s. Perhaps the addict was indeed nonviolent. Or perhaps the findings were the result of the long-standing tradition in drug-abuse research to study only captured populations and to assess criminality on the basis of arrest records alone.

In 1972, in an obscure paper published in what may be the most remote corner of the social science–criminology literature, a New York University graduate student challenged the position that heroin users were nonviolent.[28] Based on the growing number of studies of poly-drug abusers, an emergent cohort of multiple-drug users that had evolved from the drug revolution of the 1960s, it was argued that a new and different breed of heroin user was living on the streets of American cities. These people not only used heroin but other drugs as well. Most importantly, their criminality was *situational* in nature. Rather than repeatedly committing burglaries, they lacked any type of criminal specialization. They engaged in a wide variety of crimes—including assaults, muggings, and armed robberies—selected according to the nuances of situational opportunity. Shortly thereafter, other research studies began reporting on the same phenomenon.[29]

Paul J. Goldstein of New York's Narcotic and Drug Research, Inc., conceptualized the whole phenomenon of drugs and violence into a useful theoretical framework.[30] The *psychopharmacological model of violence* suggests that some individuals, as the result of short-term or long-term ingestion of specific substances, may become excitable, irrational, and exhibit violent behavior. The *economically compulsive model of violence* holds that some drug users engage in economically oriented violent crime to support costly drug use. The *systemic model of violence* maintains that violent crime is intrinsic to the very involvement with any illicit substance. As such, systemic violence refers to the traditionally aggressive patterns of interaction within the systems of illegal drug trafficking and distribution.

The early statements attributing violent behavior to drug use generally focused on the psychopharmacological argument. More recently this model has been applied to cocaine, barbiturates, and PCP, with a major focus on the amphetamines. In study after study, it was reported that the chronic use of amphetamines produced paranoid thought patterns and delusions that led to homicide and other acts of violence.[31] The same was said about cocaine. The conclusion is correct but likely applies only to isolated individuals and situations. The studies that drew the conclusion were based on limited clinical observations of just a few individuals who had already manifested violent behavior. This should not suggest, however, that the psychopharmacological model is without merit. There *have* been episodes of violence that were generated by the effects of these drugs—however infrequent they have been.

Contrary to everything that has been said over the years about the quieting effects of narcotic drugs, *there may be more psychopharmacological violence associated with heroin use than that of any other illegal drug.* Goldstein's studies of heroin-using prostitutes in New York City during the 1970s found a link between the effects of the withdrawal syndrome and violent crime.[32] The impatience and irritability caused by withdrawal motivated a number of prostitutes to rob their clients rather than provide them with sexual services. This phenomenon was found common in Miami, and not only among prostitutes but with other types of criminals as well. For example, one prostitute declared:

> . . . there are lots of shortcuts to get the john's money without having to go down on him. Sometimes you can con him out of it. Sometimes you just rob them outright. . . . Most of the time when me and the other girls are feeling sick and we just want to get back out in the street to fix . . . somethin' just seems to come over us. More than one time we felt so bad that I just cut a guy just to get out'a there and get straight. One time I was so crazy I just cut this guy and didn't even take his money.

A methadone patient stated:

> Many times when you're sick you might do things you don't normally [do] . . . you can get so desperate and uptight that you don't see straight. . . . I cut a connection more than once just so I didn't have to argue over the price of shit.

A low-level street dealer added:

> I'm just talkin' to this guy and all of a sudden, *bam!* He hits me. I know he wasn't feelin' too good, but the cocksucker just hits me and walks away.

The economically compulsive model of violence best fits the aggressive behavior of contemporary heroin and cocaine users. Among the 573 narcotics users interviewed in Miami, more than a third engaged in a total of

5,300 robberies as a source of income. Although some of these were "strong-arm" robberies or muggings where the victim was attacked from the rear and overpowered, the majority occurred at gunpoint. In fact, over a fourth of the respondents used a firearm in the commission of a crime. A similar phenomenon was found among the cohort of 429 non-narcotics users, with weapon use most common among those who were primarily cocaine users.

In early August 1985, the Associated Press news wire carried a report of what appeared to be a "new" variety of crime in Miami, committed by modern-day highwaymen. Suddenly, motorists on segments of Interstate 95 in downtown areas were being attacked and robbed. Rush-hour commuters stalled in expressway traffic had become the victims of young thieves who climbed up embankments, smashed car windows with bricks, and snatched wallets and handbags. Some drivers were robbed and beaten after their automobiles had been ambushed and disabled by thrown rocks or objects placed on the road.[33] Yet to members of the drug community, the practice of highway robbery was not new. In response to the sudden national publicity, a former heroin addict stated:

> I remember doing that 20 years ago when I was running the streets shooting dope. Only then, I—95 wasn't built yet and we'd do it on the Palmetto Expressway. We'd find a disabled car late at night waiting for a service wagon. We'd stick them up and sometimes strip the car.

An active criminal—addict also stated:

> You're right, it's been going on for years. What's changed is the magnitude. Also, now I think its more of a white—black thing.

Just three weeks after Miami's highway-robbery problem had received national attention, state and local law-enforcement agencies had tried various measures to control the situation—increased patrols, helicopter surveillance, decoy police, attack dogs. Numerous arrests were made, but the attacks continued and Miami motorists were given a green light to run down highwaymen who threatened them.[34] A former heroin user living in the community from which most of the highway robbers came explained:

> Now it's become a challenge. They've got cops in stalled cars out there, helicopters overhead, dogs sniffing around, and all kinds of other things. With all that, any of the renegades down here that can still pull off a stickup become heroes in the

neighborhood. Anybody who can still get away with it is considered something real special.

Among the women in the Miami study, there seemed to be a more focused link between drug use and economically compulsive violence. Before pursuing this point, however, some distinctions in the criminal activity of the men and women in the study seem necessary. Although the 573 narcotics users averaged 370 offenses each during the year before the interviews, the mean for the women was 415 and for the men 356. Thus, it appears that the women users committed crimes with greater frequency. However, their offenses fell into only a few areas. Of a total of 77,149 offenses, three-fourths were shoplifting, drug sales, and prostitution—crimes that generate little income and must be committed with considerable frequency to make them economically viable. Consider the addict–prostitutes in the sample. The 124 of them turned more than 25,000 tricks, an average of just a little over 200 each in one year's time. One such prostitute explained:

> Let's face it, a junkie whore is not the most desirable lady of the street. Some do lots of johns, but most don't. And moneywise you take what you can get. If all a john has is $10, I'm not going to let him walk. . . . So what happens is you really have to hustle. You work the streets some, you do a lot of dealing and *boosting* [shoplifting]. Today if I'm not lucky on the streets I'll hit a few stores and maybe run a few bags around town.

In terms of violence, most of the prostitutes supplemented their incomes periodically by assaulting and robbing, or unobtrusively stealing from their clients. In fact, of the more than 25,000 instances of prostitution, 1 in 7 also involved a theft or robbery. Among the nonnarcotics-using group of women, although there were fewer prostitutes, there was an almost identical pattern. Moreover, in both of the groups, almost *all* of the violent crimes were associated with prostitution. Yet, on the other hand, there was also a small core of women of both drug-using types that participated in a wide variety of crimes. Much like the "new female criminals" described by sociologist Freda Adler a decade ago,[35] these women had gone beyond the traditional limits of prostitution and shoplifting into major-league drug trafficking, extortion, auto theft, loan-sharking, and hijacking.

In the systemic model, acts of drug-related violence can occur for a variety of reasons: territorial disputes between rival drug dealers; assaults and homicides committed within dealing and trafficking hierarchies as means of enforcing normative codes; robberies of drug dealers, often followed by unusually violent retaliations; elimination of informers; punishment for selling adulterated, phony, or otherwise "bad" drugs; punishment for failing to pay one's debts; and general disputes over drugs or drug paraphernalia.[36]

Although these varieties of systemic violence are apparent wherever illegal drugs are distributed and used, drug violence has become legion in Miami. It received national attention for the first time in 1979 with what Miami locals still refer to as the "shoot-out at Dadeland Mall." Dadeland, a large indoor shopping complex in the Kendall section of South Dade County, rated as the most successful shopping mall in the world, attracts tens of thousands of customers on any given business day. On July 11, 1979, an armor-plated "war wagon," equipped with gunports, one-way windows, 30-caliber carbines, pump shotguns, 9-mm Browning automatics, and Ingram submachine guns, pulled up to a liquor store at the edge of the mall. The occupants of the "hit van" leveled their weapons and proceeded to spray the store with machine-gun fire, attempting to execute everyone in sight. Two Colombian nationals—both suspected of being cocaine traffickers—were killed and two bystanders were wounded.[37] For Miami residents, the shoot-out at Dadeland Mall and the other murders within the gangland of the "cocaine cowboys" had turned their "Magic City" into a deadly parody of the outlaw days of the Old West. Moreover, the Dadeland killings had pushed the 1979 death rate for drug dealers in the Miami area up to one a week. Through the first half of the 1980s, the level of drug-related deaths remained high, with the result that in 1984 Miami led the nation in homicides.[38] Although the drug-related violence in Miami that received media attention was concentrated within the cocaine-trafficking and distribution networks, street users of both heroin and cocaine reported that there were especially high rates of systemic violence. Among those studied, almost all reported having been either the perpetrator or victim of drug-related violence. A heroin dealer commented regarding one of his street-level sellers:

> Just the other day we caught this dumb junky nigger stiff with his hand in the till messin' with the money. We took care of him outright so as the word would get around quick. . . . We cut three of the stupid motherfucker's fingers off and fed them to his dog.

A number of women users reported that they were the victims of rape at the hands of drug dealers. One 24-year-old cocaine and marijuana user stated:

In the last few years I've been beaten and raped at least 10 times when I was trying to make a buy. One time this Cuban pimp drug dealer smacked me across the mouth, tied me to a bed, and then had all his friends try to fuck me to death—all the time sayin', "pretty white girl, ya just love it don't ya." If I ever find the bastard I'll blow his fucking brains out.

Many of the narcotics users indicated that they experienced violence at the hands of the police. Said one:

When they roust you they're not often all that gentle. Sometimes they just want information, sometimes they take your stuff and let you go, sometimes they give you a kick in the balls just for the fun of it. What pisses me off the most is when they hit you just to get your attention.

Violence associated with disputes over drugs has been common to the drug scene probably since its inception. Two friends come to blows because one refuses to give the other a *taste*. A husband beats his wife because she raided his *stash*. A woman stabs her boyfriend because he didn't *cop* enough drugs for her too. And as Goldstein pointed out:

The current AIDS scare has led to an increasing amount of violence because of intravenous drug-users' fear of contracting this fatal disease from contaminated "works." Some sellers of needles and syringes claim that the used works they are trying to sell are actually new and unused. If discovered by would-be purchasers, violence may ensue. A recent incident led to the death of two men. A heroin user kept a set of works in a "shooting gallery" for his exclusive use. One day another man used these works. The owner of the works discovered what had happened and stabbed this man to death. He later stabbed a friend to death who was present when the stranger had used the works, had done nothing to stop him, and had failed to inform the owner of what had happened.[39]

In short, systemic violence seems to be endemic to the parallel worlds of drug dealing, drug taking, and drug seeking.

POSTSCRIPT

Researchers in the drug field have held that narcotics addicts are responsible for as many as 50 million crimes each year in the United States.[40] In addition, an unknown and perhaps as great a level of crime is committed by cocaine users and other drug users. The Miami study discussed here certainly lends support to such an estimation. The 1,002 narcotics and nonnarcotics users were directly involved in over 340,000 offenses—in just one year, and in only one city. Although the majority of the offenses fall into the category of "victimless crime," these users nevertheless participated in some 95,000 criminal events that the FBI defines as "serious crime"—homicide, forcible rape, robbery, aggravated assault, burglary, larceny, vehicle theft, and arson. Too, the level of drug-related crime is out of control, well beyond the scope of contemporary policing.

How are these data best interpreted? Are drug users—and particularly heroin and other narcotics users—*driven to crime*, driven by their enslavement to expensive drugs that can be afforded only through continuous predatory activities? Or is it that *drugs drive crime*, that careers in drugs intensify already existing criminal careers? Contemporary data, in Miami and elsewhere, tend to support the latter position more than any other explanation.

Notes

1. *Reader's Digest*, June 1956, p. 21.
2. President's Commission on Law Enforcement and Administration of Justice, *The Challenge of Crime in a Free Society* (Washington, D.C.: U.S. Government Printing Office, 1967).
3. Task Force on Narcotics and Drug Abuse, President's Commission on Law Enforcement and Administration of Justice, *Task Force Report: Narcotics and Drug Abuse* (Washington, D.C.: U.S. Government Printing Office, 1967), p. 11.
4. Edward J. Epstein, *Agency of Fear* (New York: G. P. Putnam's, 1977), p. 8.
5. Epstein, pp. 148–151.
6. *New York Times*, 23 Apr. 1972, p. 23.
7. *Washington Post*, 16 Jan. 1973, p. A3.
8. Cited by Carl D. Chambers and James A. Inciardi, "Forecasts for the Future: Where We Are and Where We Are Going," in *Drugs and the Criminal Justice System*, ed. James A. Inciardi and Carl D. Chambers (Beverly Hills: Sage, 1974), p. 221.
9. Chambers and Inciardi, p. 222.
10. Epstein, pp. 179–181.

11. For a complete discussion of the operations of the "panel" on drug abuse and crime and the structuring of the federal drugs–crime research agenda, see Richard R. Clayton, "Federal Drugs–Crime Research: Setting the Agenda," In *The Drugs–Crime Connection,* ed. James A. Inciardi (Beverly Hills: Sage, 1981), pp. 17–38; Research Triangle Institute, *Report of the Panel on Drug Use and Criminal Behavior* (Springfield, Va.: National Technical Information Service, 1976).

12. John C. Ball, Lawrence Rosen, John A. Flueck, and David N. Nurco, "The Criminality of Heroin Addicts: When Addicted and When Off Opiates," in Inciardi, pp. 39–65; John C. Ball, John W. Shaffer, and David N. Nurco, "The Day-to-Day Criminality of Heroin Addicts in Baltimore—A Study in the Continuity of Offense Rates," *Drug and Alcohol Dependence,* 12 (1983), 119–142.

13. David N. Nurco, John C. Ball, John W. Shaffer, and Thomas E. Hanlon, "The Criminality of Narcotic Addicts," *Journal of Nervous and Mental Disease,* 173 (1985), 98.

14. See Bruce D. Johnson, Paul J. Goldstein, Edward Preble, James Schmeidler, Douglas S. Lipton, Barry Spunt, and Thomas Miller, *Taking Care of Business: The Economics of Crime by Heroin Abusers* (Lexington, Mass.: Lexington, 1985). See also Paul J. Goldstein, "Getting Over: Economic Alternatives to Predatory Crime Among Street Heroin Users," in Inciardi, pp. 67–84.

15. See James A. Inciardi, "Heroin Use and Street Crime," *Crime and Delinquency,* July 1979, pp. 335–346; Susan K. Datesman and James A. Inciardi, "Female Heroin Use, Criminality, and Prostitution," *Contemporary Drug Problems,* 8 (1979), 455–473; James A. Inciardi, "Women, Heroin, and Property Crime," in *Women, Crime, and Justice,* ed. Susan K. Datesman and Frank R. Scarpitti (New York: Oxford University Press, 1980), pp. 214–222; James A. Inciardi, "The Impact of Drug Use on Street Crime" (Paper presented at the Thirty-third Annual Meeting of the American Society of Criminology, Washington, D.C., 11–14 Nov. 1981); Anne E. Pottieger and James A. Inciardi, "Aging on the Street: Drug Use and Crime Among Older Men," *Journal of Psychoactive Drugs,* Apr.–June 1981, pp. 199–211; Charles E. Faupel, "Drugs and Crime: An Elaboration of an Old Controversy" (Paper presented at the Thirty-third Annual Meeting of the American Society of Criminology, Washington, D.C., 11–14 Nov. 1981); Susan K. Datesman, "Women, Crime, and Drugs," in Inciardi, ed., *The Drugs–Crime Connection,* pp. 85–105; Carl D. Chambers, Sara W. Dean, and Michael Pletcher, "Criminal Involvements of Minority Group Addicts," in Inciardi, ed., pp. 125–154; Anne E. Pottieger, "Sample Bias in Drugs/Crime Research: An Empirical Study," in Inciardi, ed., pp. 207–238; James A. Inciardi, Anne E. Pottieger, and Charles E. Faupel, "Black Women, Heroin and Crime: Some Empirical Notes," *Journal of Drug Issues,* Summer 1982, pp. 241–250; James A. Inciardi, "The Production and Detection of Fraud in Street Studies of Crime and Drugs," *Journal of Drug Issues,* Summer 1982, pp. 285–291; James A. Inciardi and Anne E. Pottieger, "Drug Use and Crime Among Two

Cohorts of Women Narcotics Users: An Empirical Assessment," *Journal of Drug Issues,* 16 (Winter 1986), 91–106.

16. See John C. Ball, "The Reliability and Validity of Interview Data Obtained from 59 Narcotic Drug Addicts," *American Journal of Sociology,* 72 (1967), 650–654; Richard Stephens, "The Truthfulness of Addict Respondents in Research Projects," *International Journal of the Addictions,* 7 (1972), 549–558; Arthur J. Bonito, David N. Nurco, and John W. Shaffer, "The Veridicality of Addicts' Self-Reports in Social Research," *International Journal of the Addictions,* 11 (1976), 719–724; Zili Amsel, Wallace Mandell, Lynda Matthias, Carol Mason, and Iris Hocherman, "Reliability and Validity of Self-Reported Illegal Activities and Drug Use Collected from Narcotic Addicts," *International Journal of the Addictions,* 11 (1976), 325–336; Thomas J. Cox and Bill Longwell, "Reliability of Interview Data Concerning Current Heroin Use from Heroin Addicts on Methadone," *International Journal of the Addictions,* 9 (1974), 161–165.
17. Nurco et al., "The Criminality of Narcotics Addicts," p. 100.
18. See note 12 above.
19. See, for example, *U.S. News & World Report,* 19 Aug. 1985, p. 27.
20. Johnson et al., pp. 139–160.
21. Lawrence Kolb, "Drug Addiction and Its Relation to Crime," *Mental Hygiene,* 9 (1925), 78.
22. Kolb, pp. 74, 79.
23. W. S. Robinson, "Ecological Correlations and the Behavior of Individuals," *American Sociological Review,* 15 (1950), 351–357.
24. American Medical Association, Council on Mental Health, "Report on Narcotic Addiction," *Journal of the American Medical Association,* 7 Dec. 1957, p. 1834.
25. Task Force on Narcotics and Drug Abuse, pp. 10–11.
26. Harold Finestone, "Use of Drugs Among Persons Admitted to a County Jail," *Public Health Reports,* 90 (1957), 553–568.
27. For a review of the issues and research on drugs and violence, see Duane C. McBride, "Drugs and Violence," in Inciardi, ed., *The Drugs–Crime Connection,* pp. 105–123.
28. James A. Inciardi, "The Poly-Drug Abuser: A New Situational Offender," in *Politics, Crime and the International Scene: An Inter-American Focus,* ed. Freda Adler and G. O. W. Mueller (San Juan, Puerto Rico: North-South Center for Technical and Cultural Exchange, 1972), pp. 60–68.
29. Richard C. Stephens and Rosalind D. Ellis, "Narcotics Addicts and Crime: Analysis of Recent Trends," *Criminology,* 12 (1975), 474–488; Margaret A. Zahn and Mark Bencivengo, "Violent Death: A Comparison Between Drug Users and Non-Drug Users," *Addictive Diseases: An International Journal,* 1 (1974), 283–296.
30. Paul J. Goldstein, "Drugs and Violent Behavior" (Paper presented at the Annual Meeting of the Academy of Criminal Justice Sciences, Louisville, Ky., 28 Apr. 1982).

31. See Everett H. Ellinwood, "Assault and Homicide Associated with Amphetamine Abuse," *American Journal of Psychiatry,* 127, (1971), 1170–1175; Roger C. Smith, "Speed and Violence: Compulsive Methamphetamine Abuse and Criminality in the Haight-Ashbury District," in *Proceedings of the International Conference on Drug Abuse,* ed. Chris Zarafonetis (Philadelphia: Lea & Febiger, 1972), pp. 435–448; S. Asnis and Roger C. Smith, "Amphetamine Abuse and Violence," *Journal of Psychedelic Drugs,* 10 (1978), 317–378.

32. Paul J. Goldstein, *Prostitution and Drugs* (Lexington, Mass.: Lexington, 1979), p. 126.

33. *New York Times,* 8 Aug. 1985, p. A12.

34. *USA Today,* 23 Aug. 1985, p. 3A.

35. Freda Adler, *Sisters in Crime: The Rise of the New Female Criminal* (New York: McGraw-Hill, 1975).

36. Goldstein.

37. *New York Times,* 12 July 1979, p. 8; *U.S. News & World Report,* 23 July 1979, p. 6; *Baltimore Sun,* 30 July 1979, p. 3A.

38. *USA Today,* 29 July 1985, p. 3A. See also William Wilbanks, *Murder in Miami* (Lanham, Md.: University Press of America, 1984).

39. Paul J. Goldstein, personal communication, 15 Aug. 1985.

40. John C. Ball, Lawrence Rosen, John A. Flueck, and David N. Nurco, "The Lifetime Criminality of Heroin Addicts in the United States," *Journal of Drug Issues,* 12 (1982), 225–239.

CHAPTER FIVE

HOOKER, WHORE, JUNKIE, THIEF; DEALER, DOPER, COCAINE FREAK
Some Comments on Prostitution and the Enslavement Theory of Addiction

When the "new chemical age" of the 1960s extended the boundaries of drug use from the marginal zones of society to the very center of mainstream American life, researchers and clinicians in the drug field asked themselves a number of difficult questions: Who are the drug users? What is the nature and extent of their use? Why are they using drugs? What are the short-term and long-term effects of their behavior on themselves and society? Can they change the behavior? There was an almost immediate reaction to these queries. Federal agencies, universities, and private foundations allocated hundreds of millions of dollars in funding for research, treatment, and prevention, and a massive effort to combat the "drug problem" was underway.

In the years hence, what has been learned about drug taking in America? Has the whole effort been worthwhile? Has drug use lessened? Has it had a negative impact on society? Can substance abuse be prevented, or at least curtailed in some populations? The answers to a number of these questions are obvious. *No*, drug use has not decreased. If anything, more people are using drugs today than ever before. And *yes*, the effects of drug use on society are numerous, in terms of crime, health problems, lost productivity, family disruptions, and general economic costs. On a more positive note, the advancement of knowledge in the drug field has been considerable, particularly in the areas of clinical, biomedical, epidemiological, and psychosocial research.

Curiously, though, despite the massive funding for research and despite all that has been learned about drug use, some of the most fundamental myths continue to endure. There still seems to be a belief in the "addiction-prone personality" as the major explanation of drug abuse. The idea that

145

marijuana use per se leads to heroin addiction is repeated continuously. On Capitol Hill and even in the sanctuary of the Oval Office, policies grounded in the notion that only a greater technological war on drugs can reduce the parameters of the drug problem are still endorsed. Yet one can excuse the general public for a persistent faith in ideas that have long since been proven false by the rigors of science. After all, most research findings are presented only to limited audiences—at scientific meetings, and in professional journals and government reports. But what explains the persistence of myth among researchers and clinicians in the drug field? Without question, there are many myths, both minor and major, that are still being repeated.

Perhaps the most curious myth to persist in contemporary drug literature relates to the emergence of methadone. In describing how this drug was first synthesized in Germany as a substitute for morphine during the early 1940s, textbook writers are still saying that the drug was first called "Dolophine," so named after Adolf Hitler.[1] The early literature on methadone, however, makes no such suggestion, but repeatedly indicates that the Germans referred to it as "compound 10820," or *Amidon*.[2] "Dolophine," however, comes from the Latin *dolor*, meaning "pain." *Dolophine* is a trade name for methadone, adopted by Eli Lilly and Co. after the end of World War II when patents for the drug were made available to U. S. pharmaceutical manufacturers. Lilly's purpose in using that particular designation was to convey the notion of "pain relief."[3] Exactly how the association between Dolophine and Hitler found such an enduring place in the drug literature is not fully clear. Perhaps it all began with Alexander King, the nonconformist editor of *Life* magazine and surrealist comedian, who made the following comment about his drug treatment at Lexington in a 1958 autobiography:

> We got shots four times a day and an additional barbiturate sedative at night. They gave us a synthetic horror called Dolofine [sic] which was invented in Germany under the Nazis and named after the great Adolph![4]

Even though the saga of Dolophine and its mythical relationship to Adolph Hitler is no more than a curious anecdote in the annals of drug abuse, there are other more significant matters. Consider what has been called the "enslavement theory of addiction."

LABOR MARKETS, BLACK MARKETS, AND ENSLAVEMENT THEORY

Over the years, "enslavement theory" has emerged in a variety of forms. It has been argued, for example, that the Chinese laborers who worked the mines and built the railroads in the nineteenth-century American West were enslaved to opium smoking by their employers. In this respect, William J. Chambliss has indicated:

> . . . an opium-addicted labor force was a highly competent labor force. The threat of withdrawing the supply of opium kept many potential labor complaints from becoming a serious threat to the employer.[5]

It has been similarly argued that heroin in the American ghetto has the same purpose—to pacify those "who might otherwise more openly fight against the oppression and despair of their position at the bottom of the scale in a class society."[6] Or more specifically:

> The worst of it—and the reason the white power structure has allowed the heroin business to thrive in the ghetto—is that *smack* makes its slaves politically helpless. It makes isolated outlaws of those who might otherwise lead the attack against injustice in American society.[7]

In a contrasting direction, there is the position that the focus and intensity of law enforcement is often a function of the condition of the labor market. More specifically, when labor is scarce and the demand for unskilled workers is high, drug use by the lower classes is ignored. When unemployment rates are high, however, and members of minority groups are willing to work for wages lower than those of the white majority, then the minorities become targets of repression. Drug enforcement becomes the instrument of repressive policy, the drugs that minority groups use become the objects of enforcement, and minority-group members are singled out for prosecution and removal from the labor force.[8]

There is no question that the drugs used by minority groups have, at times, been singled out for suppression, but the labor market theories and their related drug-enslavement perspectives tend to be somewhat irresponsible and without the slightest historical or empirical support. It appears that those who espouse such ideas have a vision of humanity and society that fits into an attractive theory and that in time, the theorists come to believe that the vision is real.

The best-known and most persistent variety of enslavement theory is associated with the complex relationship between drug abuse and criminal behavior. Again, the theory suggests that essentially law-abiding individuals become criminals as the result of drug use. That is, the high price that the drug black market imposes forces users to commit crimes to support their habits. Thus, criminality is the result of enslavement to drugs and the drug black market.

Although the origins of the theory date back to nineteenth-century America with the early clinical writings about morphine dependence, its most complete statement appears in the writings of David W. Maurer and Victor H. Vogel. In the third edition of *Narcotics and Narcotic Addiction*, Maurer and Vogel stated:

> *First,* the potential addict begins to take very small doses of some addicting drug, let us say morphine, or heroin. He either does not realize what the drug will do to him, or he knows that others have become addicted but believes that it will never happen to him. . . .
>
> *Second,* the addict notices that the amount of the drug he has been taking does not "hold" him, and, if he is addiction-prone, he no longer experiences the intense pleasure which he felt in the very early stages of the use of the drug. If he has been "pleasure-shooting" (taking small doses at intervals of several days or several weeks) he notices that he must increase these in size to continue to get any pleasure from the drug; eventually, of course, he will also increase the frequency until he is taking a shot four to six times daily. . . .
>
> *Third,* as the habit increases in size over a period of weeks or months, the addict who must buy his drugs from bootleg sources finds that more and more of his wages go for drugs and that he has less and less for the other necessities; in fact, other things come to mean less and less to him, and he becomes heavily preoccupied with simply supporting his habit. . . .
>
> *Fourth,* it becomes obvious to him that he must have increasing amounts of money on a regular basis, and that legitimate employment is not likely to supply that kind of money. . . . *Therefore, some form of crime is the only alternative.*[9]

The theory, of course, is not without some logic. As already pointed out in Chapter 1, during the latter part of the nineteenth century and the early years of the twentieth, the use of narcotics was fairly widespread, and both morphine and heroin were readily available through legal channels. When the Harrison Act made narcotics a socially created evil, users *had* to embrace the black market to obtain their drugs. Since that time, the possession of heroin has remained a crime, and most users seem to have criminal records.

The theory also has a basis in empirical research. From the 1920s through the 1970s, the findings almost overwhelmingly indicated that narcotics use preceded criminal activity. Hence, as the enslavement theorists suggested, the inference of causality was clear—*drug use caused crime*. Perhaps it *was* so, but probably it was an outgrowth of research biased by the reliance on arrest records as indicators of criminality. For it is clear, at least within highly criminal populations, that only an insignificant proportion of the offenses committed actually result in arrest.

METHADONE, THE "BRITISH SYSTEM," AND THE MAGIC BULLET APPROACH TO HEROIN ADDICTION

An outgrowth of a spirited belief in "enslavement theory" is the call for establishing in the United States the United Kingdom's approach to the treatment of addiction. Popularly known as the "British System," it began in 1926 when a Ministry of Health committee headed by Sir Henry Rolleston recommended that narcotic addicts should receive narcotic prescriptions in the hope that they would eventually be withdrawn from their drugs.[10] For decades the system was simply a policy that permitted private physicians to prescribe maintenance doses to heroin and morphine users. Addicts were "registered" in that their names were kept in a file at the Home Office, and at any time it appeared possible to readily calculate the rate of heroin addiction by simply counting the names on file. It did seem to work. In the mid-1950s Britain had but a few hundred known addicts, and "crime in the streets" by heroin users was unheard of.[11]

Not too long after the American post-World War II heroin epidemic had begun, some argued for bringing the British system to the United States. Almost always, the frame of reference was reducing the crime problem. New York neurologist Hubert S. Howe contended before the American Association for the Advancement of Science in 1957:

> After more than 40 years of diligent enforcement, the Harrison Act has failed to accomplish its purpose. Instead, we have a black market, with its insidious train of crime.[12]

Dr. Howe went on to suggest implementation of the British approach, adding that "the only way to get rid of the black markets is to undersell them." [13]

There were others who favored what was going on in Britain, but the issue received only minimal publicity. This all changed with the publication of Edwin M. Schur's *Narcotic Addiction in Britain and America* in 1962.[14] Professor Schur presented a thorough and rational argument, contrasting the punitive laws and enforcement procedures in the United States with the solution in Great Britain that appeared to be considerably more sane, humane, and successful. As the debates over the alternative narcotics policies began to gear up, however, methadone-maintenance treatment was introduced in New York City. To many on both sides of the issue, the new approach was not altogether unlike that in England, and the debates subsided—at least for a time.

Methadone, a synthetic narcotic with all the characteristics of other opiate drugs, had traditionally been used for heroin and morphine withdrawal. By substituting methadone for the drug of addiction, followed by decreasing doses of the methadone, withdrawal was gradual, allowing physical dependence to drop an increment at a time rather than suddenly.[15] Methadone was the drug of choice because it was effective in oral doses, its action lasted up to 24 hours, and many addicts viewed it as a "medicine" rather than a drug of abuse.

The first methadone-maintenance treatment program began in the early 1960s when New York research physicians Vincent P. Dole and Marie E. Nyswander began a study of the metabolism of heroin addicts. Their plan began with the maintenance of two hard-core criminal addicts on morphine, in a manner similar to the British approach. Soon after the experiment began it was evident that the results were going to be less than impressive. Their patients were practically immobile, spending their time idly waiting for their next injection of the narcotic. Standard detoxification procedures with methadone were begun, and because the two patients had been maintained on high doses of morphine, they were given similarly high doses of methadone.[16]

Dole and Nyswander quickly noticed that under the influence of high-dose methadone, dramatic changes in their patients' behavior and appearance were occurring. One took a serious interest in painting and the other considered completing his education. The doctors also observed that when their patients were *maintained* on the high doses of methadone, the pattern of improvement continued, narcotic hunger was abated, and supplementary doses of heroin failed to produce a euphoric high. They labeled this latter phenomenon the "methadone blockade." [17]

From this rather serendipitous experience, the Dole–Nyswander theory of methadone maintenance emerged. It was conceived as a viable treatment for heroin addiction because it could free addicts from their fears of withdrawal and the pressures of drug-taking and drug-seeking activities. This would enable addict–patients to work out their problems, such as securing employment, restoring family relationships, and solving personal problems, by using psychotherapeutic help if necessary. Only after emotional and life-style stabilization had been achieved would efforts be made to reduce a patient's methadone intake.

Dole and Nyswander treated a small number of additional patients during the months that followed, and their apparent success led to a $1.4 million commitment from New York City in June 1965 for a large-scale test of their "apparent treatment breakthrough." [18] When the new experimental program was evaluated in 1968, the findings were favorable. [19] Most of the patients had remained in treatment, their employment rates had gone up, none of those still in treatment had become readdicted to heroin, and rearrest on criminal charges decreased. Although there was considerable criticism of the techniques used to evaluate the Dole–Nyswander approach, [20] methadone maintenance was deemed to be the answer to the heroin problem in the United States. Dr. Dole even became a contender for the Nobel Peace Prize in 1970.* On the basis of the New York experience, methadone treatment began to proliferate: by 1970 there were 12,000 patients in New York City alone, and within four years there were more than 75,000 patients nationally. [21]

To a great extent, the sudden political popularity of the new treatment technique was an outgrowth of the folklore spread, inadvertently or otherwise, by the methadone patriarchs. *First,* there was the "heroin blockade:"

> When properly stabilized, the patient is permanently buffered in a zone of normal function. He is protected against both abstinence and euphoria. If he takes heroin, he does not get "high," as he otherwise would. . . . [22]

> Methadone appears to be unique, among narcotic drugs available for prescription, in its capacity to maintain a steady blockade without narcotic effects. [23]

The *second* matter was the low abuse potential of methadone when the drug was administered orally:

---

* Rather than to Dole, the Nobel Peace Prize went to Dr. Norman E. Borlaug, an Iowa crop expert who had developed new strains of high-yield grains that spurred food production in Mexico, India, and Pakistan.

> . . . methadone, when diluted in fruit juice (as we dispense it), can be taken only by mouth, and in this form has a lower abuse potential than when available for injection. Addicts seeking a narcotic effect have little interest in the diluted preparation.[24]

It turned out that methadone was not the panacea that everyone hoped it would be. As early as the 1950s, Nyswander had observed that in some patients methadone was the primary drug of addiction,[25] a situation that was more fully documented a decade later.[26] Then in 1971, Carl D. Chambers of the New York State Narcotic Addiction Control Commission introduced two new terms to the methadone literature—"dirty urines" and "methadone cheaters." Based on analyses of urine samples taken from methadone-maintenance patients at the Philadelphia General Hospital, Chambers found a significant number to be using illicit drugs in conjunction with their therapeutic doses of methadone:

> The extent of drug abuse among these stabilized patients was greater than anticipated. Heroin was being abused 35.3% of the time, the other narcotics were being abused 9.5% of the time; barbiturates were being abused 11.5% of the time and amphetamines were being abused 14.4% of the time. "Clean urines," specimens in which no drug abuse was detected, occurred only 41.1% of the time. Of marked significance, urines in which *no* methadone was detected occurred 17.4% of the time.[27]

At least one clinician castigated Chambers for his use of the terms "dirty urines" and "methadone cheaters," arguing that these terms be stricken from the drug lexicon because they are negatively judgmental and of no value in the management of patients.[28] Nevertheless, the terms became a formal part of the methadone literature as other researchers began to find methadone cheating elsewhere.[29] There was also methadone supplementation, a practice involving the self-administration of additional doses of the drug beyond what was being provided in the maintenance program.[30] The *dirty urines, cheating,* and *supplementation* combined to suggest that something was amiss with the "treatment breakthrough" of methadone maintenance: that methadone did not suppress "drug hunger," not even for heroin or other narcotics; that the so-called "heroin blockade" was not a blockade at all; and that for some, methadone was becoming a drug of choice. Equally serious was the fact that, somehow, methadone was being diverted from legitimate treatment programs and making its way to the streets.

Subsequent studies demonstrated that methadone diversion was widespread, having been channeled to the street community by both patients and staff of the treatment program.[31] Moreover, in some cities methadone had become a prominent street drug that was being sold on the black market and becoming responsible for a growing number of overdose deaths.[32] In spite of these problems, methadone maintenance as a treatment technique still had a strong basis of defense: It *had* cut down on the heroin intake of tens of thousands of addicts. Since it is a long-acting drug, patients needed it only once every 24 hours, as opposed to heroin, which called for "fixing" every 4 to 6 hours. Since it is orally effective, users could avoid the rituals associated with intravenous drug use.* Furthermore, evaluation studies demonstrated that many patients were indeed leading productive lives. Given these pluses, methadone treatment continued to prosper, but since heroin addiction and crime were still in the streets, some also continued to argue in favor of the British system. They pointed out the large number of addicts for whom methadone was not working, and the even greater number who refused to seek treatment, suggesting that *heroin* maintenance was what was really needed. A recent argument on this behalf appeared in a little volume entitled *Myths That Cause Crime,* a rather curious title for a series of essays that to some extent support the persistence of myth. Criminologists Harold E. Pepinsky and Paul Jesilow argue for the legalization of heroin as a mechanism for dealing with the crime and health problems associated with narcotic addiction:

> . . . maintenance of an opiate addiction should be legalized, even if we are not ready to legalize all drugs. Addicts certified by a physician should be allowed to obtain a daily amount of narcotic sufficient to prevent the onset of withdrawal. England, for example, uses a system of clinics where certified addicts were able to purchase their daily dose. The addict can easily and safely obtain the drug at an affordable price and

---

* In this regard, there are many "needle freaks" who are often more psychologically dependent on the ritualistic aspects of "shooting-up" than they are physically dependent on heroin. As a former addict in Miami explained it:

> There was a time when I was just one of those crazy needle freaks. It was really nutty. *Copping* [buying the drug], going to the basement to shoot up, getting out the needle and cleaning it, *cooking* [dissolving the drug in a teaspoonful of water], *tying off* [applying a tourniquet to the arm just above where the drug is to be injected to build up pressure in the vein], drawing the stuff into the syringe, and sticking the needle into my arm was more exciting than the rush. One time I got high just shooting sugar and water. I heard about one real freak that can get off on peanut butter.

thus no need to turn to crime or suffer poor health to support a habit. The addict and society both benefit from such an arrangement.[33]

Going beyond the authors' apparently unshakable belief in enslavement theory, they assume that the "British system" still works. It would appear that protagonists of the system haven't checked up on it since Edwin M. Schur first publicized it more than 20 years ago.

In actuality, the British approach to narcotic addiction got into trouble quite some time ago. It had worked for a good many decades because the addiction rate in England was low, and most patients were medically addicted. Moreover, there was no street subculture of addicts. As such, the system was tailored to fit a favorable addiction situation and for that reason, and probably for that reason alone, it was successful. When the cultural and drug revolutions emerged in the United States during the 1960s, they arrived in England at the same time. New populations of drug users began to surface, and the heroin-addiction rate began to increase, as did the abuse of other drugs and the presence of a drug subculture and black market. Because of this, in 1967 the system was adjusted. No longer could addicts obtain opiate prescriptions from private physicians. A government-sponsored program took charge, putting strict controls over opiates and requiring addicts to be registered officially and treated through clinics or specially licensed physicians.[34]

As the British system moved into the 1970s, addiction continued to increase, the drug black market prospered, and the "system" began shifting its patients from heroin to methadone. Moreover, some peculiar things were happening. At the beginning of 1976, for example, 1,954 individuals were listed on the British "addict register,"[35] but of these, 926 were *new* cases and 532 were former patients who had abandoned the clinic system and reregistered again. Moreover, of the 1,954 cases, only 496 (some 25.4%) had been on the rolls at both the beginning and end of 1975. That raises the question of where the other 1,458 addicts went. Where indeed *did* they go? Actually, 69 were dead, 483 were in jail, and the balance had simply stopped seeking treatment. Thus, during 1976 there was a 50% dropout rate and a 25% penalization rate—figures that would hardly suggest that the program was overly effective. Those who had left treatment and dropped from sight were likely living within Britain's drug subcultures (although it is also probable that a number of these were successful cases no longer in need of treatment). The fact is that most heroin users were not registering because the clinic system was not providing them with the amount of heroin and other drugs they desired. By 1980, England's thriving black market in heroin, cocaine, and other illegal drugs had become a major enterprise. One needed only to walk the back streets of London's East End to draw that conclusion.

Then, in 1982, Arnold S. Trebach's monograph *The Heroin Solution* was published.[36] Trebach had undertaken a thorough examination of both the American and British drug scenes. He was aware that the treatment system in England was failing, that there was an active drug black market, that rates of addiction and drug abuse were on the rise, and that there was the growing problem of drug-related street crime. Nevertheless, and perhaps because like Napoleon and Henry Ford he too had no faith in the lessons of history, he made the startling prediction:

> . . . Nor do I see the English addiction problem coming even close to the dimensions or character of the American. In comparative ornithological terms, I still see a gentle English addiction sparrow and, across the ocean, a predatory American heroin eagle.[37]

There was more. Trebach went on to argue that the British had given up prematurely on their original system, that the prescribing of heroin and cocaine to drug users by private physicians should have been left intact, and that physicians in the United States should be given a free hand to do the same:

> . . . by extending to many doctors the power to prescribe narcotics, including heroin, for addicts, we would be taking addicts off the streets, out of police lockups, out of prisons, and placing them in doctors' offices.[38]

Although Trebach's proposal was unquestionably humanitarian, it was also, at the very best, naive. The British system was adjusted in 1967 to shift away from the private physician for some very good reasons. It had worked for the small cohort of addicts that represented England's "drug problem" for decades, but when the 1960s witnessed the spread of drug abuse on a worldwide scale, drug taking in Britain began to increase sharply with a new breed of user—one who was part of a growing drug subculture that purchased its drugs on an already developed black market.

There are also more pragmatic issues. So many cultural differences exist between England and the United States that a successful transplant is anything but assured. Moreover, the heroin-using population in the United States is a highly criminal population. In all likelihood, most American physicians would prefer that addicts remain out of their communities—not to speak of their offices. Most importantly, the success of the transplant is grounded in a belief in the enslavement theory of addiction—that the high cost of drugs leads to crime.

There is something to consider in response to Trebach's comparison of the gentle English addiction sparrow and the predatory American heroin eagle, as well as his prediction that the addiction problem in England would never reach the dimensions existing in the United States. In 1985, British government officials quietly agreed that there were some 50,000 heroin addicts in their country, representing a quadrupling since 1980.[39] Assuming that these figures are no less accurate than estimates of the U.S. addict population, the addiction rate in Great Britain went from 22.3 to 88.6 per 100,000 population, a 297% rate increase over the five-year period. In the United States, where the number of heroin addicts has remained relatively stable at 500,000, the addiction rate actually declined by 3%, from 215.3 per 100,000 population in 1980 to 209.3 five years later.*

PROSTITUTION AND ENSLAVEMENT THEORY

As early as the 1860s, the conception of the female drug user as a member of the "oldest profession" had begun to develop. Prostitution had been cited as a major cause of morphine addiction, and in later decades the etiology of drug dependence among women was repeatedly examined within the framework of prostitution.[40]

With the onset of the twentieth century, the characterization of the "woman addict as prostitute" had become well established. In 1911, for example, the Vice Commission of Chicago commented:

> It is generally recognized that immoral women and their "cadets" are addicted to the use of cocaine and morphine as well as other drugs and liquor.[41]

Similarly, as noted by Bingham Dai in his investigation of drug addiction in Chicago in the 1930s:

> That the pimp in his attempt to entice a girl to his service not seldom "dopes" her and makes her an addict so that she will have to depend on him for her drug and thereby becomes his woman is a matter of common knowledge.[42]

---

* The population figures used to compute these rates are based on the Population Reference Bureau estimates: England—56.093 million and 56.400 million; United States—232.195 million and 238.900 million.

In addition, there was the issue of "enslavement." As one commentator noted:

> Logically, criminality is bound to begin in a case of morphinism the moment the economic margin above living expenses is not sufficient to cover the purchase of the habitual amount of the drug . . . prostitution in women, stealing in one form or another among men, are the rule.[43]

More currently, an extensive body of literature offers a strong empirical basis for the notion that prostitution is a major means of economic support for narcotics-using women.[44] Enslavement theory is, however, at best an unsettled issue. Research findings have suggested a variety of conclusions on the drugs–prostitution connection. *First,* some hold that the inference of causality (prostitution causes narcotics dependence, or narcotics dependence causes prostitution) can be belabored to no avail because of the lack of conclusive evidence on either side of the issue.[45] *Second,* others suggest that once "in the life," the isolation and emotional deprivation of prostitutes drive them to employ the same chemical remedies as other alienated segments of society.[46] *Third,* still others argue in favor of enslavement theory. As Marsha Rosenbaum stated in *Women on Heroin:*

> Initial and short-range heroin use is generally not costly to women, but ultimately she must begin to support her heroin habit and generally resorts to illegal means to do so.[47]

From 1983 through 1985, the research described in Chapter 4 focused exclusively on women, and a total of 980 face-to-face interviews were conducted in New York and Miami. An analysis of a subsample of 397 women who were then using drugs and had engaged in prostitution during the six-month period before the interview can provide some insights into the enslavement theory issue of drugs, crime, and prostitution. Of these 397 drug-using prostitutes, three-fourths had histories of current or past opiate use (heroin, illegal methadone, Dilaudid, and/or other narcotics), whereas the remaining women were nonopiate users.*

Both the opiate and nonopiate users reflected early onset patterns of

---

* More specifically, the opiate users included those women who, during their last 60 days on the street, had used heroin one or more times, illegal methadone one or more times, other opiates 20 or more times, and/or had a previous history of regular heroin use. The nonopiate users were those women who, during their last 60 days on the street, had used no heroin or illegal methadone, had used other opiates for no more than 5 days, and had never used either heroin or methadone regularly.

drug use, but the two groups differed somewhat in their progression into drugs. The opiate users initiated drug use with alcohol at a median age of 13.7 years, followed almost immediately by marijuana and/or organic solvents and inhalants. Experimentation with heroin began at a median age of 17.3 years, with the drug's regular use occurring just over a year later. Involvement with tranquilizers, sedatives, narcotics other than heroin, cocaine, "speed" (amphetamines and amphetamine-like stimulants), and hallucinogens *all* generally began after the onset of heroin use. By contrast, the nonopiate users initiated their drug use slightly later, at a median age of 14.1 years, but their patterns of experimentation and regular use of a wide variety of substances were more rapid. In general, however, the opiate users reflected the greater drug involvement of the two groups.

Follow-up interviews with a number of drug-using prostitutes in Miami during 1985 suggested a possible explanation for these differences. Once heroin use begins, the user may tend to focus almost exclusively on that particular drug. After a time, however, when tolerance to heroin's euphoric effects develops, a variety of stimulants and sedatives are sought out and used in combination with heroin in pursuit of a "high." As one heroin-using prostitute stated:

> When I first started heroin that's all I wanted. It did what I wanted it to do, and that was that. . . . I didn't need nothin' else. . . . But it's been a long time since I got a *rush* from *junk*. It don't do much by itself any more. . . . Pills, coke, and speed do for me what the big H used to do.

A second factor relates to the very nature of narcotics use and the uncertainties of the heroin black market. Users physically dependent on opiate drugs are well aware of the cross-tolerance of heroin with other narcotics. This situation, combined with the fact that heroin is periodically in scarce supply on the streets, results in the use of substitutes—typically methadone, Dilaudid, or some other synthetic narcotic. As another prostitute suggested:

> When ya need to get down, ya need to get down. Don't matter what it is as long as it gets ya down. . . . In this town they're always makin' big busts. The stuff dries up and ya can't get down. So ya look around and take what ya can get. Don't matter if it's medicine or somethin' else.

In terms of current drug use, the opiate users were heavily involved with alcohol, marijuana, heroin, and cocaine. The majority of these indi-

Table 5.1 The Drugs–Crime Sequence at Selected Median Ages of 397 Drug-Using Prostitutes, New York and Miami, 1983–1985

Sequence-Related Indicator	Opiate Users ($n = 311$)	Nonopiate Users ($n = 86$)
Age at first use		
Alcohol	13.7	14.1
Other drug	14.5	14.6
Heroin	17.3	18.4
Any opiate	17.2	N/A
Prostitution	19.2	17.8
Any crime	16.1	15.9
Age at start of regular use[a]		
Alcohol	16.7	16.0
Other drug	15.8	15.2
Heroin	18.6	N/A
Any opiate	18.6	N/A
Prostitution	19.5	17.8
Any crime	18.0	16.5
Sequence: prostitution and use of drugs other than alcohol		
Prostitution first	3.5%	7.0%
Same age	3.5%	10.5%
Drugs first	91.6%	82.6%
Missing data	1.3%	0.0%
Sequence: prostitution and opiate use		
Prostitution first	17.4%	N/A
Same age	15.1%	N/A
Opiates first	65.6%	N/A
Missing data	1.9%	N/A

[a]"Regular" means three or more times a week except for robbery, which is considered "regular" at the occurrence of the tenth offense.

viduals used all these substances and did so on a daily or almost-daily basis. Among the nonopiate users, by contrast, the heaviest involvement occurred with respect to marijuana, followed by alcohol and cocaine.

The sequential patterns of initiation into drugs and crime within this sample of prostitutes suggest some interesting implications for enslavement theory. Initially, the data in Table 5.1 tend to support the myth. For example, the opiate-using group began heroin use at a median age of 17.3

years, regular heroin use at 18.6 years, prostitution at 19.2 years, and prostitution on a regular basis at 19.5 years. Also, more specifically, the data indicate that of these 311 prostitutes, only 17.4% were involved in prostitution prior to heroin use. Moreover, only 3.5% had engaged in prostitution prior to the onset of their drug-using careers. As such, the data indeed suggest that drug use, and heroin use in particular, may indeed have something to do with pursuing prostitution as a means of supporting a narcotics habit.

Among the nonopiate users, both experimental and regular drug use *also* came before prostitution. Within this group, as Table 5.1 indicates, first drug use (other than alcohol) came at a median age of 14.6 years, followed by regular drug use (15.2 years), and prostitution (17.8 years). *Again,* drug use preceded prostitution for the vast majority of the subsample.

How, then, can one still argue that drug use, and particularly narcotics use, has little, if anything, to do with initiating a career in prostitution? After all, the sequential patterns seem to be quite clear. The answer can be found in several ways. *First,* the opiate users had initiated their criminal careers a full year prior to any experimentation with narcotics. Moreover, they were committing crime on a regular basis prior to their regular use of heroin. As such, the opiate-using prostitutes were meshed within their criminal careers well before the beginning of heavy narcotics use. This would suggest that rather than a simple cause-and-effect connection between narcotics and prostitution, individuals prone to heavy drug use on a regular basis are also prone to criminal activity on a regular basis. *Second,* and as shown later in this chapter, the *dynamics* of the heroin marketplace may have had more to do with a career in prostitution than the fact of drug taking. *Third,* the criminality of many drug users may be more related to their general social circumstances than to their narcotics use.

PROSTITUTION, ENSLAVEMENT THEORY, AND SOCIAL MARGINALITY

Within the ecological perspective of the Chicago School of Sociology in the 1920s, early studies of the prevalence of narcotic addiction in urban areas found the phenomenon to be concentrated in certain sections of the city.[48] Theory contemporary to that time conceived of the city as a series of concentric circles and zones, each containing divergent types of areas differentiated with respect to processes of urban expansion. Within the central portion of the city, high rates of abnormalities in the social metabolism were observed to exist:

> . . . within the central business district or on an adjoining street is the "main stem" or "hobohemia," the teeming Rialto of the homeless migratory man of the Middle West. In the zone of deterioration encircling the central business section are always to be found the so-called "slums" and "badlands," with their submerged regions of poverty, degradation, and disease, and their underworlds of crime and vice.[49]

A high incidence of drug addiction was readily observed to be in these centrally located, deteriorated sections, even in the pioneer studies of Chicago. Nels Anderson noted that many addicts were concentrated in the areas of the hobo, tramp, and bum.[50] Harvey Zorbaugh described the role played by drug addiction in the slum.[51] Decades later rates of addiction were still found to be highest in Chicago in those disadvantaged areas where the heaviest concentration of other types of social problems endured.[52] Similarly, in an empirical study of the distribution of crime in Seattle in the 1950s, most narcotics law violators were found to reside in the city's central and most heavily deteriorated portions.[53] Although recent research has set aside the concentric circle theory of urban structure, there is little argument that the highest concentrations of narcotic addiction and other social problems are to be found in the deteriorated "inner cities."

More than a decade ago, in what is now a relatively unknown and defunct drug journal, the relation between narcotics use and the presence of other social problems in inner cities was presented with some rather dramatic statistics.[54] In 1969, researchers at the New York State Narcotic Addiction Control Commission compiled comprehensive statistical data on opiate-use rates for New York City's 30 health center districts (aggregations of geographically and demographically contiguous census tracts). Each district was ranked in terms of its rate of opiate use, as well as its rates of other social problems such as poverty, financial assistance, unemployment, illegitimacy, and juvenile delinquency. The rates of opiate use for the 30 given areas were then correlated with the rankings of the statuses of other social problems. The results were some of the highest correlation coefficients ever encountered in social science research. For example:

opiate use/poverty	$r = 0.92$*
opiate use/unemployment	$r = 0.88$
opiate use/illegitimacy	$r = 0.81$
opiate use/financial assistance	$r = 0.78$
opiate use/delinquency	$r = 0.75$

It was clear from the data that *opiate use* was not causing poverty, unemployment, illegitimacy, financial assistance, and juvenile delinquency. Rather, the implication was that in those areas where opiate-use rates were high, high rates of other social problems tended to exist side by side.

The argument being offered here is that narcotics use and crime tend to evolve contemporaneously among certain individuals residing in areas where rates of opiate use and criminal behavior are high; this was articulated most decisively by a 22-year-old heroin-using prostitute interviewed in 1983:

> I've often thought that if I'd never started with the drugs I'd never had ended up turning tricks every day. But the more you make me think about it, the more I think that one had nothing to do with the other. You grow up in a place where everything is a real mess. Your father's a thief, your mother's a whore, your kid sister gets herself some new clothes by fucking the landlord's son, your brother's in the joint, your boyfriend gets shot tryin' to pull down a store, and everybody else around you is either smokin' dope, shooting stuff, taking pills, stealing with both hands, or workin' on their backs, or all of the above. All of a sudden you find that you're sweet sixteen and you're doin' the same things.
>
> I can't really say why I started stealing, using *shit*, and walking the streets. It all seemed to happen at once. It was all around me and it was an easy way out. It all came on kind of naturally.

---

* For those unfamiliar with statistics of this type, the highest possible r value is 1.00, meaning a perfect correlation.

PROSTITUTION, CRIME, AND
THE DRUG BLACK MARKET

There are additional points that the data suggested and subsequent interviews tended to support. In contrast to the contention of enslavement theory—that the onset of prostitution is a function of the high cost of heroin on the drug black market—it would appear, at least within the population being considered here, that *the regular use of heroin may have actually delayed the introduction to prostitution careers*. Referring back to Table 5.1, the nonopiate users began prostitution earlier than the opiate users. For example, once again using median ages of onset:

	Opiate Users	Nonopiate Users
First prostitution	19.2	17.8
First "regular" prostitution	19.5	17.8

Extensive questioning in 1983 combined with follow-up interviews conducted in 1985 suggested some curious and interesting implications. Perhaps the key variable to understanding the connection between drugs, heroin, crime, and prostitution is drug selling. Among the opiate users, 71.7% had been involved in drug dealing at one time or another. Yet more importantly, 69.1% had sold drugs on a regular basis, with the onset of this activity at a median age of 18.3 years—before the onset of regular heroin use. The majority of those questioned about their involvement in drug sales stated that the decision to pursue *dealing* over prostitution was a fully conscious one—a decision made on purely economic grounds. Experimentation with heroin and association with the heroin subculture brought them into contact with the narcotics-distribution network. Although street-level selling is not a particularly profitable endeavor for the user–dealer, most involved parties recognize it to be among the least visible and troublesome mechanisms for obtaining drugs. Moreover, it is a business that is easy to set up yet relatively risk-free. On this latter point, in an earlier study of 149 women heroin users in Miami, for example, it was found that some three-fourths of the group had been involved in almost 16,000 drug sales during a one-year period, and that less than 1% of these transactions ($n = 26$) had resulted in arrest.[55] Comments by a number of the informants supported this perspective. A 27-year-old prostitute from Miami's Liberty City section who had been using heroin since age 18 revealed:

> I did a lot of sleeping around, sometimes even for money, but I never considered myself a hooker, and turning tricks was just not for me. To bring in money or pass the time it is just too much time, work, dirt, and hassle. . . . Stealing is easy, but it too has its risks. Dealing drugs or copping for someone else was always the best way to do things. . . . For every $200 worth of *garbage* [heroin] I'd sell I'd end up with 10 *nickel bags* [$50 worth of heroin] and some small change for myself.

Similarly, a 21-year-old heroin-using prostitute from New York commented:

> If I had it to do all over again and was smart I'd stick with selling drugs instead of my ass. It's easier and cleaner. . . .

Although most of the prostitutes contacted viewed drug selling as the economic path of least resistance, most of them eventually shifted to prostitution as their main source of earnings. The reasons were numerous. Some lost their source of supply when their "connection" was arrested, moved to another part of the city, or was killed by another dealer or user. Others were caught skimming, were beaten severely for their indiscretion, and were refused any further involvement in the drug trade. A few were stuck with "bad" drugs or were suspected to be police informants, and thus lost their clientele. The major reason, however, was associated with the transitory nature of the heroin market. It is not uncommon, as noted earlier, for heroin supplies to "dry up" for short periods of time because of either increased police activity or general interruptions in drug-supply networks. The consequences were many. One prostitute reflected:

> All of a sudden there's nothin' out there on the streets—nothin' to sell or buy either. How can you make a living on the street dealin' if there's nothin' anywhere to deal?

To cope with the situation, another explained:

> If you can't deal drugs, you deal with the situation. There was no heroin out there but ya heard tell that there was lots of Dilaudid comin' in off of a lot of trucks from New York. . . . So ya go for Dilaudid, because it's what ya want—maybe even better. But it costs money and the connection is tight. Nobody

wants t' let ya sell—only buy. So ya do what ya have t' do. Instead of fuckin' for fun ya start fuckin' for money. . . .

Of the 27 opiate-using prostitutes with whom these contingencies were discussed, 23 had shifted from drug selling to prostitution as a primary source of income at a time when heroin supplies were low. It appears, then, that the onset of careers in prostitution were most directly linked to the dynamics of the heroin marketplace. As heroin supplies disappeared, selling became impossible. Substitute narcotics were available but expensive. Moreover, unconnected with the usual narcotics-distribution networks, availability of the substitutes for street sales was limited to a few entrepreneurs. As a result, many of the opiate-using women found themselves shifting to prostitution and various forms of theft to secure the economic base necessary for their overall support.

Invariably, however, most of the opiate users who were interviewed continued in prostitution even after the heroin shortages disappeared. The reason? As one long-term heroin user/prostitute put it:

> In the long and the short there's much more money. You don't really like it, but it gets you what you want. Dealing on the street brought me, oh, let's say, maybe enough drugs to keep me going plus another 20–30 dollars a day—on a good day. . . . Now sometimes I can make 50 to 75 dollars in an hour's time. Sometimes there are tips, too. . . . Sometimes if the john isn't careful I can slip a few extra bucks from his wallet. While he's busy pokin' you with his prong you're reachin' for his pants to bag his money.

Another explained:

> There's no way I can ever be a high-price girl, not with the way I been usin' lately. But I can take off a dozen blow jobs in a couple hours' time at $10 a head and you can always threaten to bite the rube's cock off if he don't come across with an extra big bill.

The greater financial rewards of prostitution over other forms of criminality are readily attested to in the structured interview data. As illustrated in Table 5.2, the 311 opiate-using prostitutes had engaged in a total of 186,857 criminal offenses during the six-month period before the interview. Although all of them had engaged in prostitution, significant

Table 5.2   Criminal Activity During the Past Six Months of 311 Opiate-Using Prostitutes, New York and Miami, 1983–1985

Crime Type	Total Crimes Committed	Type as % of Total	% of Sample Involved	% of Crimes Resulting in Arrest
Drug trafficking	951	0.5	6.4	0.2 ($n = 2$)
Drug street sales	41,987	22.5	32.8	0.1 ($n = 6$)
Prostitution	113,238	60.6	100.0	0.1 ($n = 105$)
Procuring	1,449	0.8	14.1	0.1 ($n = 1$)
Prostitute's theft	7,109	3.8	46.9	0.0 ($n = 0$)
Pickpocketing	1,324	0.7	9.3	0.3 ($n = 4$)
Confidence games	3,189	1.7	15.8	0.0 ($n = 0$)
Shoplifting	8,760	4.7	51.8	0.3 ($n = 27$)
Checks/credit cards	1,212	0.6	19.3	0.3 ($n = 4$)
Forged prescriptions	637	0.3	10.9	0.0 ($n = 0$)
Burglary	680	0.4	15.1	1.0 ($n = 7$)
Motor vehicle theft	125	0.1	7.1	1.6 ($n = 2$)
Theft from vehicle	181	0.1	7.7	0.0 ($n = 0$)
Sneak theft	280	0.1	5.1	0.0 ($n = 0$)
Other theft	10	<0.1	1.6	0.0 ($n = 0$)
Stolen-goods offenses	5,072	2.7	27.3	0.3 ($n = 16$)
Loan-sharking	38	<0.1	1.0	0.0 ($n = 0$)
Extortion	34	<0.1	1.3	0.0 ($n = 0$)
Arson–vandalism	0	0.0	0.0	N/A ($n = 0$)
Robbery	87	<0.1	11.6	9.2 ($n = 8$)
Assault w/other crime	330	0.2	13.2	0.3 ($n = 1$)
Other assault	164	0.1	7.1	1.8 ($n = 3$)
Totals	186,857	100.0	—	0.1 ($n = 186$)

proportions had also been involved in drug dealing, confidence games, robbery, and various forms of theft. When questioned about the top money-making offense, prostitution was indicated by 72.3%. For example:

drug sales and trafficking	13.5%
prostitution	72.3%
procuring	0.3%
prostitute theft from johns	2.3%
shoplifting	3.5%

burglary	1.3%
other property crimes	4.8%
robbery	1.6%
no data	0.3%

Some final points remain, and those involve the differences in drug use and criminal behavior between the opiate-using and nonopiate-using prostitutes. It would be rather tenuous to suggest that the nonopiate users were driven into prostitution through enslavement to drugs. Their major drugs of abuse were marijuana and cocaine; 62.8% were daily users of marijuana, and 43.0% were daily users of cocaine. Although cocaine is considered to be an "expensive" drug having the potential for causing someone to resort to crime to afford its regular use, this is less the case in New York and Miami because of the pivotal positions of those cities in the cocaine-trafficking and refining networks. The street price of cocaine reportedly ranged from $50 to $120 a gram in early 1985, depending on purity and potency.[56] In Miami during March of 1985, however, cocaine could be had for as little as $25 per gram. But more importantly, it must be remembered that prostitution on a regular basis for this group came *before* the regular use of cocaine. That is, for the nonopiate users, regular prostitution came at a median age of 17.8 years, whereas the regular use of cocaine began at a median age of 18.3 years. The only drugs of any significance that were regularly used prior to prostitution were marijuana and alcohol, and neither of these is particularly costly. More than likely, the reasons for the women's entry into careers in prostitution were as varied as the personalities and goals of the women involved—including the numerous ecological, psychological, sociological, and utilitarian explanations that have been offered in the prostitution literature.[57]

A second point differentiating the opiate users from the nonopiate users is their relative levels of criminality. As is already apparent from Table 5.2, the opiate-using prostitutes were heavily involved in crime. During the six-month period prior to interview, these 311 women had reportedly engaged in 186,857 criminal offenses—a mean of 601 per respondent. Although 84.4% of these events were the "victimless crimes" of prostitution, procuring, and drug law violations, the opiate users had also participated in 22,870 property crimes (prostitute theft, pickpocketing, confidence games, shoplifting, the use of stolen checks/credit cards, burglary, vehicle theft, theft from vehicle, sneak theft, and other theft), 5,072 stolen-goods offenses, and 581 robberies and assaults—a mean of 92 per subject.

Table 5.3   Criminal Activity During the Past Six Months of 86 Nonopiate-Using Prostitutes, New York and Miami, 1983–1985

Crime Type	Total Crimes Committed	Type as % of Total	% of Sample Involved	% of Crimes Resulting in Arrest
Drug trafficking	142	0.5	3.5	0.7 ($n = 1$)
Drug street sales	2,094	7.2	18.6	0.1 ($n = 2$)
Prostitution	22,260	77.1	100.0	0.3 ($n = 69$)
Procuring	578	2.0	15.1	0.2 ($n = 1$)
Prostitute's theft	1,527	5.3	36.0	0.1 ($n = 2$)
Pickpocketing	0	0.0	0.0	N/A ($n = 0$)
Confidence games	398	1.4	12.8	0.0 ($n = 0$)
Shoplifting	912	3.2	29.1	0.3 ($n = 3$)
Checks/credit cards	186	0.6	3.5	0.5 ($n = 1$)
Forged prescriptions	71	0.2	2.3	0.0 ($n = 0$)
Burglary	186	0.6	4.7	1.1 ($n = 2$)
Motor vehicle theft	8	<0.1	8.1	25.0 ($n = 2$)
Theft from vehicle	4	<0.1	3.5	0.0 ($n = 0$)
Sneak theft	1	<0.1	1.2	0.0 ($n = 0$)
Other theft	2	<0.1	2.3	0.0 ($n = 0$)
Stolen-goods offenses	469	1.6	10.5	0.0 ($n = 0$)
Loan-sharking	0	0.0	0.0	N/A ($n = 0$)
Extortion	4	<0.1	2.3	0.0 ($n = 0$)
Arson–vandalism	11	<0.1	4.7	0.0 ($n = 0$)
Robbery	17	0.1	7.0	17.6 ($n = 3$)
Assault w/other crime	8	<0.1	5.8	25.0 ($n = 2$)
Other assault	8	<0.1	5.8	37.5 ($n = 3$)
Totals	28,886	100.0	—	0.3 ($n = 91$)

By contrast, and as illustrated in Table 5.3, the nonopiate users were involved in a mean of 336 offenses during the same period of time. Some 86.8% of this group were related to prostitution and drug sales, and the mean number of property crimes, stolen-goods offenses, robberies, and assaults came to 43 per subject. As such, the opiate users were not only more criminally involved, but they were considerably more violent as well.

Moreover, not only did the opiate users tend to be the more violent of the two groups (respective means of 1.9 versus 0.4 robberies and assaults per subject), but also their potential for violence was significantly greater. For example, 62.1% of the opiate users carried weapons on at least one offense occasion, and 51.4% possessed a weapon of some kind on 150 or more offense occasions. In addition, some 21.5% used a weapon at least once. By contrast, 59.3% of the nonopiate users *never* carried a weapon of any type, and more than 90% never used a weapon during the commission of an offense.

POSTSCRIPT

Over the decades, the "enslavement theory of addiction" has suggested that once addicted to narcotics, otherwise law-abiding citizens are forced into lives of crime to support their habits. With regard to women, this view holds that the economics of heroin addiction precipitate careers in prostitution. Although recent research has suggested that the drugs—crime connection is a complex one and that drug use and crime probably emerge side by side within certain deviant populations, the enslavement perspective tends to persist.

By contrast, this discussion suggests that at least within this population of opiate- and nonopiate-using prostitutes immersed in the street worlds of drug use and crime, enslavement theory does not seem to apply. The opiate users had established patterns of criminality before their involvement with heroin, and the nonopiate users had moved into careers in prostitution before the onset of any "expensive" drug use.

Beyond this, the data suggest some additional perspectives on the relationship between heroin use and street crime among women. Rather than initiating careers in prostitution, heroin use may actually serve to delay the onset of this criminal life-style. The tendency of many female opiate users was to become enmeshed within the subculture of drug selling before their initial heroin use. Once they became involved with heroin and other narcotics on a regular basis, they remained primarily drug sellers because selling was a relatively easy and safe economic pursuit. Prostitution began only after some disruption in the women's drug-dealing activities, typically the unavailability of heroin. Yet after careers in prostitution had become firmly established, the opiate users tended to remain in them because of the greater economic rewards that prostitution offered.

The female opiate-using prostitutes also tended to be more criminally involved and more violent and potentially violent than their nonopiate counterparts. It has already been demonstrated in Chapter 4 that narcotics use tends to intensify criminal behavior. All this would suggest that although the use of heroin and other narcotics may not initiate criminal careers, it tends to intensify and perpetuate them. In this sense, *narcotics use freezes its users into patterns of criminality that are more acute, dynamic, violent, unremitting, and enduring than those of other drug-using offenders.*

Notes

1. See, for example, Patricia Jones-Witters and Weldon Witters, *Drugs & Society: A Biological Perspective* (Monterey, Calif.: Wadsworth Health Sciences, 1983), p. 242.
2. Charles C. Scott and K. K. Chen, "The Action of 1,1-diphenyl-1-(dimethyl-aminoisopropyl),butanone-2, a Potent Analgesic Agent," *Journal of Pharmacology and Experimental Therapeutics,* 87 (1946), 63–71; Nathan B. Eddy, "A New Morphine-Like Analgesic," *Journal of the American Pharmaceutical Association,* Nov. 1947, pp. 536–540; H. B. Haag, J. K. Finnegan, and P. S. Larson, "Pharmacologic Observations on 1,1-diphenyl-1-(dimethylaminoiso-propyl),butanone-2," *Federation Proceedings,* 6(1947), 334.
3. Personal communication with Dr. Ivan Bennett of Eli Lilly and Co., 14 Jan. 1976.
4. Alexander King, *Mine Enemy Grows Older* (New York: Simon & Schuster, 1958), p. 39.
5. William J. Chambliss, "Markets, Profits, Labor and Smack," *Contemporary Crises,* 1 (1977), 63–64.
6. Chambliss.
7. *The Opium Trail: Heroin and Imperialism* (Somerville, Mass.: New England Free Press, 1972), pp. 14–19.
8. See J. Helmer, *Drugs and Minority Oppression* (New York: Seabury Press, 1974); J. Helmer and T. Vietorisz, *Drug Use, the Labor Market and Class Conflict* (Washington, D.C.: Drug Abuse Council, 1974).
9. David W. Maurer and Victor H. Vogel, *Narcotics and Narcotic Addiction,* 3rd ed. (Springfield, Ill.: Chas. C. Thomas, 1978), pp. 286–287 (italics added).
10. See D. J. West, ed., *Problems of Drug Abuse in Britain* (Cambridge: Institute of Criminology, 1978); Horace Freeland Judson, *Heroin Addiction in Britain* (New York: Harcourt Brace Jovanovich, 1974).
11. Alfred R. Lindesmith, *The Addict and the Law* (New York: Vintage, 1965), p. 166.
12. *Newsweek,* 7 Jan. 1957, p. 66.
13. *Newsweek,* p. 66.
14. Edwin M. Schur, *Narcotic Addiction in Britain and America* (Bloomington: Indiana University Press, 1962).
15. Harris Isbell, "Medical Aspects of Opiate Addiction," *Bulletin of the New York Academy of Medicine,* Dec. 1955, pp. 806–901.
16. Ron Miller, "Towards a Sociology of Methadone Maintenance," in *Sociological Aspects of Drug Dependence,* ed. Charles Winick (Cleveland: CRC Press, 1974), pp. 169–198.

17. Vincent P. Dole, Marie E. Nyswander, and Mary Jeanne Kreek, "Narcotic Blockade," *Archives of Internal Medicine,* Oct. 1966, pp. 304–309.

18. R. E. Trussel and H. Gollance, "Methadone Maintenance Treatment Is Successful for Heroin Addicts," *Hospital Management,* Oct. 1970, p. 110.

19. Methadone Maintenance Evaluation Committee, "Progress Report of Evaluation of Methadone Maintenance Treatment Program as of March 31, 1968," *Journal of the American Medical Association,* 206 (1968), 2712.

20. Carl D. Chambers and Henry Brill, eds., *Methadone: Experiences and Issues* (New York: Behavioral Publications, 1973), pp. 175–177; Peter G. Bourne, *Methadone: Benefits and Shortcomings* (Washington, D.C.: Drug Abuse Council, 1975), pp. 4–12; E. J. Epstein, "Methadone, the Forlorn Hope," *The Public Interest,* 36 (1974), 3–24.

21. Miller, pp. 175–177.

22. Dole, Nyswander, and Kreek.

23. Vincent P. Dole and Marie E. Nyswander, "The Use of Methadone for Narcotic Blockade," *British Journal of the Addictions,* 63 (1968), 55–57.

24. Dole and Nyswander, pp. 55–57.

25. Marie Nyswander, *The Drug Addict as a Patient* (New York: Grune & Stratton, 1956), p. 22.

26. Joseph D. Sapira, John C. Ball, and Emily S. Cottrell, "Addiction to Methadone Among Patients at Lexington and Fort Worth," *Public Health Reports,* 83 (1968), 691–694.

27. Carl D. Chambers and W. J. Russell Taylor, "The Incidence and Patterns of Drug Abuse Among Long-Term Methadone Maintenance Patients" (Paper presented at the Thirty-third Annual Meeting of the Committee on Problems of Drug Dependence, National Academy of Sciences, Toronto, Canada, 16–17 Feb. 1971). See also Carl D. Chambers, W. J. Russell Taylor, and Arthur D. Moffett, "The Incidence of Cocaine Abuse Among Methadone Maintenance Patients," *International Journal of the Addictions,* 7 (1972), 427–441.

28. Frances R. Gearing, "People Versus Urines" (Paper presented at the Fourth National Conference on Methadone Treatment, San Francisco, 8–10 Jan. 1972).

29. Richard C. Stephens and Robert S. Weppner, "Patterns of 'Cheating' Among Methadone Maintenance Patients," *Drug Forum,* Summer 1973, pp. 357–366; Richard C. Stephens and Robert S. Weppner, "Legal and Illegal Use of Methadone: One Year Later," *American Journal of Psychiatry,* Dec. 1973, pp. 1391–1394.

30. Carl D. Chambers and Janet J. Bergen, "Self-Administered Methadone Supplementation," in Chambers and Brill, eds., pp. 131–142; Barry S. Brown, Robert L. DuPont, and Ronald J. Nolfi, "Reexamination of the Use of Illicit Drugs by Methadone Maintenance Patients" (Paper presented at the Fourth National Conference on Methadone Treatment, San Francisco, 8–10 Jan. 1972).

31. See James A. Inciardi, *Methadone Diversion: Experiences and Issues* (Rockville, Md.: National Institute on Drug Abuse, 1977).

32. Mark H. Greene, Barry S. Brown, and Robert L. DuPont, "Controlling the

Abuse of Illicit Methadone in Washington, D.C.," *Archives of General Psychiatry,* Feb. 1975, pp. 221–226.

33. Harold E. Pepinsky and Paul Jesilow, *Myths That Cause Crime* (Cabin John, Md.: Seven Locks Press, 1984), p. 108.

34. See Griffith Edwards and Carol Busch, *Drug Problems in Britain: A Review of Ten Years* (London: Academic Press, 1981).

35. C. E. Mauge and D. K. Dragan, "Heroin Maintenance: The Second Time Around," *Drug Abuse and Alcoholism Review,* 3 (1978).

36. Arnold S. Trebach, *The Heroin Solution* (New Haven, Conn.: Yale University Press, 1982).

37. Trebach, p. 173.

38. Trebach, p. 269.

39. *New York Times,* 11 Apr. 1985, p. A15.

40. F. E. Oliver, "The Use and Abuse of Opium," *Third Annual Report of the State Board of Health of Massachusetts,* Jan. 1871; L. L. Stanley, "Morphanism," *Journal of the American Institute of Criminal Law and Criminology,* 6 (1915–1916), 586. See also H. Wayne Morgan, ed., *Yesterday's Addicts: American Society and Drug Abuse, 1865–1920* (Norman: University of Oklahoma Press, 1974).

41. The Vice Commission of Chicago, *The Social Evil in Chicago* (Chicago: Gunthrop-Warren, 1911), p. 84.

42. Bingham Dai, *Opium Addiction in Chicago* (Shanghai:Commercial Press, 1937), p. 136.

43. E. W. Adams, *Drug Addiction* (London: Oxford University Press, 1937), p. 37.

44. Everett H. Ellinwood, W. G. Smith, and George E. Valliant, "Narcotic Addiction in Males and Females: A Comparison," *International Journal of the Addictions,* 1 (1966), 33–45; Carl D. Chambers, R. Kent Hinesley, and Mary Moldestad, "The Female Opiate Addict," in *The Epidemiology of Opiate Addiction in the United States,* ed. John C. Ball and Carl D. Chambers (Springfield, Ill.: Chas. C. Thomas, 1970), pp. 222–239; Karen N. File, Thomas W. McCahill, and Leonard D. Savitz, "Narcotics Involvement and Female Criminality," *Addictive Diseases: An International Journal,* 1 (1974), 177–188; Paul Cushman, "Methadone Maintenance in Hard-Core Criminal Addicts," *New York State Journal of Medicine,* 72 (1972), 1752–1769.

45. Jennifer James, "Prostitution and Addiction," *Addictive Diseases: An International Journal,* 2 (1976), 601–618.

46. Freda Adler, *Sisters in Crime: The Rise of the New Female Criminal* (New York: McGraw-Hill, 1975), p. 77.

47. Marsha Rosenbaum, *Women on Heroin* (New Brunswick, N.J.: Rutgers University Press, 1981), p. 5.

48. Robert E. L. Faris and H. Warren Dunham, *Mental Disorders in Urban Areas* (Chicago: University of Chicago Press, 1939).

49. Robert E. Park, Ernest W. Burgess, and Roderick D. McKenzie, *The City* (Chicago: University of Chicago Press, 1925).

50. Nels Anderson, *The Hobo: The Sociology of the Homeless Man* (Chicago: University of Chicago Press, 1923).
51. Harvey Zorbaugh, *The Gold Coast and the Slum* (Chicago: University of Chicago Press, 1923).
52. Illinois Institute for Juvenile Research and the Chicago Area Project, *Report of the Chicago Narcotics Survey.* Unpublished manuscript, Chicago, 1953.
53. Calvin F. Schmid, "Urban Crime Areas: Part II," *American Sociological Review,* Oct. 1960, pp. 655–678.
54. James A. Inciardi, "The Villification of Euphoria: Some Perspectives on an Elusive Issue," *Addictive Diseases: An International Journal,* 1 (1974), 241–267.
55. James A. Inciardi, "Women, Heroin, and Property Crime," in *Women, Crime, and Justice,* ed. Susan K. Datesman and Frank R. Scarpitti (New York: Oxford University Press, 1980), pp. 214–222.
56. *U.S. News & World Report,* 25 Feb. 1985, p. 17.
57. For an extensive bibliography on prostitution, see Paul J. Goldstein, *Prostitution and Drugs* (Lexington, Mass.: Lexington Books, 1979), pp. 155–169.

商標　　　　　帆船

FROM TINGO MARIA TO TEHERAN
The Domestic and International Implications of Drug Trafficking

Narcotic addiction and drug abuse are generally understood in terms of a limited number of issues. *First,* there are public health considerations. Illicit drugs, whether they be narcotics, stimulants, depressants, or hallucinogens, have been found to cause a range of physical and/or psychosocial complications. As such, the abuse of drugs can place the productivity and well-being of a potentially large segment of the population at risk. The *second* issue is the connection between substance abuse and crime, a link that has become better understood in recent years. The drug-taking and drug-seeking activities of heroin and other types of users has indeed affected rates of burglaries, larcenies, robberies, and other crimes. Too, the drug-trafficking and drug-distribution marketplace has increased the profits and power of organized criminal syndicates. Furthermore, violent death has come to be associated with the competition that exists at all levels of drug-selling and drug-distribution networks.

To foreign observers, particularly those in South America, where U.S. antidrug efforts have been politically visible in recent years, these public health and criminal issues facing U.S. citizens seem to represent the overwhelming public conception of the international drug scene. Moreover, since the flow of North American "narcodollars" into these countries has seemingly bettered the economic lot of many local farmers and peasants, there has been considerable opposition to most U.S.-backed drug-control initiatives. For example, as one Bolivian media representative put it in 1982:

> . . . drug abuse is a North American problem, a U.S. vice that Bolivia has no responsibility for. Therefore, Bolivia has no responsibility for drug control. There is no drug problem here.

175

It is in the United States. Why, then, does your DEA come down here? *

Similarly, a military police official in Lima, Peru commented:

The North American appetite for cocaine has done more to feed the children of Simón Bolívar and the descendants of the Inca empire than most government programs. Why not just let it be?

And an editorial in a Colombian newspaper asked the question:

Why is the Drug Enforcement Administration aiming its guns outside the United States, after production? Why not go inside the United States, after consumption? [1]

Finally, numerous local politicians, media representatives, educators, and concerned citizens in many cities in the coca-growing nations of South America have expressed the sentiment that the United States should solve its drug problem *within its borders*. Why, they ask, should they and their governments cooperate with control efforts that will only hurt their interests? These same questions have been asked in other parts of the world when U.S. proposals to limit the cultivation of the opium poppy have been advanced over the years.

The reasons for the United States supported drug-control efforts in Latin America and Asia are no doubt numerous: in behalf of the stateside public health and crime problems; in the interests of good foreign policy and effective international relations; in response to the long-range needs of many developing nations; and for the sake of various other political and economic considerations. More specifically:

1. Attempts have been made to reduce both the demand and the supply of illegal drugs in the United States. The effectiveness of these demand- and supply-reduction strategies has only been minimal. The logical alternative is to combine these initiatives with an assault on drug production at its source.

2. Many have held that when drug production and trafficking become pervasive problems in nations with weak governments and faltering

---

* Note here that all undocumented quotations and observations were drawn from the author's field research in Colombia, Bolivia, Ecuador, and Peru during 1982.

economic systems, both politics and economics become further de-stabilized. Those who support this position maintain that these conditions can lead to the emergence of dictatorships, aggressive and/or communistic governments, and even war. In a hemisphere where communism—the antithesis of democratic political dogma—has already gained a foothold, there is no question that the United States would support initiatives that might undermine such policies and influence.

3. As developing countries, many nations of the Third World receive aid from the United States in the interests of stimulating agricultural and industrial growth and upgrading standards of living. Drug production and trafficking can have counterproductive effects on any potential for growth.

There are probably other political, economic, and even humanitarian reasons as well. Yet, whatever the reasons, the intention here is neither to decipher nor defend U.S. international drug-control policies, nor to preach to foreign nations regarding any benefits of a broad-based support of American interests. Perhaps that is best left to the politicians, diplomats, and specialists in foreign affairs who have a better understanding of such matters. Rather, the idea is to identify and examine the implications of drug trafficking at both broad and discreet levels and to illustrate how these can have an impact on the economic, social, political and other sectors of life in both drug-producing and "corridor" nations and communities.* The primary focus here is on South America, the continent from which virtually all the cocaine consumed in the United States originates. However, the various implications for other sectors of the world are also referenced.

BACK TO AMAZONIA AND THE ANDES

Historically, the chewing of coca leaves has been a dominant cultural pattern among the Indian peasant laborers of the Andes Mountains of South

---

* *Corridor,* as it refers to foreign nations, is a U.S. State Department term. It relates to those countries in which the cultivation of the raw materials for illicit drugs plays only a limited role in the trafficking complex. Rather, the major effort is directed at the conveyance of raw materials from one producer to another, or the transportation of the intermediate or final product to some port of embarcation.

America. The mild stimulation engendered by the low cocaine-content leaves enables workers to endure the burdens of their 12- to 14-hour days at hard labor in the mines and in the fields.[2] Both Bolivian and Peruvian law permits controlled licit production of coca for domestic consumption—about 12,000 kilograms in Bolivia and 14,000 kilograms in Peru (which also includes production for international pharmaceutical use). As such, a substantial part of the Andean economy has always depended on the cultivation, transport, and sale of coca leaves. The growers of illegal coca are the thousands of farm families who have shifted away from the cultivation and harvest of more traditional crops. One can readily understand the reasons for such a transition, given the realities of the economic, political, and geographical conditions that dominate South American life.

Bolivia

Straddling the Andes, Bolivia is a land of gaunt mountains, cold desolate plains, and semitropical lowlands. Its 424,162 square miles occupy an area about the size of Texas and California combined. It is a big country, but with a population of only 6 million. About 15% are of European heritage; the balance are Aymara Indians or *mestizos* (mixed Indian and European ancestry). Most live on the bleak, treeless, windswept Altiplano, a lofty plateau more than 13,000 feet above sea level. Despite the fact that the Altiplano is a harsh, strange land, it is also the most livable part of the country.

Rising from the floor of a shallow canyon in the middle of the Altiplano is the city of La Paz, Bolivia's capital and major urban area. Living in La Paz is in many ways like living on the moon. The city rests in a barren crater of naked land, at an altitude of more than two miles, where the air is so thin that newcomers find it difficult to breathe. In fact, there is so little oxygen in the city's rarified atmosphere that fires almost never occur.

La Paz is unusual in other ways as well. The city's nearly 1 million residents are packed into but a few square miles. There is a small population of financial elites—merchants, professionals, and politicians who see to the needs of the city and country; executives and landowners made affluent by Bolivia's rich mineral resources; and "narcotrafficantes," whose extravagant wealth has come from the cultivation of the coca leaf and its processing into cocaine. Yet the majority of the people of La Paz are impoverished Aymara Indians. The men wear work clothes, often the type that laborers in the United States wear, but the few who can find jobs are typically employed at the most menial of tasks. The Aymara women present a striking contrast. Jamming the streets and sidewalk stalls to sell the few fruits and vegetables that can be grown on the Altiplano waste-land, they are always dressed in the most colorful of costumes. Their typi-cal dress includes a large skirt of brilliant color under which there are six or more *polleras* (petticoats), a striped or embroidered shawl in an in-finite rainbow of pinks, blues, reds, and yellows, crowned with either bowlers or white top hats. Many are carrying babies, each tied into a bundle of striped blankets, on their backs.

For the Indians and mestizos of Bolivia life is spare and bitter, with al-most no comforts. Those who reside in La Paz actually live in the sur-rounding hills where the air is even thinner. Their homes, at the edge of the city and throughout the Altiplano, are shanties made of discarded signboards, doors, and other debris, or mud that has been shaped into bricks and dried in the sun. The houses have no windows, electricity, or plumbing; they are dark, dank, musty, and unpleasant. The life expec-tancy of the Indians in some parts of Bolivia is only 33 years; there is never any financial security; and tuberculosis and other diseases take a tremendous toll on children and adults. Most Indian mothers expect to have two out of three children die in their first few years of life.

Although Bolivia is rich in natural resources—petroleum, natural gas, tin, lead, zinc, copper, and gold—it is in a state of economic chaos. Most of the population works in agriculture, which is generally unrewarding. Those who do toil in the mines spend much of their time on strike. The country has a national debt of $5.3 billion,[3] a trifling sum compared to the staggering U.S. budget deficits, but Bolivia's gross national product was only $3.2 billion during the mid-1980s (as compared with $2.6 tril-lion for the United States). In an attempt to pay its debts, the Bolivian government printed more pesos. The results were catastrophic. Whereas the "official" exchange rate in 1982 was 44 *pesos bolivianos* to 1 Ameri-can dollar, by March 1986 a $1 bill could buy 1,552,950 pesos—and that was the "official" rate. On the black market, the dollar was valued at more than double the official rate.[4] This level of currency devaluation re-minds one of complaints about the double-digit inflation at the beginning of the Reagan administration. But the American citizen has little under-standing of what *real* inflation can be. There was such an inflationary spi-ral in Bolivia during 1985 that by the end of the year inflation had hit more than 25,000%.[5] In view of such vast natural resources amidst ap-parently uncontrollable economic chaos, it is no wonder that many Boli-vians refer to their country as "a beggar sitting on a throne of gold."

Bolivia is also in a shambles politically. Since gaining its independence from Spain in 1825 under the leadership of Simón Bolívar, the country has had more than 60 revolutions, 70 presidents, and 11 constitutions; the government has changed hands by coup a total of 189 times; and from 1978 through 1985 there had been 12 presidents, with the eleventh resigning out of sheer frustration.[6] Part of the problem has been corruption, a problem endemic to many regimes. Another has been poor economic planning and management at times when world markets were unfavorable to Bolivian production.[7] Many citizens of Bolivia feel, however, that they have difficulties because their people just cannot seem to get along with one another. In fact, indicative of this self-denigrating attitude, there are stories in Bolivian folklore which hold that the quarrelsome nature of the peoples of that country is the result of a deliberate act of God.

Peru

Lying in western South America, Peru extends nearly 1,500 miles along the Pacific Ocean. In land area, it is almost the size of Alaska, with a population of some 19 million. Peru is divided by the Andes Mountains into three sharply differentiated zones. To the west are the coastal plains, mostly arid and extending 50 to 100 miles inland. The central area is mountains, some reaching to heights of 20,000 feet, and plateaus and deep valleys. Beyond the mountains to the east lie the high and low jungles—the heavily forested slopes leading to Amazonia.

Economically, Peru is not much better off than Bolivia. Large segments of its predominantly Indian and mestizo population are either unemployed or underemployed; triple-digit inflation has plagued the economy for a number of years; there is a rapidly declining per capita income; and the value of the currency has declined drastically—from 289 *soles* to the dollar in 1980 to almost 14,000 by late 1985, placing the country on the verge of bankruptcy.[8]

Peru's precarious condition is due partially to natural disasters and world economic trends but primarily to inappropriate political decisions. Agriculture, which accounts for 40% of the country's working population, suffered a variety of setbacks during the early 1980s when there were heavy rains and flooding in northern Peru, landslides in central Peru, and drought in the south. The prosperous mining sector was affected by widespread strikes and declining silver and copper prices on world markets. Moreover, at one time Peru's fishing catch—primarily anchovy—was the fourth largest in the world. In 1976, however, it was virtually halted because of depleted stocks; it resumed in 1982, but was suspended again when the meandering *El Niño* current brought exceptionally warm waters to the Peruvian fishing grounds.

In the political sphere, a military coup in 1968 gave power to a pro-

Marxist military government. In its attempt to create a "nationalist—socialist" system, the military took over many locally and foreign-owned industries and large agricultural estates. The result was inefficient and low-output production. Moreover, rather than using the national treasury for economic development, the ruling junta used much of it for the purchase of Soviet fighter planes.[9]

When Peru changed back to democratic rule in 1980, another set of problems was added. President Fernando Belaunde Terry, apparently a well-meaning visionary who had hoped to build a "new Peru," shifted the country's development emphasis from the nation's somewhat thriving Pacific coast to the jungle-covered Amazonia. The effort, after consuming the country's limited savings and billions of dollars borrowed from abroad, proved to be a costly failure.[10]

The most visible signs of the economic changes over the last two decades can be seen in Lima. Once a quiet city of impressive Spanish-style buildings, stately museums, and world-class restaurants, its 2 million residents seemed to feel confident about the future of their city and country. After the military junta took power and began to dismantle the rural economy, Lima experienced explosive urbanization—accumulating almost 3 million additional residents over a 20-year period. Most were displaced peasants in search of work. Now, the streets are broken and littered with garbage. Many new business and residential structures, although occupied on their first and second floors, remain unfinished, their construction halted for lack of funds. Also, as in La Paz, there are the *pueblos jovenes*—the squalid shantytowns.

Adding to the problems of Peru is the *Sendero Luminoso,* or "Shining Path," a corps of fanatic guerilla terrorists who wish to purify Peru by violence and establish a "paradise" dominated by the now very repressed Indian population. The Shining Path has spawned violence, both by the *Senderista* terrorists and the military. Moreover, the activities of the Senderista Luminoso have required the use of scarce government resources in an attempt to keep terrorism under control.

Colombia

Situated in the northwestern part of South America and occupying a land area almost the size of Bolivia, Colombia is the only country on the continent that borders both the Atlantic and Pacific oceans. It has a population of almost 28 million, 98% of which is concentrated in the mountainous sections of the country. These highland regions, which account for 45% of the land, are composed mainly of high peaks, narrow valleys where many of the cities are clustered, and isolated intermontane basins. The rest of the country is in the *Orinoco Llanos,* the almost uninhabited lowlands to the east.

The population of Colombia is considerably varied, ranging from pure white, pure Indian, and pure black to blood mixtures of all three. In fact, Colombia, as a whole, is considerably varied, fitting few patterns that are typically associated with South America. Military coups have been infrequent, and many Colombian people are not poor, nor are they all coffee growers peripherally associated with the drug trade. Economically, the country is prosperous in many ways. Agricultural products and natural resources are numerous, but its foreign debt has become unmanageable. Moreover, health and sanitation are growing problems that have resulted in high rates of infant mortality. Furthermore, with 50% of the population living in urban areas and a high birthrate, there are growing numbers of the inevitable *barrios clandestinos*—the shantytowns. Although these are a common feature of city landscapes throughout South America, they seem to be more pronounced in Colombia—lacking drinking water, electricity, and sanitation facilities.

In general, the combination of at least the geography and economics of Bolivia, Peru, and Colombia has made them opportune for the development of the illicit drug trades. Although the topography and climate are the best in the world for the cultivation of coca, the vast areas of almost inaccessible mountain slopes make these countries difficult to police. Their sliding economic situations provide further incentives to drug trafficking.

For many peasants, the cultivation of marijuana and coca, the refining of coca leaves into paste or cocaine hydrochloride, and the trafficking in these substances have served as a way out of poverty. In Bolivia, where the per capita income is but a few hundred dollars for the laborer working at traditional crops earning $5 a day, the opportunities in the coca fields are significant. Just caring for the crop and picking and hauling the leaves can bring a tripling of income. For the farm family that can actually grow and process the coca, there is the lure of modest wealth. For government leaders who see vast amounts of trafficking dollars infused into their faltering economies, it appears that the illicit drug trades have their positive qualities. Yet in the short run and the long run, these activities can have serious negative implications. *In the economic sphere,* there have been effects on inflation, government economic planning, wages and property values, and the availability of traditional goods and services. *In the social sphere,* there is drug use, violence, and street crime. *In the political sphere,* there is corruption and the destabilization of government power. There can also be effects on the cultural traditions of entire groups and on the ecology of entire regions.

NARCODOLLARS, COFFEE BEANS, AND "TROUBLE IN PARADISE": THE ECONOMIC IMPLICATIONS OF DRUG TRAFFICKING

The sudden infusion of large sums of money into any country or community can be inflationary. It has been estimated that in 1979 alone, more than $3 billion entered the Colombian economy as the result of illicit crop cultivation and drug trafficking. Almost one-third of these funds entered directly in the form of U.S. dollars.[11] The investment of these drug dollars was generally limited to construction of luxury housing and resort hotels. The result was the bidding up of prices in the construction industry well beyond already inflationary levels, thus pushing lower- and middle-income families out of the housing market.

In the Peruvian jungle town of Tingo Maria, the effects of the drug-related inflationary spiral were of a different sort. As already noted in Chapter 2, the primary business activity of this remote town is the trafficking in coca products. The drug trades infused great sums of money into this little community over a short period of time, making many local peasants and farmers virtual millionaires. Along with the instant wealth came a sudden demand for automobiles, trucks, and various luxury items. Auto dealers moved in, but the demand was much greater than the supply. As a result, in 1981 Chevrolet Chevettes were selling for $25,000; small pickup trucks went for $35,000; Cadillacs and Lincolns were $100,000; and a Corvette or Mercedes could fetch as much as $350,000. Many legitimate business operators were either priced out of the market or drawn into trafficking in order to survive. Then a most curious thing happened. Since the auto dealers were more interested in sales than service, there were no facilities for parts or repair. Thus, when a vehicle broke down, it was simply abandoned in the jungle and replaced with a new one. A similar phenomenon occurred in parts of Bolivia.

Miami, the major cocaine-corridor community in the United States, also experienced inflated real estate values as the result of cocaine trafficking. As a real estate broker indicated in 1983:

> Part of the problem was the South American economy as a whole. Legitimately wealthy families were flying up for the day just to invest their money in something safe, to protect their savings. They'd buy luxury condos almost sight unseen and then go home. That tended to push up prices. Then the cocaine cowboys would walk in with suitcases full of money. They'd

buy a house for $1 million and pay all cash up front. . . . Canal-front houses that were selling a year earlier for $300,000 were suddenly $1 million.

The sudden infusions of money into some communities had effects on currency exchange rates. During the early 1980s in several Colombian cities, there was a glut of American dollars on the streets and in the banks. To convert these into pesos, traffickers worked with black-market foreign-exchange entrepreneurs who would discount the value of the dollar. This had a ripple effect on legitimate businesses that had to accept U.S. currency. A Bogotá hotel manager stated in 1982:

> *Officially,* the dollar was stable, but on the street it was constantly floating. We tried to get our U.S. customers to pay in pesos or credit card, which was fine. But every time they settled a bill with dollars or traveler's checks we took about a 15% loss on the transaction. After a few weeks of this, the owners insisted that we raise the rates for all visitors from the United States.

Trafficking has also had an economic impact on agriculture. As arable lands became more profitable from the cultivation of marijuana and coca, their value increased dramatically. Furthermore, traditional crops were replaced with coca, causing a decline in legitimate crop output. For example, from all over Bolivia during the 1970s and early 1980s, Aymara and Qulchua Indians crisscrossed the Andes with new trails leading to the coca-growing regions, leaving wheat and rice fields behind.[12] Most of the settlers living along the banks of Colombia's Putumayo, Cauca, and Caquetá rivers no longer planted yucca, corn, and pineapples. They abandoned their fields to work in the coca trade, eliminating economically significant crops from that part of the country.[13] A similar experience served to reduce the level of Colombian coffee exports.[14]

In a number of corridor communities that have historically been known as major winter resorts, the presence of drug trafficking has resulted in significant declines in tourism. Miami, where tourism is a $10 billion annual industry, has been particularly affected in this way. The increased attention given to the drug scene there during the late 1970s resulted in losses of billions of tourist dollars, capped by a 25% drop in hotel occupancy rates during 1981. This problem was further compounded when *Time* magazine, with its weekly circulation of 4.6 million copies, published its "Trouble in Paradise" issue on September 23, 1981, which detailed the Miami drug-related violence.[15] During the week following, hotel managers and travel agents were inundated with cancellations. A motel owner commented in 1984:

> The day after the "Trouble in Paradise" story hit the streets, I lost 10% of my bookings, followed by another 20% the following week. Some of my regular customers who have been staying here every winter since the 1960s have never come back. Now they go to the west coast of Florida where the drug scene is less visible.

A similar situation has become apparent in Cartagena, Colombia, on the Caribbean coast. Cartagena's Bocagrande beach, one mile from the historic colonial city, is an expanse of fine restaurants, luxury hotels, and picturesque markets that has lured North and South American tourists for decades. Although Cartagena is a safe city, seemingly untouched by Colombia's position in international drug trafficking, hotel managers have noticed a drop in the number of tourists coming from the United States. In this regard, a tour director stated:

> . . . we still have the South Americans coming in year round, but most of the others [from the United States] don't come down any more. They see us as a nation of outlaws.

AL PACINO, MAXIMUM JOHN, AND CAPTAIN KIDD: THE SOCIAL IMPLICATIONS OF DRUG TRAFFICKING

So the feds in Miami ask this guy Tony Montana where he picked up his good English, and Tony says, "My father ta'e me to da movies. I watch da guys like Humphrey Bogart, James Cagney. I learn to spe' from dose guys. I li'e dose guys." And so begins Brian De Palma's *Scarface*, a 1983 intended epic, portraying the rise and fall of a Cuban refugee turned cocaine cowboy. Played by actor Al Pacino, Tony works his way through the violent world of the Miami cocaine-trafficking scene, making it to the top, for a while at least. Ultimately, like almost every other character in the film, Tony falls in a hailstorm of bullets.

The reviews of *Scarface* were decidedly mixed.[16] One critic called it "a limp allegory of impotence"; others praised it as a gruesome morality play that accurately depicted the violent world of cocaine trafficking. Good or bad, *Scarface* was an interesting oddity. It was only the second time in motion-picture history that a major production received an "X" rating (the first having been *Last Tango in Paris,* a decade earlier). The reasons for the poisonous rating were two. The first was the vulgar language. One common four-letter obscenity was uttered, by consecutive count, a total of 181 times. In that sense, the rating seemed to be a bad rap, for after all, that is no worse than Richard Pryor or Eddie Murphy, even on one of their good days. The second reason was the gruesome violence, chain-saw executions and all. On appeal, the rating was reduced to "R" and *Scarface* made it to the neighborhood picture show. What was curious here was the fact that even with the grisly circus of horrors that was so furiously presented, the film did not even begin to approach the actual magnitude of violence that characterizes the real-life world of cocaine trafficking.

Described earlier as "systemic violence," the large profits associated with drug trafficking instigate brutal aggression against people, property, and institutions. Throughout the trafficking regions of South America, killings are quite common. A typical pattern involves the execution of not only the rival dealer but of his entire family as well to serve as a warning to others. A characteristic case in this behalf occurred in New York City during 1984. Years earlier, Enrique Bermudez, a low-level dealer in the East Coast drug world, had pleaded guilty to selling a half-ounce of cocaine to an undercover police officer. Under the New York drug laws, the strongest in the nation, Bermudez could have received a life sentence. Instead, he chose to cooperate with the authorities in return for a shorter sentence. He served five years in prison, and his testimony resulted in the incarceration of several other dealers. However, Bermudez apparently failed to understand the laws of retribution in the Colombian cocaine industry. On Palm Sunday in 1984, while Bermudez was at work, several traffickers entered his home to exact their revenge. Two women and eight children, ranging in age from 2 to 14 years, were executed. All had been either held in their chairs while being shot in the head or later propped up into positions that made the scene resemble the house of horrors in London's famous Madame Tussaud's Wax Museum. As one investigator described the mode of execution:

> Colombian killers leave no witnesses. They kill the maid, the
> TV repairman, the child. They kill anyone who is around.[17]

An agent of the Drug Enforcement Administration, working in Medellín, Colombia, a major refining and exchange point in the South American cocaine network, described the two most common methods of execution in that city:

> The first way is by simple machine gunning. Two hit men will ride through the traffic on a motorcycle. When they get up to the victim's car, the guy on the back of the bike levels a cannon and sprays the car. The second way is a bit messy. They'll carve him up with hatchets and chain saws and feed the pieces of meat to pigs that run free in the neighborhood.

Moreover, a Colombian military official added:

> The Colombian drug-assassination ethic also features what some call the "necktie killing." The target's throat is slit open so his tongue can hang through it like a tie. . . . It is a gruesome sight to see this—men, women, and children, all lined up in chairs like soldiers with their tongues coming out their necks. . . .

The violence is not restricted to traffickers. In Sierra Nevada de Santa Marta, Colombia, the people of the Arhuacos tribe had grown coca for generations, using it for the mild stimulant effects. In 1982, however, the men of the tribe were murdered and their women raped by traffickers seeking the aborigines' coca plantings.[18] Also in 1982, a team of Bolivian narcotics agents seized 60 kilos of coca paste in the Chapare growing region. That night, a mob of 200 peasants tortured, mutilated, and murdered the agents involved.[19] In 1983, while on patrol along the Maracas River some 400 miles north of Bogotá, Colombian soldiers found the remains of 60 peasants who had refused to cooperate with drug traffickers.[20] In 1984, near Tingo Maria, a band of cocaine traffickers burst into a jungle campsite and opened fire with automatic weapons, killing the 17 members of the Peruvian civil guard employed by a United States-financed program to destroy coca crops.[21]

Killings occur in other sectors as well. In Medellín and other Colombian drug centers, prosecutors and judges seeking convictions of traffickers have been systematically executed. One of the victims was that nation's justice minister, Rodrigo Lara Bonilla, assassinated in 1984 after he had made the mistake of publicly demanding stronger measures against local "narcotrafficantes."[22] Even the president of Colombia has been threatened.[23]

Drug-related assassinations have not been limited to foreign nationals. Many American judges and prosecutors have been threatened, and in 1982 federal judge John H. Wood was executed in Texas. Known as "Maximum John" for the stiff sentences he handed down, a $200,000 bounty was placed on his head to prevent him from presiding over a drug-trafficking case.[24] The American diplomatic corps in Colombia was targeted. First, the U.S. Embassy in Bogotá was bombed in late 1984.[25] Then a $350,000 reward was offered by Colombian cocaine traffickers for the kidnapping of any high-ranking agent of the Drug Enforcement Administration (DEA).[26] Finally, in early 1985, American diplomats and their families residing in Colombia were threatened with execution. For every alleged trafficker extradited to the United States, the warning said, five U.S. citizens would be executed.[27] More recently, there was the 1985 kidnap-murder of DEA agent Enrique Salazar in Guadalajara, Mexico, an episode in the drug war engineered by traffickers but actually carried out by Mexican police officers.[*,28]

Drug trafficking can also be credited with the current rise of piracy in the Caribbean, the Bahamas, and the Gulf of Mexico. Interestingly, it was in these same waters that piracy in the grand manner of Captain Kidd and Henry Morgan flourished several centuries ago. The voyages of Columbus had provided Spain with an early start in seeking the treasures of the New World. The ensuing territorial conquests gave that nation an almost total claim on the Americas, as well as the financial strength to construct the most powerful navy in Europe. Trade, often with cargoes in excess of $100 million per ship, found a natural right-of-way through the Caribbean, made highly navigable by the Gulf Stream currents, prevailing winds, and sheltering islands of the West Indies. During the seventeenth and eighteenth centuries, moreover, the West Indies became a depository for transported convicts; social and political refugees from France, Spain, and Great Britain; and vagrant sailors when the Treaty of Utrecht in 1713 brought an end to the War of the Spanish Succession.[29]

The grand era of piracy began in 1714 when Captain Henry Jennings of Jamaica and 300 seamen descended upon the salvage crew of a grounded

---

* The killing of agent Salazar had an immediate effect on the Guadalajara tourism industry. Within days after Salazar's body was found, Americans were suddenly absent from the city's glistening new hotels and fashionable restaurants and discotheques. They had simply packed up and left. (See the *New York Times*, 20 Mar. 1985, p. A3.) Three months later, a Miami travel agent commented:

> I can't even *give* tickets away to Guadalajara. I haven't had one new booking for that place in three months, and the nine I already had before the murder either went somewhere else in Mexico or canceled altogether. They all said they just wouldn't feel safe down there.

The problems in Mexico were further compounded on October 30, 1985 when 17 police officers and 5 other members of an antidrug group were executed in a remote region of the Gulf Coast state of Veracruz by a large band of drug traffickers armed with high-powered automatic weapons. Some had been tortured and most had been killed by a single bullet through the head. (See the *New York Times*, 10 Nov. 1985, p. E2; *Time*, 18 Nov. 1985, p. 60.)

Spanish galleon, looting the vessel of some 300,000 "pieces of eight." News of the event proved inspirational to the social pariah and displaced mariner on the Caribbean waterfronts, and ships were seized, manned, and turned pirate. It was the topography of the Indies that made piracy a lucrative pursuit. Located along the heavily traveled Gulf Stream routes, the islands provided landside strongholds close to the illicit maritime ventures. The endless number of coves offered natural opportunities for ambush, and with the area's scattered habitation and development, the marine bandits could swiftly retreat to the security and sanctuary of unobserved seclusion.

Many of the reasons that spawned piracy in the Caribbean during the 1700s also contributed to its reemergence in the contemporary era of drug trafficking. Much of the smuggling during the 1970s was by sea. According to the head of Colombia's *Guardacostas,* the shuttles would begin along the Caribbean coast from secluded ports between the cities of Cartagena, Barranquilla, and Santa Marta. Shipments bound for Key West and Gulf Coast ports followed a northwesterly bearing, passing to the west of the Cayman Islands and Cuba, and through the Yucatan Channel into the Gulf of Mexico. Those heading toward Atlantic Coast ports went in a more northerly direction, selecting the Windward Passage between Cuba and Haiti and then sailing northwest in a straight line through the Bahamas. Another route they took was the Mona Passage between Puerto Rico and the Dominican Republic, followed by sea routes meandering through or along the east side of the Bahamas until their South Florida destinations were close at hand. These passages provided relative seclusion, combined with relative ease of navigation. Moreover, with some 700 islands and no less than 2,000 cays within the Bahama chain alone, there were many isolated locations where drug transactions could take place.

The piracy of pleasure craft, or "yachtjacking" as some have called it, began during the early 1970s. Some vessels were pirated and used for transporting drugs. Others were seized because they had come too close to drug-transaction areas or were mistaken as rival drug craft. In all instances, the passengers and crew of the stolen craft were killed, tossed overboard, and likely devoured by sharks and other sea creatures. So prevalent had the problem become that warnings to mariners repeatedly appeared in U.S. Coast Guard bulletins and respected yachting publications.[30]

By 1981, the problem seemed to have peaked. Aircraft had become a more popular form of smuggling transport. More effective enforcement efforts in Bahama and Caribbean waters had shifted traffickers' sea routes east through the Leeward Passage, well away from the areas frequented

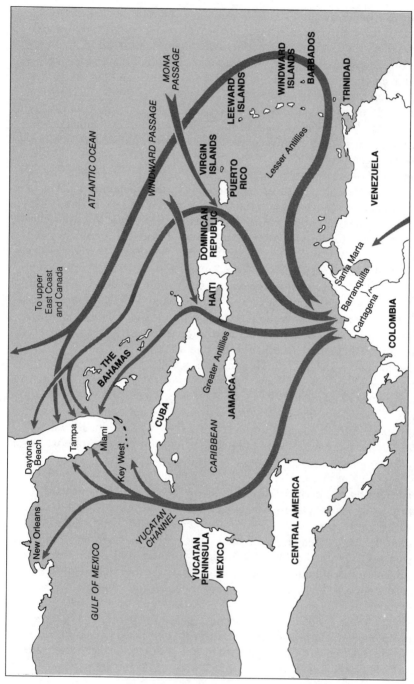

Drug-Trafficking Sea Routes in the Caribbean

by recreational boaters. Drug trafficking as a whole had become better-financed, and the theft of vessels was no longer necessary. Perhaps most importantly, boat owners took more care in avoiding reported "trouble spots" and began to arm themselves heavily. Yet in 1985, the piracy of pleasure craft in waters off the coast of Florida had not disappeared.[31] At national boat shows and local exhibitions catering exclusively to Florida boaters, dealers in security equipment are prominent.* Moreover, as one Miami gun shop owner stated in June of 1985:

> Although the homeowner is the major buyer of guns here, yachtsmen and fishermen probably rank second. So many of them cruise those lonely waters from Grand Bahama Island and Bimini down through Andros, the Exumas, Deadman's Cay, and the Inagua islands that there's no way they're going without at least a .38 or .45 handgun. . . . Corrosion-proof firearms are the most popular. . . .

Similarly, the dockmaster at a Key West marina commented:

> . . . Nobody seems to take any chances any more. Just about every serious boater crossing the Gulf Stream or headed for the Bahamas carries firearms.

Finally, a Miami firearms instructor stated in December of 1985:

> I have two kinds of students—home owners and boat owners. The home owners want to know how to shoot pistols, while the boat owners are into heavy artillery. By and large, when they're out on the high seas in the no-man's-land of the cocaine cowboys, they want something that will let bullets fly like water spraying from a hose. In fact, they want training with the same things that the drug runners carry—automatics and semiautomatics like the UZI and MAC-10—something that can crank out at least 600 rounds per minute.

However, violence is not the only social problem that emerges as the result of trafficking in drugs. Through a natural-history process, as soon

---

* By the end of 1985, yachting magazines were still addressing, however subtly, the issue of self-protection in the waters off the coast of South Florida. In the November 1985 issue of *Boating* magazine, for example, a feature story on cruising the Bahamas listed nine tips, the last of which was "guns and ammo." (See *Boating*, Nov. 1985, p. 31.)

as trafficking becomes firmly established in drug-producing and corridor nations, these locales begin to develop drug-use and street-crime problems of their own. Producing countries initially export the raw materials they have cultivated, such as coca leaves, for refining and distribution elsewhere. In time, to maximize profits, refining operations begin to move closer to cultivation areas, and quickly, what was once only a growing area has suddenly been transformed into a refining and distributing area as well.

The presence of illicit drugs in any trafficking nation increases their availability to local citizens, not only because the drugs are readily at hand but also because any surpluses must be sold somewhere. Thus, the emergence and growth of a local drug-use problem. Drug traffickers are very enterprising people. As soon as a drug culture has begun to develop, traffickers bring in other drugs not indigenous to the area. Thus, nations that were once simple suppliers of drugs evolve into primary consumers. This historical pattern has repeated itself throughout the world in recent years: in Brazil,[32] Peru,[33] Bolivia and Colombia,[34] Nigeria,[35] the Bahamas,[36] Jamaica and the Caribbean;[37] in Nepal[38] and throughout Western Europe, India, Pakistan,and almost all of Southeast Asia.[39] Islamic students who are enrolled in American universities yet return to Iran each summer report that even in Teheran under the repressive regime of Ayatollah Ruhollah Khomeini, narcotics use is widespread—not simply confined to the poppy-growing regions.*

Perhaps the most acute example of this evolutionary process emerged in the Golden Triangle regions of Burma, Laos, and Thailand. Historically, most of the heroin that entered the United States originated as raw opium in that part of Southeast Asia. Then the Golden Crescent countries of Iran, Pakistan, and Afghanistan began to produce a cheaper and more potent opium, leading to a decline in opium exports from the Golden Triangle nations. In an attempt to compete, jungle laboratories sprang up in Thailand, Burma, and Laos, where the opium was refined into heroin and routed to the outside world by way of Bangkok. During the early 1980s, at a time when the increasing popularity of cocaine and the stabilized population of narcotic addicts in the United States reduced the demand for heroin, the Golden Triangle had bumper opium harvests, 600 tons annually—enough to make some 120 metric tons of heroin. The result was a surplus of the drug, at cheap prices, much of which found its way to

---

* Heroin addiction is apparent even in Communist Poland. Opium poppies are grown for the use of their seeds in Polish pastries, and the rest of the plant is purchased from farmers and transformed into heroin. According to an "NBC Nightly News" telecast on March 24, 1985, there are an estimated 300,000 heroin addicts in Poland.

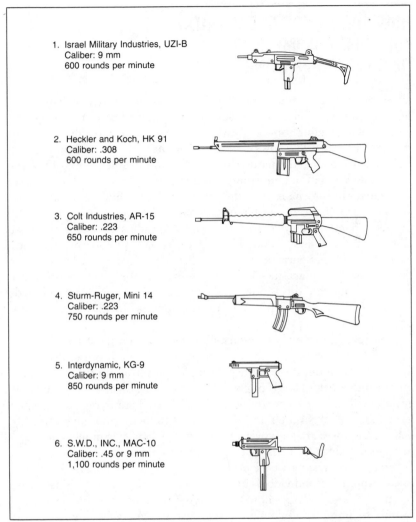

1. Israel Military Industries, UZI-B
   Caliber: 9 mm
   600 rounds per minute

2. Heckler and Koch, HK 91
   Caliber: .308
   600 rounds per minute

3. Colt Industries, AR-15
   Caliber: .223
   650 rounds per minute

4. Sturm-Ruger, Mini 14
   Caliber: .223
   750 rounds per minute

5. Interdynamic, KG-9
   Caliber: 9 mm
   850 rounds per minute

6. S.W.D., INC., MAC-10
   Caliber: .45 or 9 mm
   1,100 rounds per minute

Weapons of Choice in the Boaters' and Drug Runners' Arms Race

the streets of Bangkok and other Thai cities. In this nation of 48 million people, as many as 600,000 people use heroin.[40] Moreover, as soon as the drug culture became firmly established, street crime began to grow, a phenomenon that has manifested itself in virtually every community in the world where the use of illicit drugs has become widespread.

HOW ARE THINGS IN ZINAHOTA?
THE POLITICAL IMPLICATIONS
OF DRUG TRAFFICKING

It is a market like no other market in the world, and it thrives in Zinahota, Bolivia. This is a village of only 300 peasants in the heart of the Chapare coca-growing region, some 120 kilometers east of Cochabamba. As far as the rest of the world knows a place by the name of Zinahota does not exist: It is so small and remote that even the most detailed maps of Bolivia fail to show it. Yet on almost any given day during the coca harvest season, Zinahota is a chaos of jostling pigs, chickens, children, traffic jams, and crowded alleys, where merchants hawk pots and pans, onions and peppers, shampoo, bicycle tires, and transistor radios. However, the most common items bought and sold are coca leaves and concentrated coca paste. Unlike other parts of the world where clandestine transfers of illicit drugs must take place in seclusion, far from probing law-enforcement agents, in Zinahota this is done in the public market, totally unmolested. The reason? The Bolivian government cannot ensure the safety of any drug agents working in the area.[41]

The situation in Zinahota, which illustrates a government's total loss of control over a region, is but one of the political implications of drug trafficking. In addition, there is the securing of power by traffickers or their representatives at all levels of government; there is the indirect control of government posts by corruption and violence; there is regime instability demonstrated through an unwillingness to arrest and imprison traffickers; and there are antigovernment threats when drug moneys are used to finance political terrorism or actual government takeovers.

Perhaps the most pervasive problem in the political arena is the wholesale corruption of individuals and institutions. In some trafficking areas, corruption is so widespread in the justice system, banking, the legal profession, military, the diplomatic corps, customs, and general government that it is often viewed as part of the natural order of things. In South Florida, drug-related corruption in law enforcement has become so common that reports of new scandals no longer receive extensive press coverage.* Elsewhere, the level of corruption has advanced to such a degree that what occurs in South Florida appears to be rudimentary.

---

* The image of the Miami police became so tarnished as a result of the drug-related corruption that in October 1985 more than 800 officers in that city volunteered for drug testing to demonstrate their integrity. (See *USA Today*, 28 Oct. 1985, p. 3A; *New York Times*, 5 Nov. 1985, p. A12; *Newsweek*, 11 Nov. 1985, p. 32.)

In Latin America, enforcement of the drug laws is so limited that U.S. officials have charged that Cuban President Fidel Castro and officials of neighboring countries actually encourage drug sales as a revenue source.[42] In Colombia, as an outgrowth of President Belisario Betancur's efforts against drug syndicates, it was found that no less than 400 judges had been corrupted by drug-related bribe money.[43] In 1985, a seizure in Paraguay of chemicals used in the manufacture of cocaine led U.S. officials to believe that senior members of the military government were directly involved in trafficking.[44] Similarly, it would appear that drug-related corruption permeated the governments of the Bahamas, Belize, and the Caribbean Turks and Caicos islands.[45] For Peru, coca is the single largest export, pumping almost $1 billion into the fragile economy—made possible by corruption in government and the military.[46] Senator Javier Valle Riestra said in 1985, regarding the criminal processing of drug traffickers in his nation, "Justice in Peru is a public auction house. Sentences are bought and sold. . . ."[47]

Corruption has long since hit the banking industry in the form of "money laundering." Money laundries have been used for decades by organized-crime figures and others wanting to keep large amounts of money from being taxed. Their widest use, however, has occurred in recent years among drug dealers and traffickers who accumulate millions of dollars each week, *in cash.* Because of the amount of funds involved, the dollars cannot be spent or invested without attracting government attention. Thus the "dirty" money must be "cleaned," giving it the appearance of legitimacy—hence, the need for its "laundering" or "rinsing."[48]

The most typical form of money-laundering operation occurs through banks in Miami, Switzerland, Panama, Hong Kong, the Bahamas, and the Grand Cayman Islands in the Caribbean. The pattern involves the depositing of, say, $10 million, in a U.S. bank, in cash. Although the federal Bank Secrecy Act requires that banks must report deposits of $10,000 or more to the Internal Revenue Service, for a 2% fee some bankers will "forget" to file the proper notice with the IRS. The American bank then wires the money to an account in the Cayman Islands, a country with strict banking laws that protect the privacy and identity of its depositors. The account to which the money is wired belongs to a bogus Cayman Islands corporation owned by the drug trafficker. The corporation, by way of the Cayman Islands bank, returns the money to the drug dealer in the form of a loan. Thus, the dealer gets his money back, "clean," in an ostensibly lawful manner, and because it is a "loan," it is not subject to taxation.

In a 1982 case, Miami's Great American Bank of Dade County was charged with laundering $96 million in South American drug profits.[49] During the same year, more than 100 crime leaders, Bahamian government officials, and international financiers became the targets of a U.S. government inquiry into the laundering of billions of "narcodollars." [50] In 1985, money laundering was found to be an $80 billion-a-year industry, with the majority of the money coming from illegal drug sales and involving major banks and brokerage houses throughout the United States. [51] Curiously, as the result of the extensive money-laundering operations involving Miami banks and with the widespread use and trafficking of cocaine in that city, virtually every piece of U.S. currency handled in South Florida is contaminated with microscopic traces of cocaine. [52]

The most threatening political aspect of drug trafficking is its impact on government institutions. Through bribery and corruption, traffickers and/or their representatives have secured judgeships and administrative appointments. Moreover, weak governments can be the focus of direct takeovers by traffickers. There is a precedent for this. In 1980, for example, the presidential election in Bolivia yielded no clear winner. Before the congress could meet to decide between the main contenders, a military junta led by army commander General Luis García Meza staged a coup. Ironically, García Meza was himself a major cocaine trafficker, and he proceeded to establish alliances between the government and civilian drug enterprises. [53] A year later García Meza was ultimately forced to resign, but not because of his involvement with the cocaine trades, but for his fiscal mismanagement. Three years later, Bolivian President Hernán Siles Zuazo, the fourth person to hold that office since García Meza's resignation, announced a war on cocaine. In 1984 Zuazo was kidnapped from the presidential palace by a group of cocaine traffickers. Although he was released unharmed and the attempted coup was aborted, the problem seems to be ever present in that nation. [54] By 1985, as a result of the pervasiveness of traffickers in official posts and the crisis in economic affairs, many considered the political system in Bolivia to be leaderless, with the government existing only on paper. [55]

The final issue in the political arena is the link between drug trafficking and terrorism. There is widespread opinion that the activities of the Palestine Liberation Organization, the Syrians in the Bakaa Valley, the communist insurgents in Burma, the M–19 leftist rebels in Colombia, and the Shining Path guerillas in Peru are financed and armed by the heroin, cocaine, marijuana, and hashish industries. [56]

POSTSCRIPT

Drug abuse, whether it involves heroin, cocaine, or other drugs, is not simply the problem of the consuming community or nation. There are implications for trafficking nations as well in their political, social, and economic sectors of life. Moreover, the impact of trafficking tends to be circular. That is, whatever influences one sphere of activity seems to rebound on all others.

There are other effects as well. In Bolivia, for example, the centuries-old custom of coca chewing by laborers is threatened by the inflated price of leaves, brought on by trafficking. Not only has a cultural tradition begun to disappear, but it has also affected the ability of many Bolivian laborers to support themselves fully. Without the gentle stimulation engendered by the leaves, many are unable to remain in the mines and in the fields for long hours at hard labor.

There are consequences in the ecological sector. Throughout the United States and Mexico, paraquat, a potent herbicide, has been used to eradicate fields of marijuana plants. Environmentalists have questioned the safety of its use, but its effects on the general ecology of the areas where it has been introduced are immeasurable. However, a different situation exists in many coca-growing regions. On the slopes of the Andes in the high jungles of Peru, for example, coca growers use paraquat heavily. They apply it to the soil surrounding each bush to inhibit any weed growth that might draw nutrients away from the coca. Better coca plants have been one result but so too have been widespread soil erosion and landslides.

Finally, any number of unanticipated consequences have occurred in the diplomatic, financial, and social sectors for those nations and peoples whose economies depend on drug trafficking. A number of Latin American nations have lost U.S. economic aid, foreign investment, and international bank loans as a result of their unwillingness to better control drug trafficking within their borders. Moreover, there is a long-term implication that is potentially more drastic. Drug abuse in the United States and Western Europe has been characterized by *change*—change over the years in the preference of one drug over another. At present, cocaine is the widespread drug of choice. Yet when cocaine becomes less appealing as a drug of abuse, or when the effects of drug enforcement and prevention efforts begin to have a noticeable impact, what will happen to those peasants who abandoned the coffee and sugar plantations to cultivate coca and marijuana? Cocaine use in the United States will likely decline by the 1990s. It is inevitable, for it has happened with all other drugs of abuse. Even heroin-use rates in the United States are declining. What will happen to those nations and communities whose economic systems are dependent on cocaine trafficking? During the latter part of 1984, Colombia began to experience the effects of such a situation. Faced with economic chaos, a multibillion dollar debt, and an inability to attract foreign loans and investment—to a very great extent, the result of its reputation as a drug-trafficking and outlaw nation—President Betancur announced a war on drugs. The American business community applauded his commitment, but his people did not. His initial efforts resulted in a shifting of many cocaine-processing laboratories from Colombia to South Florida. In consequence, there was further economic inactivity, pressure from leftist rebels, and dissention among peasants that caused widespread disenchantment with Betancur's entire regime.

Notes

1. Bogotá *Chromos,* 25 Aug. 1981, p. 45.
2. See June Nash, *We Eat the Mines and the Mines Eat Us: Dependency and Exploitation in Bolivian Tin Mines* (New York: Columbia University Press, 1979).
3. *USA Today,* 31 July 1985, p. 4A.
4. Bankers Trust, Foreign Exchange Division, 4 Mar. 1986.
5. *New York Times,* 5 Aug. 1985, p. A4; *Latin American Regional Reports, Andean Group Report,* 24 Jan. 1986, p. 2.
6. *New York Times,* 21 July 1985, p. E5.
7. *Christian Science Monitor,* 13 Aug. 1985, p. 14.
8. *U.S. News & World Report,* 15 July 1985, p. 49; *New York Times,* 18 Aug. 1985, p. F25.
9. Thomas S. Skidmore and Peter H. Smith, *Modern Latin America* (New York: Oxford University Press, 1984), pp. 187–224.
10. *U.S. News & World Report,* 11 Mar. 1985, p. 39.
11. Peter A. Lupsha, "The Political Economy of Drug Trafficking" (Paper presented at the Annual Meeting of the Latin American Studies Association, Bloomington, Ind., 16–20 Oct. 1980).
12. *New York Times,* 12 Sept. 1984, p. A16.
13. Bogotá *El Tiempo,* 18 Apr. 1982, p. 1A.
14. Bogotá *El Tiempo,* 29 May 1981, p. 1A.
15. *Time,* 23 Sept. 1981, pp. 22–32.
16. *New Statesman,* 3 Feb. 1984, p. 28; *New Yorker,* 26 Dec. 1983, pp. 50–53; *Time,* 5 Dec. 1983, p. 96; *Newsweek,* 12 Dec. 1983, p. 109; *Commonweal,* 24 Feb. 1984, p. 116.
17. Bogotá *El Tiempo,* 28 Apr. 1982, p. 3A.
18. *Newsweek,* 30 Apr. 1984, p. 24.
19. *Miami Herald,* 14 Nov. 1982, p. 24.
20. *Miami Herald,* 17 Apr. 1983, p. 26A.
21. *New York Times,* 19 Nov. 1984, p. 1A.
22. *USA Today,* 2 May 1984, p. 7A; *Newsweek,* 14 May 1984, p. 48.
23. *Wilmington* (Delaware) *News-Journal,* 25 July 1984, p. A8; *Newsweek,* 3 Sept. 1984, p. 17; *USA Today,* 2 May 1984, p. 7A.
24. *Miami Herald,* 18 Nov. 1982, p. 1; *Miami Herald,* 15 Dec. 1982, p. 10A; *New York Times,* 14 Mar. 1982, p. 31.

25. *Time,* 10 Dec. 1984, p. 46.
26. *New York Times,* 18 Feb. 1985, p. A7.
27. *Newsweek,* 1 Jan. 1985, p. 37.
28. *New York Times,* 12 Feb. 1985, p. A6; *USA Today,* 18 Feb. 1985, pp. 1A, 3A; *USA Today,* 21 Feb. 1985, p. 3A; *USA Today,* 15 Mar. 1985, p. 5A; *New York Times,* 17 Mar. 1985, p. E2; *U.S. News & World Report,* 18 Mar. 1985, p. 13.
29. See James Burney, *The History of the Buccaneers of America* (New York: W. W. Norton, 1950); Philip Gosse, *The History of Piracy* (New York: Tudor, 1932); P. A. Means, *The Spanish Main* (New York: Scribner's, 1935); Hugh F. Rankin, *The Golden Age of Piracy* (New York: Holt, Rinehart & Winston, 1969); George Woodbury, *The Great Days of Piracy in the West Indies* (New York: W. W. Norton, 1951).
30. G. O. W. Mueller and Freda Adler, *Outlaws of the Ocean* (New York: Hearst Marine Books, 1985), p. 139. See also *Time,* 22 Sept. 1980, p. 24.
31. Wilmington (Delaware) *News-Journal,* 25 Apr. 1985, p. A10.
32. Rio de Janeiro *O Globo,* 23 July 1982, p. 5.
33. Lima *El Comercio,* 30 Dec. 1981, p. D-3.
34. F. Raul Jeri, "Coca-Paste Smoking in Some Latin American Countries: A Severe and Unabated Form of Addiction," *Bulletin on Narcotics,* Apr.–June 1984, pp. 15–31.
35. *USA Today,* 26 Dec. 1984, p. 3A.
36. *New York Times,* 18 Dec. 1984, p. A20.
37. *New York Times,* 10 Sept. 1984, p. A1; *Christian Science Monitor,* 13 Aug. 1985, p. 36.
38. *USA Today,* 9 Dec. 1983, p. 9A.
39. *New York Times,* 13 Nov. 1983, p. 24; C. P. Spencer and V. Navaratnam, *Drug Abuse in East Asia* (New York: Oxford University Press, 1981).
40. *U.S. News & World Report,* 24 May 1982, p. 49; *Time,* 19 Mar. 1984, p. 35. See also Spencer and Navaratnam.
41. See *Miami Herald,* 14 Nov. 1982, pp. 1A, 22A; *Paris AFP,* 1637 GMT, 16 Dec. 1985 (a radio news service).
42. *U.S. News & World Report,* 6 Feb. 1984, p. 49.
43. *Time,* 28 May 1984, p. 62.
44. *New York Times,* 3 Jan. 1985, p. A1.
45. *New York Times,* 6 Jan. 1985, p. 8; *New York Times,* 9 Apr. 1985, p. A15; *USA Today,* 11 Mar. 1985, p. 3A; *Manchester Guardian Weekly,* 17 Mar. 1985, p. 7; *New York Times,* 6 Mar. 1985, p. A1; *National Law Journal,* 29 July 1985, p. 6.
46. *New York Times,* 1 Sept. 1985, p. 1.
47. *Latin America Regional Reports, Andean Group Report,* 26 July 1985, p. 4.
48. *New York Magazine,* 31 Oct. 1983, pp. 30–36.
49. *Miami Herald,* 14 Dec. 1982, p. 1.
50. *Miami Herald,* 7 Nov. 1982, p. 21A.
51. *American Banker,* 15 Feb. 1985, pp. 4–6; *American Banker,* 22 Feb. 1985, pp. 4–7; *American Banker,* 28 Feb. 1985, pp. 4–12; *Business Week,* 11 Mar.

1985, p. 37; *Wall Street Journal,* 12 Mar. 1985, pp. 1, 26; *USA Today,* 15 Mar. 1985, p. 3A; *Business Week,* 18 Mar. 1985, pp. 74–82; *World Press Review,* Nov. 1985, p. 58; *Christian Science Monitor,* 18 Oct. 1985, p. 21; *Newsweek,* 23 Sept. 1985, p. 52.

52. *Miami Herald,* 19 Feb. 1985, pp. 1–2C.
53. Department of State, Bureau of International Narcotics Matters, *International Narcotics Control Strategy Report, 1985* (Washington, D.C.: Department of State, 1 Feb. 1985), p. 49.
54. *USA Today,* 2 July 1984, p. 6A; *Richmond* (Virginia) *Times Dispatch,* 1 July 1985, p. 1.
55. *Latin America Regional Reports, Andean Group Report,* 1 Mar. 1985, p. 8.
56. *Latin American Regional Reports, Andean Group Report,* 8 Nov. 1985, pp. 2–3; *New York Times,* 22 May 1984, p. A8; *New York Times,* 9 Sept. 1984, p. 12; *Newsweek,* 25 Feb. 1985, p. 15; *USA Today,* 15 Feb. 1985, p. 5A; *Miami Herald,* 24 Mar. 1983, p. 22A; *U.S. News & World Report,* 11 Mar. 1985, p. 38; Bogotá *El Tiempo,* 1 June 1981, p. 6A; Harvey F. Kline, "New Directions in Colombia?" *Current History,* Feb. 1985, pp. 65–68.

BACK TO THE FUTURE
Coping with the Worlds of
Heroin, Cocaine, and Crime

Just over a decade ago, the noted psychiatrist Thomas Szasz commented in his book *Ceremonial Chemistry:*

> The plain historical facts are that before 1914 there was no "drug problem" in the United States; nor did we have a name for it. Today there is an immense drug problem in the United States, and we have lots of names for it. Which came first: "the problem of drug abuse" or its name? It is the same as asking which came first: the chicken or the egg? All we can be sure of now is that the more chickens, the more eggs, and vice versa; and similarly, the more problems, the more names for them, and vice versa. My point is simply that our drug abuse experts, legislators, psychiatrists, and other professional guardians of our medical morals have been operating chicken hatcheries: they continue—partly by means of certain characteristic tactical abuses of our language—to manufacture and maintain the "drug problem" they ostensibly try to solve.[1]

Szasz certainly does have a way with words. He is suggesting something that nominalists have been saying for centuries: that a thing does not exist until it is imagined and given a name. For Szasz, a hopeless believer in this position, the "drug problem" in the United States did not exist before the passage of the Harrison Act in 1914, but became a reality when the behavior under consideration was *labeled* as a problem. If one were to read Szasz's entire volume, despite the numerous errors of fact combined with his caustic abuse of the English language, his point would be clear: the drug problem in America was created in great part by the very policies

203

designed to control it. On the other hand, one could save a good bit of time by just glancing at the subtitle of the Szasz book: *The Ritual Persecution of Drugs, Addicts, and Pushers*—it seems to convey the same message.

THE CIA, MASTURBATION, AND SOLVING THE DRUG PROBLEM

The position Szasz has taken has been fashionable for quite some time. Others have attacked American drug-control policies with equal vigor. Washington attorney Rufus King has described the issue as a 50-year folly, a misguided and ineffective endeavor.[2] David F. Musto's classic *The American Disease* offers a similar perspective, although accomplished with considerable scholarship.[3] We then have the social scientists, among the first to speak out against the federal approach to drug control. Alfred R. Lindesmith, who probably spent a good part of his professional career condemning federal policies, summed it up in 1956 in *The Nation:*

> For 40 years the United States has tried in vain to control the problem of drug addiction by prohibition and police suppression. The disastrous consequences of turning over to the police what is an essentially medical problem are steadily becoming more apparent as narcotic arrests rise each year to new records and the habit continues to spread, especially among young persons. Control by prohibition has failed; but the proposed remedies for this failure consist mainly of more of the same measures which have already proved futile.[4]

Then there is the Marxist perspective. Even though the social scientists suggest that federal drug policies are simply an outgrowth of the government's practiced benign stupidity, many Marxists hold that they are based on something quite insidious. Criminologists D. Stanley Eitzen and Doug A. Timmer argue that the American approach is deliberately structured to fail because the political economy of the United States needs the private accumulation of capital and profit that drug trafficking provides. For that reason, they state, the drug trades are not only tolerated, but condoned as well.[5] How Eitzen and Timmer reached this conclusion is somewhat difficult to decipher since there are no historical or empirical data to support their argument. Apparently convinced that the political and economic order of monopoly capitalism is the handmaiden of almost all repression, it seems that they read far too much into an erroneously documented statement that William J. Chambliss made some years ago. In his *On the Take,* Chambliss stated:

> . . . the heroin traffic from Southeast Asia, especially from the Golden Triangle of northern Thailand, Burma, and Laos, expanded production as a new source of heroin for the incredibly lucrative American market. . . . It is not known whether this new heroin source was linked to Republican politicians, but the fact that the CIA and the South Vietnamese governments under generals Ky and Thieu actively aided the development of this heroin source suggests that such a link is not beyond the realm of possibility.*,[6]

This notion is based on material found in Alfred W. McCoy's *The Politics of Heroin in Southeast Asia,* published in 1972.[7] Although McCoy's work is somewhat flawed by the point that some of his statements are first offered as probabilities and later accepted as fact, and by his falling victim to the fad of blaming everything that is wrong in the world on American foreign policy, his well-documented conclusion cannot be denied: that the heroin trade in Southeast Asia grew to some extent with the complicity of U.S. government representatives in that part of the world. But McCoy also points out that this was a product of American anticommunist zeal.[8] To translate all this into the "private accumulation of capital and profit" argument that Eitzen and Timmer offer requires a considerable leap of the imagination and represents little more than Marxist pontification.

Those who have supported federal approaches to drug control have been labeled as "law and order" conservatives, or simply ignored. But what would the others have done? What would the drug scene in the United States look like if Thomas Szasz or Rufus King or Alfred Lindesmith were in charge of the policies of national control?

For Dr. Szasz, the solution is simple. Ignore it, and it will no longer be a problem. After all, he maintains, there is precedent for it:

---

* As a source for this idea, Chambliss cites pages 52–75 in Alfred W. McCoy's *The Politics of Heroin in Southeast Asia.* On these pages, however, there is no mention of the CIA, generals Ky and Thieu, or even the Republicans. Rather, they include a discussion of the decline of the European heroin trade in the 1960s followed by a historical sketch of opium use in Southeast Asia. What Chambliss actually wanted to cite was pages 149–217.

What does this larger view show us? How can it help us? It shows us that our present attitudes toward the whole subject of drug use, drug abuse, and drug control are nothing but the reflections, in the mirror of "social reality," of our own expectations toward drugs and toward those who use them; and that our ideas about and interventions in drug-taking behavior have only the most tenuous connection with the actual pharmacological properties of "dangerous drugs." The "danger" of masturbation disappeared when we ceased to believe in it: when we ceased to attribute danger to the practice and to its practitioners; and ceased to call it "self-abuse." [9]

What Szasz seems to be suggesting is that heroin, cocaine, and other "dangerous drugs" be legalized; hence, the problems associated with their use would disappear. In part, he may be right. Illegal trafficking in drugs and the systemic violence associated with it would indeed pass into obscurity. After all, if the enormous profits associated with the drug black markets were eliminated, traffickers would be forced to seek out other ventures. Moreover, new industries that focus on the legal production and sale of heroin and cocaine would emerge, a segment of the underground economy would vanish, and tax revenues would increase. But what about the health problems associated with drug use? Would they too disappear? Would drug use itself cease to exist? Masturbation certainly did not. What about drug-related crime? Would that too vanish? Would the criminal populations who also use drugs stop committing burglaries and robberies simply because the chemicals they enjoy were no longer considered "dangerous"?

Rufus King, Alfred Lindesmith, and most others who oppose contemporary drug-control policies favor the British system as the answer to the problem. [10] Even Lindesmith, whose endorsement of this approach came before drug abuse spread across Western Europe, causing the British clinic system to falter, cannot be excused for such an indiscretion. It was apparent well before the drug revolution of the 1960s that the addict population in Great Britain was unique—small, and composed primarily of medical addicts. As for Rufus King and the others, the best that can be said is that they were armchair crusaders who had little direct contact with life in the street worlds of heroin, cocaine, and crime. Moreover, even if the British system worked, that would solve only the heroin problem.

If not these solutions, what then?

POSSE COMITATUS, FAT ALBERT, AND *BLUE THUNDER:* FIGHTING THE WAR ON DRUGS

Historically, the federal approach to drug abuse and drug control has included a variety of avenues for reducing both the supply of, and the demand for, illicit drugs. At the outset, the supply-and-demand reduction strategies were grounded in the classic deterrence model: through legislation and criminal penalties, individuals would be discouraged from using drugs; by setting an example of traffickers, the government would force potential dealers to seek out other economic pursuits. For most people who had a significant investment in the social system, the model worked—at least for a time. Other components were then added: treatment for the user; education and prevention for the would-be user; and research to determine how to best develop and implement plans for treatment, education, and prevention. Ultimately, two additional components were added to the supply–demand reduction strategies. There were the federal interdiction initiatives: the Coast Guard, Customs, and Drug Enforcement Administration operatives were charged with intercepting drug shipments coming to the United States from foreign ports; in the international sector there were attempts to eradicate drug-yielding crops at their source. On the surface, none of these strategies seemed to have any effect, and illicit drug use continued to spread.

The problems were many. Legislation and enforcement alone were not enough, and early education programs of the "scare" variety quickly lost their credibility. For social scientists, clinicians, and most other people who had humanitarian ideals—which probably included the majority of the American people—treating drug abuse as a medical problem seemed to be the logical answer. The difficulty was that for the most part, the medical model of treatment was structured around a belief in an addiction-prone personality. However, all drug abusers were not the same. The result was high program-failure rates, regardless of the method of treatment. Moreover, research technologies for assessing program effectiveness were weak. Even today, an overview of the various drug-abuse treatment strategies suggests that everything is working and everything is failing. This overview means that all therapeutic approaches—whether they involve methadone maintenance, group therapy, psychotherapy, simple detoxification, or even penitence through prayer—seem to be working for somebody. However, the strategies of clinical and social science research do not seem to be capable of determining *what* rehabilitative technique is most effective for *whom*. The difficulty seems to be in the selection of drug abusers for the delivery of treatment services. Particularly poor achievements appear in the screening of patients into treatment, the focusing of the most appropriate programs upon those who need them most, the failure to admit that there are some who cannot be helped, and the determination of when a patient has received the maximum benefits from any given therapeutic technique.[11]

Given the perceived failure of the traditional approaches to drug-abuse control, during the late 1970s federal authorities began drawing plans for a more concerted assault on drugs, both legislative and technological. It began with the RICO (Racketeer-Influenced and Corrupt Organizations) and CCE (Continuing Criminal Enterprise) statutes. What RICO and CCE accomplish is the forfeiture of the fruits of criminal activities. Their intent is to eliminate the rights of traffickers to their personal assets, whether these be cash, bank accounts, real estate, automobiles, jewelry and art, equity in businesses, directorships in companies, or any kind of goods or entitlements that are obtained in or used for a criminal enterprise.

Something then had to be done about the Posse Comitatus Act, originally passed by the Forty-fifth Congress on June 18, 1878. The act had been a response to post-Civil War reconstruction policies that permitted U.S. marshals in occupied southern states to call upon federal troops to enforce local laws. It was the goal of southern congressmen to prevent such a practice, and the Posse Comitatus Act accomplished exactly that. It prohibited the army (and eventually other branches of the military) from enforcing federal, state, and local civilian law, and from supplementing the efforts of civilian law-enforcement agencies.[*,12] But the Posse Comitatus Act was never a constitutionally mandated statute. In fact, its very wording permitted the assistance of the military if specifically authorized by an act of Congress.[†] As a result, when President Reagan signed the Department of Defense Authorization Act of 1982 into law, it included several amendments to the century-old Posse Comitatus Act. Although military personnel were still prohibited from physically intercepting suspected drug vessels and aircraft, conducting searches and seizures, and making arrests, the entire war chest of U.S. military power did become available to law enforcement—for training, intelligence gathering, and detection. Moreover, members of the U.S. Army, Navy, Air Force,

---

* The Posse Comitatus Act did not, however, prevent the U.S. Coast Guard from intercepting and seizing vessels at sea that were transporting contraband to American ports.

† Over the years, Congress has authorized the use of the military to control civil disorder. For this reason, Chicago's Mayor Daley was able to call in the Illinois National Guard, as well as regular army troops, at the Democratic National Convention in 1968.

and Marines could operate military equipment for civilian agencies charged with the enforcement of the drug laws.

Beginning in 1982, the "war on drugs" had a new look. Put into force was the Bell 209 assault helicopter, more popularly known as the Cobra. There was none in the military arsenal that was faster, and in its gunship mode it could destroy a tank. There was the navy's EC-2, an aircraft equipped with a radar disk capable of detecting other aircraft from as far as 300 miles away. There were "Fat Albert" and his pals—surveillance balloons 175 feet in length equipped with sophisticated radar and listening devices. Fat Albert could not only pick up communications from Cuba and Soviet satellites but also detect traffic in Smugglers' Alley, a wide band of Caribbean sky that is virtually invisible to land-based radar systems. There were NASA satellites to spy on drug operations as far apart as California and Colombia, airborne infrared sensing and imaging equipment that could detect human body heat in the thickest underbrush of Florida's Everglades, plus a host of other high-technology devices. The U.S. Coast Guard also strengthened its equipment and U.S. Customs put *Blue Thunder* into service, a vessel specifically designed to outrun the high-performance speedboats that traffickers use in Florida waters. A 39-foot catamaran with 900 horsepower, *Blue Thunder* cut through 6-foot seas at speeds better than 60 mph. In all, drug enforcement appeared well-equipped for battle.[13]

IS THE WAR ON DRUGS BEING WON?
CAN THE WAR ON DRUGS BE WON?
SHOULD THE WAR ON DRUGS BE FOUGHT?

To these three questions, one could answer, respectively, "no, not really," "perhaps, at least to some degree," and "yes, why not?"

The high-tech/military-assistance/asset-forfeiture approach to drug enforcement has had some successes, but it does have its critics.[14] Some hold that the expenditures involved outweigh the gains achieved. Others argue that the war cannot be won at all, so why squander military and other government resources. Such criticisms do make some sense. After all, the borders of the United States present a difficult control problem. There are 96,000 miles of land border and coastline in addition to the many internal ports of arrival for international air cargo and travelers. Large numbers of people and conveyances cross these borders each year: 309 million legal travelers, 50,000 vessels, 13 million tons of containerized cargo, and thousands of small vessels and general aviation aircraft.[15] Finally, there are many who continue to argue that drug abuse is either a medical problem or a definitional issue and should not even be a matter dealt with by the government. Given these varying opinions, what then?

In answering this question, one is reminded of Sir Winston Churchill's well-known comment about democracy: that it is the worst system devised by the wit of man "except for all the others." What are the alternatives for dealing with the drug problem? There is the *South American model,* one Thomas Szasz might subscribe to, which holds that *there is no problem.* Yet there *is* a burgeoning problem in South America, particularly in Colombia. Furthermore, since the opium poppy is now being grown in Colombia's remote Orinoco Llanos, heroin use will soon begin to emerge in that part of the world.* There is the *British model,* but that situation too has gotten out of control.

Finally, there is legalization, or what might be called the *Trebach model.* Arnold S. Trebach, author of *The Heroin Solution* and director of the Institute on Drugs, Crime and Justice at American University in Washington, D.C., has stated that:

> As long as there is demand for drugs, traffickers will find a way to circumvent any conceivable drug-control strategy. We just don't have the power to solve the problem.[16]

Dr. Trebach goes on to suggest that drugs be legalized, heavily taxing their sale and using the tax receipts to pay for treatment programs for those harmed by drugs. There is, however, precedent for the failure of this approach both in England with heroin and in the United States during the heydays of the patent-medicine industries. Moreover, amphetamines during the 1960s and Quaaludes during the early 1970s were so loosely controlled that, in effect, they were legal. Also, 60 million people in the United States use tobacco even though they are aware of its potential consequences, and 100 million use alcohol. What would happen if cocaine, a drug that is considerably more pleasant to many individuals than are cigarettes or alcohol, were legal? Dr. William Pollin, former director of the National Institute on Drug Abuse offered an answer:

---

* It should be noted here that the opium poppy is once again being grown in the United States. During the course of a marijuana raid in northern Vermont in September 1985, more than 2,000 opium plants were discovered with their pods sliced open and prepared for the extraction of the raw opium. (See the *New York Times,* 22 Sept. 1985, p. 55.)

If there were no law enforcement, then the number of cocaine users would be up there in the same numbers with smokers and drinkers.[17]

Although one runs the risk of being ignored, or being called "fascist" or "arch-conservative" by atavistic liberal thinkers, *it would appear that contemporary American drug-control policies, with some very needed additions and changes, would be the most appropriate approach.* Heroin addiction is far from being solved, and perhaps it never will be. At least it has been contained to some degree, and rates appear to be declining. In fact, it is very probable that of all the nations in the world where a heroin problem exists, the United States may be the only country where the rates of heroin use are actually going down.*

Although the University of Michigan's annual survey of high school marijuana use showed a slight increase at the close of 1985, on the whole, rates of marijuana use are also in a downward trend,[18] and as pointed out elsewhere in this discussion, student attitudes have begun to shift away from legalization of the drug. One might wish to argue that marijuana use in the 1980s, at least in some parts of the country, has become de facto legal as a result of reduced enforcement of the laws prohibiting it; hence, the removal of the prohibition has made the drug less attractive to risk takers. But there are no indications that marijuana use has been de facto legalized. As illustrated in Table A, the number of marijuana arrests in the United States from 1974 through 1984 has not changed significantly.

In the treatment field, although failure rates are high, there are positive indicators. For those heroin users who were in treatment for periods longer than 90 days, regardless of the particular therapeutic modality, their rates of substance abuse and criminal activity declined somewhat.[19] Thus, contemporary drug-control approaches indeed manifest a level of success, particularly education and prevention.

Yet there is something very wrong with the current U.S. approach to drug-abuse control. It lacks a true commitment! Federal funding for the prevention and treatment of drug abuse was reduced by the Reagan administration, and in the area of interdiction, many efforts appear to be only halfhearted. There have been times, for example, when major South American traffickers were arrested, that relatively low bail levels were established, with the consequence that bail jumping followed almost immediately. Other defendants have returned to their homelands while

---

* This would be the case if the number of heroin users in the United States has indeed been 500,000 since the mid-1970s. As such, the declining rate of heroin use becomes a function of population growth.

Table A Marijuana Arrests in the United States, 1974–1984

Year	Total Arrests
1974	445,600
1975	416,100
1976	441,100
1977	457,600
1978	445,800
1979	391,600
1980	405,600
1981	400,300
1982	455,600
1983	406,900
1984	419,400

SOURCE: Federal Bureau of Investigation, *Uniform Crime Reports,* 1974–1984 (Washington, D.C.: U.S. Government Printing Office, 1974–1984).

awaiting trial, never to be seen again—a phenomenon that Miami prosecutors now refer to as the "Colombian acquittal."

When it was announced that the Posse Comitatus Act would be amended to permit military assistance in the war on drugs, who was the first to balk at the proposal? The American Civil Liberties Union was—and understandably so, since there was the potential for the erosion of private rights. But joining the ACLU view was the Pentagon—rather strange bedfellows. The real issue the Department of Defense had in mind was that interagency cooperation might detract from military preparedness.[20] There has also been the continuing vacillation over the withholding of foreign aid from those drug-producing countries that make no substantial efforts to control cultivation and refining within their own borders. The State Department has reversed its position on this matter on more than one occasion.

The government of the United States seems to have all the tools in place to launch a more effective drug-control strategy, and with a greater commitment, significant gains might be had.

1. Interdiction efforts at U.S. borders should move ahead with the full assistance of the military, despite Pentagon concerns. Since the Justice Department and the White House use the rhetoric of a "war" on drugs, the matter should be dealt with as if it were indeed a war. The intelligence-

gathering potential of military hardware, combined with concentrated surveillance and patrol of territorial waters and air space, could provide excellent training experiences for the military.

Asset forfeiture has been effective, but it could be carried further. On February 15, 1985, for example, agents of the Customs Service seized a Boeing 747 cargo jet used to smuggle more than a ton of cocaine into the United States.[21] Owned by Colombia's Avianca Airlines, the plane was valued at $119 million. It was the thirty-fourth time in five years that an Avianca plane had been found to have cocaine shipped with un-manifested cargo, yet the fate of the aircraft was uncertain. If the Customs Service and the DEA had begun to fully exercise their statutory rights to seizure at the outset, Avianca would probably have begun long since to inspect its cargoes before allowing them to leave Colombian air-fields. Either that or much of the airline would have been confiscated by now, thus making Customs and the DEA the new owners of Avianca, allowing interdiction strategies to continue at considerably less cost to American taxpayers.

More concerted interdiction efforts, combined with asset forfeiture and more stringent foreign-aid policies designed for those nations that fail to make better drug-control efforts and refuse to extradite traffickers wanted in the United States, might have an impact. Considerably less in the way of illegal drugs would reach the streets of rural and urban America. An immediate result would be a dramatic rise in the prices of cocaine and pills. But if cocaine suddenly went from $150 a gram to over $1,000, who would it effect? In all probability, it would price the experimenters and social–recreational users out of the market. They account for the vast majority of users. Also, from this population of social–recreational users the dysfunctional cocaine users emerge. Moreover, the new price structure would serve to reduce the number of new users.

2. There would still be criminal and noncriminal, but nevertheless dys-functional, users of heroin, cocaine, and other drugs. For these a treatment system is in place, however shaky it may be. Nevertheless, it exists and it has been effective for some. Moreover, researchers and clinicians continue to examine patient performance. Eventually, therapeutic approaches will improve. Here too, federal policy needs a greater commitment.

As for the criminal addict, research on the relationship between drug use and crime has demonstrated that the whole question of which comes first, drugs or crime, is a trivial issue. Drug users, and particularly heroin users, commit millions of predatory crimes each year, and it is surprising that American society is so willing to let such a drain on its resources continue. Most probably, the society is unwilling to let it continue but has also recognized the lack of commitment on the part of the government. For the user seriously involved in crime, however, there is incarceration; for the rest, there is treatment. This, of course is easier said than done. As New York's Dr. Bruce D. Johnson and others have pointed out, not all heroin users are serious criminals, and the task of identifying those most intensively involved in crime is a difficult one.[22]

3. The education, prevention, and research initiatives must continue, perhaps at an even faster rate. Moreover, running the risk of being accused of fostering Yankee imperialism, nations involved in the cultivation and trafficking of illicit substances must come to understand the implications of such practices on their own economic, political, and social systems. The international effort in this behalf should not be undertaken by diplomats, State Department officials, or other government representatives. They always run the risk of being perceived as offering "the official U.S. government position," thus reducing their credibility. Rather, there should be "citizen ambassadors"—clinicians, researchers, and educators in the drug field who can speak objectively about U.S. policy and experience.

4. Finally, even when it appears that strides are being made, the approaches ought not be allowed to slacken. If anything has been learned from the history of drug taking in the United States, it is that drug use is a changing phenomenon. There are fads. Different drugs come and go. Already, new potential drugs of abuse are appearing on the horizon. "Basuco," the coca paste of Colombia, has made its way to the streets of both the East Coast and the West Coast. There will be new "designer drugs" that simulate the effects of opiates, stimulants, and hallucinogens. From a small tree of Colombian forests there is "epadu," a cocalike alkaloid that is 40% less active than cocaine but 60% less in price. Soon a stimulant 100,000 times more potent than caffeine will be available. It is under development by Nova Pharmaceuticals in Baltimore and is intended for the treatment of asthma and heart problems, but the potential for its abuse is quite high. And finally, there is "black tar" heroin, processed from Mexican poppies and having greater purity but a lower price than other forms of heroin.[23]

Without question, a number of these proposals would have significant domestic and international implications. There are many economic and budget-deficit issues that make the wholesale support of drug-abuse treatment, prevention, research, and enforcement initiatives tenuous. There are foreign policy issues. Although American foreign policy should not be founded solely on an antidrug-trafficking argument, Attorney General

Edwin Meese's "last resort" philosophy is equally inappropriate.* There are issues in civil liberties and constitutional rights. Although police powers of arrest, search, and seizure in drug cases tend to be often abused, a variety of U.S. Supreme Court decisions since the early 1960s have provided defendants with avenues for excluding illegally obtained evidence from court proceedings. Moreover, numerous citizens have been awarded damages in suits against the police for abuses of their law-enforcement powers. On the other hand, some new laws enacted to handle drug cases (and organized and white-collar crime cases as well) require close scrutiny. The new legislation includes RICO and CCE mentioned earlier and, in 1984, the Comprehensive Crime Control Act and a provision of the Tax Reform Act. Under these new statutes, defendants' assets can be seized upon conviction, and included in these forfeitures can be the fees paid to the attorneys who represented them. Moreover, since the Tax Reform Act of 1984 requires attorneys to report cash payments of $10,000 or more, attorneys can be brought before grand juries to testify about fees and other information that is privileged. In consequence, many attorneys are not accepting drug-trafficking cases, with the result that the integrity of the Sixth Amendment right to counsel has been called into question.[24]

On the other hand, and keeping these sensitive issues in mind, drug abuse tends not to disappear on its own. It hasn't in the past, and it probably will not in the future. Moreover, by the close of 1985, the State Department found that most drug-producing nations were still doing little or nothing to control coca and opium-poppy crops,[25] and at least one nationwide poll found drug abuse to be the most often cited of problems that should be among the government's top priorities.[26]

Notes

1. Thomas Szasz, *Ceremonial Chemistry: The Ritual Persecution of Drugs, Addicts, and Pushers* (Garden City, N.Y.: Anchor Press, 1974), pp. 11–12.
2. Rufus King, *The Drug Hang-Up: America's Fifty-Year Folly* (New York: W. W. Norton, 1972).
3. David F. Musto, *The American Disease: Origins of Narcotic Control* (New Haven, Conn.: Yale University Press, 1973).

---

* Speaking before the Senate Foreign Relations Committee in September 1985, the attorney general stated that a policy of cutting off foreign aid to drug-producing countries should only be "a last resort." (See the *New York Times,* 17 Nov. 1985, p. 47.)

4. *The Nation*, 21 Apr. 1956, p. 337. See also Alfred R. Lindesmith, *Addiction and Opiates* (Chicago: Aldine, 1968).

5. D. Stanley Eitzen and Doug A. Timmer, *Criminology: Crime and Criminal Justice* (New York: Wiley, 1985), p. 276.

6. William J. Chambliss, *On the Take: From Petty Crooks to Presidents* (Bloomington: Indiana University Press, 1978), pp. 165–166.

7. Alfred W. McCoy, *The Politics of Heroin in Southeast Asia* (New York: Harper & Row, 1972).

8. For reviews and analyses of McCoy's work, see *Atlantic Monthly*, Nov. 1972, pp. 112–122; *The Nation*, 4 Dec. 1972, pp. 568–570; *New Yorker*, 30 Sept. 1972, pp. 126–127; *Library Journal*, 15 Nov. 1972, p. 3696; *Saturday Review*, 23 Sept. 1972, pp. 72–76.

9. Szasz, p. 180.

10. King, p. 350; Lindesmith, p. 234.

11. James A. Inciardi, "The Effectiveness of Addiction Treatment," *Addiction Therapist*, Autumn 1975, pp. 2–5.

12. *Drug Enforcement*, Summer 1984, p. 33; *United States Statutes at Large*, 45th Cong., 1877–1879, vol. 20, p. 152.

13. For descriptions of the military involvement and high technology approaches to drug enforcement, see *Wall Street Journal*, 5 Aug. 1982, pp. 1, 8; *Newsweek*, 9 Aug. 1982, pp. 14–15; *Motor Boating & Sailing*, Sept. 1982, pp. 46–49, 107–109; *National Law Journal*, 1 Nov. 1982, pp. 3, 17; *Miami Herald*, 23 Jan. 1983, p. 11A; *Miami Herald*, 17 July 1983, p. 1A; *National Law Journal*, 13 Feb. 1984, pp. 1, 27–28; *Time*, 13 May 1985, p. 27; *New York Times*, 30 June 1985, p. E4.

14. *U.S. News & World Report*, 4 Oct. 1982, pp. 54–55; *Miami Herald*, 31 Mar. 1983, p. 4B; *New York Times*, 13 Sept. 1984, pp. A1, A16; *Wall Street Journal*, 9 Apr. 1985, p. 30.

15. The White House, Drug Abuse Policy Office, Office of Policy Development, *National Strategy for Prevention of Drug Abuse and Drug Trafficking* (Washington, D.C.: U.S. Government Printing Office, 1984), p. 52.

16. *New York Times*, 14 Sept. 1984, p. A12.

17. *New York Times*, p. A12.

18. *U.S. News & World Report*, 18 Nov. 1985, p. 16; *USA Today*, 7 Nov. 1985, p. 3A.

19. David N. Nurco, John C. Ball, John W. Shaffer, and Thomas E. Hanlon, "The Criminality of Narcotics Addicts," *Journal of Nervous and Mental Disease*, 173 (1985), 94–102.

20. *New York Times*, 4 July 1981, p. 8.

21. *New York Times*, 15 Feb. 1985, p. 6.

22. Bruce D. Johnson, Paul J. Goldstein, Edward Preble, James Schmeidler, Douglas S. Lipton, Barry Spunt, and Thomas Miller, *Taking Care of Business: The Economics of Crime by Heroin Users* (Lexington, Mass.: Lexington, 1985), p. 187.

23. National Institute on Drug Abuse, *NIDA Notes*, 2 (May 1986), 6–7.

24. *New York Times,* 21 Nov. 1985, p. A20.
25. Committee on Foreign Relations, Bureau of International Narcotics Matters, *International Narcotics Control Strategy Report: Mid-Year Update* (Washington, D.C.: Department of State, 1985).
26. *USA Today,* 29 Sept. 1985, p. 1A.

NAME INDEX

219

SUBJECT INDEX

ABOUT THE AUTHOR

James A. Inciardi is Professor and Director of the Division of Criminal Justice at the University of Delaware. He received his Ph.D. in sociology at New York University, and has extensive research, teaching, field, and clinical experience in the areas of substance abuse, criminal justice, and criminology. He has been director of the National Center for the Study of Acute Drug Reactions at the University of Miami School of Medicine, vice-president of the Washington, D.C.–based Resource Planning Corporation, and Associate Director of Research for the New York State Narcotic Addiction Control Commission and the Dade County Comprehensive Drug Abuse Treatment System. Dr. Inciardi is a former editor of *Criminology: An Interdisciplinary Journal.* He has done extensive consulting work both nationally and internationally and has published more than one hundred articles, chapters, and books in the areas of substance abuse, history, folklore, criminology, criminal justice, medicine, and law.